This much is certain, that we have no theological right to set any sort of limits to the loving-kindness of God which has appeared in Jesus Christ. Our theological duty is to see and understand it as being still greater than we had seen before.

Karl Barth, *The Humanity of God*

RECONCILED HUMANITY

Karl Barth in Dialogue

Hans Vium Mikkelsen

WILLIAM B. EERDMANS PUBLISHING COMPANY
GRAND RAPIDS, MICHIGAN / CAMBRIDGE, U.K.

© 2010 Hans Vium Mikkelsen

Published 2010 by
Wm. B. Eerdmans Publishing Co.
2140 Oak Industrial Drive N.E., Grand Rapids, Michigan 49505 /
P.O. Box 163, Cambridge CB3 9PU U.K.

Printed in the United States of America

15 14 13 12 11 10   7 6 5 4 3 2 1

Library of Congress Cataloging-in-Publication Data

Mikkelsen, Hans Vium, 1966-
Reconciled humanity: Karl Barth in dialogue / Hans Vium Mikkelsen.
p.   cm.
Revision of the author's thesis (Ph.D.) — Theological Faculty of Aarhus.
Includes bibliographical references (p.   ) and index.
ISBN 978-0-8028-6363-8 (pbk.: alk. paper)
1. Barth, Karl, 1886-1968.   2. Revelation — Christianity.
3. Atonement.   I. Title.

BT127.3.M55   2010
231.7′4 — dc22

2009044732

www.eerdmans.com

To Inge

Contents

Preface

The theology of Karl Barth has been an inspiring — and at times also provoking — source within my study of theology. To read him is to enter into dialogue not only with him, but also with his way of using the tradition as a source for theological knowledge today. However, this does not mean that Barth always agreed with the tradition — or that he hijacked it for his own purposes. Rather, he uses the tradition as his dialogue partner in his attempts to raise and answer fundamental theological issues and questions of his own time.

The aim of this book is to present Karl Barth as a worthwhile dialogue partner for theology today — with special emphasis on two topics: *revelation* and *atonement*. My reading is not only concerned with what Barth did say, but also with how one can use the thought of Barth today in a constructive way. The latter asks for more than a "translation" of the theology of Barth into our time and context. In this book I also want to work the other way around, to interpret the theology of Barth starting from the fundamental theological issues and questions in our time and context. Hopefully this will help to avoid a dogmatic stigmatization of Barth's theology, which can take the form of either an apologetic reading where the theology of Barth is described as "the golden age of theology," or a purely critical approach where his theology *a priori* is doomed to be outdated. In this way I hope to be able to skip the all-too-often established dichotomy between Barthians and non-Barthians.

On the topic of revelation I try to show how Barth in his understanding of the relation between Scripture and revelation establishes an alternative to the two major traps within both theology and church life today: *fundamentalism* and *relativism*. I find that Barth's theology of revelation demonstrates how it is possible to state that the Bible at one and the same time is the word of God to human beings, and human words of God. In fact, Barth's understanding of revelation asks for a continued reinterpretation of the scriptures into the context of the reader.

On the topic of atonement I demonstrate how Barth, despite his traditional language, is establishing an alternative to the often-used typology between an objective, a subjective, and a classical approach to the atonement. Barth is special in the way he demonstrates how the life, death, and resurrection of Jesus Christ must be seen *in interaction with each other* to understand the depth and the content of the atonement. The act of atonement cannot be reduced to the cross. The incarnation is so much more than the necessary prelude to the death of Jesus. The latter tends, unfortunately, often to be the actual result, when the death of Jesus is interpreted as a necessary sacrifice to God: Why did he live? So that he could die. One can see the impact of Barth's teaching of the atonement even more clearly, when it is read in the light of René Girard's theory of *mimetic desire* and the *scapegoat*. Jesus did not die as the final sacrifice to God. In both his life and death, Jesus was the personification of the presence of God's kingdom. The Christian God is not a God who wants sacrifices from human beings as a kind of payment or act of redemption, nor is the reason for the death of Jesus to be found in an internal conflict between the mercy and the righteousness of God. Rather God sacrifices himself on the cross for the life of human beings. The combination of Girard and Barth is inspiring in several ways. The anthropological aspects of Barth's theory of atonement become clearer; the theological perspectives of Girard's thinking ditto.

My claim that Barth is an inspiring dialogue partner for theology today demands a material exploration. Throughout this book I use various philosophers and theological thinkers to discuss, explore, develop, and criticize the theology of Barth — and I hope in this way to open the theology of Barth so that in a fruitful way it can interact with other ways of thinking and practicing theology.

Finally, I try in this book to establish a connection between tradition and modernity, one of the central challenges for systematic theology today. One cannot just skip tradition because one does not like it; nor can one refer to the tradition as the final and unambiguous key to the theological questions of today. Theological work consists in integrating tradition and modernity in a way that (perhaps) changes both. To establish this connection has been a central aim of my constructive reading of Barth. The reader must judge if this mission has been completed.

Abbreviations

CD	*Church Dogmatics*
DBW	Dietrich Bonhoeffer Werke
DBWE	Dietrich Bonhoeffer Works
KD	*Die Kirchliche Dogmatik*
LW	Luther's Works. American Edition
Rev. trans.	Revised translation

INTRODUCTION

In the Church there are fathers: father Luther, father Calvin, other fathers. Why should a free theologian not be their son and disciple? But why should he insist on complete agreement with them?

Karl Barth, *The Humanity of God*

CHAPTER 1

Introductory Remarks

Aim

This book is an attempt to show how vital a dialogue partner Barth is for contemporary theology. The main issues I will investigate in this book are those of revelation and atonement. How do we use and refer to revelation today — and what do we mean when we say that Jesus died for the sake of the human race? I have not only chosen these two subjects because they are important in understanding the theology of Barth, but also because they are vital for understanding the scope and the challenge for theology today.

The perception of revelation relates first and foremost to the perception of Scripture: How, at one and the same time, do we claim that the Bible is the Word of God and that the Bible is composed of human words about God? This double statement is to be read as an attempt to avoid the two pitfalls of theology today: fundamentalism and relativism. Fundamentalism claims that the authority of the Bible is based on a literal understanding of the Bible, where the Bible is read as the answer to all our questions in a way that does not take its own context and historical embeddedness into account. This approach can be made in more or less sophisticated ways. One common feature is that interpretation is abandoned, or when allowed, is really used as a synonym for translation. The question of interpretation is then narrowed down to a question of translating the message of there and then, to a message that can be understood here and now. Translation regards form, not content. Thus, the message is the same, from eternity to eternity. No space is allowed for changes, either in the message or in God. Relativism states, on the other hand, that no religion can claim to be the true religion. Such a claim is looked upon as a variety of imperialism. Instead the buzzword is tolerance. The distinction between true and false is no longer looked at from the perspective of essence or reference; instead the touchstone is whether it functions or not. If it works, it is truth; if not, it is false. The inherent truth-claim of the Bible (and any other holy scripture) is thereby reduced to a question for the individual participant: Does he or she find comfort in the religion or not? Is Barth's dialectic between the perception of the Bible as the Word of God and the Bible as human words about God a practicable road between the abysses of fundamentalism and relativism? Does Barth's perception of the revelation avoid too heavy an emphasis on the literal content of the Bible?

The revelation of God in Jesus Christ is at the very center of Barth's theology — both noetically and ontologically. God is both the subject and the object of revelation. The emphasis on this double structure is well known and thoroughly described in several analyses. Less known is the fact that Barth's theology of revelation includes a positive understanding of the human being's experience of revelation. Revelation has to have an actual impact, which means that the reality of revelation cannot be fully explored with a description of the dialectic between God as both subject and object. This remains within the objective aspects of revelation. In my analysis I will therefore focus on a description of what I define as the subjective aspects of revelation. Revelation must be experienced as such to have an impact on the individual, which again implies that revelation includes involvement of the self. One cannot remain neutral toward the revealed revelation. If that is the case, nothing has been revealed. Barth's structural understanding of revelation here is very close to the structure of the encounter within the I-Thou philosophy, which inspired Barth more than he himself gives away in the *Church Dogmatics*.[1] In fact, it seems as if this is mere coincidence. However, by means of an investigation of Barth's lecture manuscript on anthropology from 1943/44, I will demonstrate the extent to which he is acquainted with Martin Buber's philosophy of dialogue. One can only guess why he does not want to admit this heritage in *CD*.

Barth's teaching of the atonement is at one and the same time in op-

---

1. Karl Barth, *Church Dogmatics* (Edinburgh: T. & T. Clark, 1956-75). Hereafter abbreviated as *CD*.

position to a traditional conservative understanding of the death of Jesus as the necessary sacrifice to God, and a modern liberal theology where God has nothing to do with the death of Jesus (pure coincidence). Neither of the two is able to deal with the importance and the meaning of the death of Jesus in an adequate way that gives a meaningful answer to the questions: Why did he die? Did he have to die?

These two questions entail a whole range of sub-questions that all relate to the relation between God the Father and Jesus, the Son of God and Son of Man. Did Jesus have to die to satisfy God? Was Jesus' death the necessary sacrifice that enables God to live out his love for human beings? How are the will of Jesus and the will of God related? Does the death of Jesus have any impact on God himself? Is it only the situation of the human being which is changed in the atonement, or is it also the situation of God? Has God bound himself to human beings in the atonement so that God no longer can be God without humanity? Or is it only human beings who are tied to God? Asking these questions helps examine the tradition in a positive way — not just for the sake of confirming or rejecting it, but also for the sake of exploring new theological insights in discussion with the tradition.

Barth's teaching of the atonement seems at first glance very close to that of Anselm, both in language and structure. Not only do they both describe God as both the subject and the object of the atonement, but they also use juridical metaphors to describe the content of Jesus' death. But does Barth really agree with Anselm on the topic of atonement? No: despite the fact that Barth maintains the structure of God as both the subject and object in the atonement, he does not describe the death of Jesus as a necessary sacrifice with the aim of overcoming an internal conflict in God between his righteousness and mercy. Further, a major difference consists in the way Barth interrelates the life, death, and resurrection of Jesus. None of them can be understood separately. Barth hereby overrules the well-known typology of Gustaf Aulén, who differentiates among the objective, the subjective, and the classical teaching of the doctrine of atonement. The first focuses on the death of Jesus Christ, the second on the life of Jesus Christ, and the third on the resurrection of Jesus Christ.

From the perspective of the liturgical cycle, Barth's teaching of the atonement can be read as an attempt to describe the connection between Maundy Thursday, Good Friday, and Easter Day. The form and content of the liturgy differs radically on each of these days. Each service must dwell with the particular issues of the specific Holy Day. Do we join the disciples celebrating the Passover with Jesus, do we stand at the back of the crowd looking at our Master hanging on the cross, judged to death for blasphemy, or do we accompany him, without knowing it, on the way to Emmaus? Nevertheless, each of the sermons must be interrelated with the other two Holy Days to be an Easter Sermon.

Barth's teaching of the atonement in *CD* IV is a major contribution to a theological re-reflection on the meaning and importance of Jesus' life, death, and resurrection, as he develops his teaching of the atonement in a dialectical perception of what I will define as a teaching of the atonement from both above and below. Jesus' death on the cross can be read as both God's judgment of the human being and the human being's judgment of God. The judgment of God entails both wrath and punishment, but how are wrath and punishment to be interpreted? In this book I will argue that the key to understanding the wrath and punishment of God is Jesus' own cry on the cross: "My God, my God, why hast thou forsaken me?" The punishment and the wrath of God are understood here as the absence of God that Jesus experiences on the cross. But Jesus' own experience of God-forsakenness is not identical with God-abandonment. Jesus was resurrected on the third day. Thus, God did not forsake Jesus, but God did absorb Jesus' experience of finitude and despair on the cross. God can suffer without emptying himself out on the cross. In the words of Barth: "God gives Himself to human beings without giving Himself away." On this topic Barth is debating with the kenosis-theology of his time, which, according to Barth, pays a price too high, as they in their emphasis on kenosis are rejecting the absolute difference between God and the human being. To focus too much on the weakness of God is just another subtle way of human projection. The suffering of Christ must be interpreted in Trinitarian terms if it is not to lead to the death of God.

In this book I will favor Barth's perception of the atonement as allowing space for a dynamic understanding of God, where God himself is changed due to the life, death, and resurrection of Jesus Christ. This is not only due to his emphasis on the relation between the life, death, and resurrection of Jesus, but also to his reinterpretation of Chalcedonian Christology, where the relation between the Father and the Son is essential. I am well aware that on this point I am reading Barth against Barth, so to speak, as Barth himself would reject the view that God is changed by the incarnation. My attempt to read Barth against Barth includes a critique of the way

Barth interrelates his reference to the eternal will of God and the absolute freedom of God. According to Barth, God should not be subjected to any kind of necessity (intrinsic or extrinsic). At times Barth stresses this point so heavily that he states that God could have acted otherwise from the very beginning. God would still have been a loving and merciful God, even if he had not created the world, or the human being in the center of the world. God is in need of neither the world nor humanity. The odd logic seems to be: the more uncertainty, the more grace. The human being is hereby left in what can at best be defined as a kind of "flashback fear." If God could have acted otherwise, can he still do so now, despite the fact that he has created the world, and human beings in its center? But this dead end is not, as I will demonstrate, a necessary consequence of Barth's emphasis on the eternal will of God.

Finally, one more question needs to be addressed. Is Barth an exponent of the idea of *apokatastasis?* He would himself have denied it. However, in the *Humanity of God* Barth asks rhetorically if his theology ends up with universalism. He does not fully answer this question, either negatively or positively. Instead he urges that the matter should be reconsidered under the rubric: Why could it not be so? I hope to demonstrate how it is possible to read Barth as a universalistic thinker. Barth is at this point in conflict with Luther and Calvin, who both teach the double outcome. Barth remains within the Reformed tradition insofar as he keeps the focus on a connection between a double predestination and a double outcome. But he nevertheless turns this doctrinal teaching upside down, as he claims that God has elected *all* human beings in Jesus Christ. In Christ both the election and the reprobation of all people have taken place substitutionally. Thus a twofold election has taken place in Christ. The election is no longer individualized, so that some are elected to eternal salvation, others to eternal reprobation. The double outcome is then no longer referring to a spatial and chronological separation between salvation and damnation. Resurrection is salvation. It is not a neutral event that can lead to either salvation or damnation.

Reading Strategy

Karl Barth's *CD* is an astonishing and huge work that can only provoke respect. To read it is to enter into a highly complex and mature way of thinking, where the reader (whether inclined to be sympathetic or antipathetic to the whole theological project as such) is astonished by the variety and the mutual coherence of the dogmatic proposals at issue. Barth's proposal is at one and the same time both highly sophisticated and quite simple. It is simple in the way the whole *CD* can be read as an exposition of the faith claim: "Jesus loves you" (a claim that in the hands of most others would have been turned into a far-too-sweet, possessive, and importunate statement).[2] It is complex in the way Barth changes between an unproblematic use of and reference to the tradition (as if the question of modernity has not touched him at all), and, at places, a sweeping critique of the tradition (forced by the insights of modernity).[3] The question of modernity often lies beneath his use, rejection, interpretation, and reinterpretation of the tradition. However, in the *CD* Barth very seldom states explicitly who he is in discussion with, who inspires him, or who he is rejecting on a particular matter. It seems as if he would claim that the matter in itself is what matters, and not so much who your discussion partners are. Instead, it is all turned into one big *Summa*, where all the themes are mutually interwoven. The same topics are taken into consideration at several places under various headings.

Reading the *CD* can be compared to the effort of reading a hiking map. The same mountain-massif is followed for a long time, but it nevertheless looks different every time you turn a corner, walk up a hill, or descend a slope. The map, with its signs and contours, has to be read carefully in order to establish the inner connection between all these signs and contours, and the reality to which they refer. The task is at one and the same time to establish an overall view of the landscape and to become confident about the actual part of the track you are on. The attempt to establish an overall view and the attempt to make a detailed analysis must at all times relate to each other. If not, you will surely lose your bearings, with one inevitable result: being lost!

2. A story says that Barth, shortly before his death, was asked to express the meaning of his theology in one sentence (which in itself is an impossible and meaningless task). His answer was nevertheless: "Jesus loves you!" I have not been able to verify the authenticity of this story, but I find that, true or apocryphal, it serves as a fine introduction to the strange combination of naïveté and subtlety that is at stake in Barth's theology.

3. On Barth's reference to the tradition see Migliore's presentation of Barth's use of Reformed Orthodoxy in *The Göttingen Dogmatics*. Daniel L. Migliore, "Karl Barth's First Lectures in Dogmatics: Instruction in the Christian Religion," in *The Göttingen Dogmatics: Instruction in the Christian Religion* (Grand Rapids: Eerdmans, 1991), pp. xv-lxii.

The same kind of reading strategy will be used in my attempt to read the *CD*. The overall interconnection between the various dogmatic themes has to be taken into account if one is to do justice to Barth's work. Another reason why the *CD* will be read in big stretches and not by the help of the index (à la "What does Barth say about so and so?") is that the *CD* in many ways — especially Volume IV, *The Doctrine of Reconciliation* — can be claimed to be written as a narrative dogmatic. In *CD* IV the story of God's entering into the world is told. Further, Barth seems more and more to develop a narrative reading of the Bible in the way he uses and analyzes the Bible. This is especially seen in his many excursuses, where the biblical reasoning for his dogmatic statements is given. Obviously it is not enough to establish the overall view. One also has to make some detailed analysis of carefully selected text-excerpts from the *CD*. If not, the interpretation will inevitably end up doing nothing more than repeating Barth's own favorite phrases.

I will opt here for a non-apologetic and constructive approach to the work of Barth.[4] This will be most evident in the second part of my study, dealing with Christology and atonement, where I will investigate whether Barth's teaching of the atonement can be opened up with the help of René Girard's social-anthropology. With this constructive way of interpreting Barth, I will aim at a reading between two typical reading strategies:

(1) A closed, internal reading that stays within Barth's own universe. The main subject here is the dogmatic content. Such a reading might be very helpful in understanding the depth of Barth's theology, but it seems very often to be either unable or perhaps just uninterested in establishing a dialogue between Barth's theology and the challenges facing theology today. Of course, this apologetic and internal approach

---

4. Of course, to advocate that Barth should be read in a constructive way is not the same as saying that anything goes. If one wants to claim that the argument given is an argument that works to prolong Barth's theology, it must be possible to verify that the center and the nerve within Barth's theology is still intact. Can the interpretation claim to be a plausible continuation of the content in Barth's theology seen in relation to the new questions, new insights, new modes of thinking, etc. that have arisen since the writing of the *CD*? Or is it "just" a particular idea in Barth's theology, which on an ad-hoc basis has inspired further thoughts and ideas on specific theological issues. Not that there is anything wrong with the latter case, except that it cannot claim to be a position in continuity with Barth's dialectical theology as such.

could be defended by the conviction that the solution of today's theological challenges should be found in a return to the theology of
Barth.

(2) A reading that is mainly interested in the methodology of Barth's dialectical theology. This is often combined with an approach from the
outside. The dogmatic content is here more or less neglected. However, if this whole exercise is limited to a structural comparison, the result of the whole analysis is already given in establishing the precondition for the comparison.

My aim is for something between these two ways of reading Barth. Both
methodology and dogmatic content will be analyzed. By doing this I hope
that it will be possible to do justice to the dogmatic content of the *CD*
without falling into a purely internal analysis. Thus, my reading strategy
will be twofold: (1) to demonstrate the plausibility of my interpretations
with the help of references to and analysis of the *CD,* and (2) to put Barth's
theology — with regard to both method and content — into perspective
with the help of various scholars, some of them Karl Barth's contemporar-
ies, others not. The main thinkers here will be Schleiermacher (1768-1834),
Hegel (1770-1831), Brunner (1889-1966), Buber (1878-1965), Pannenberg
(1928-), Girard (1923-), and Frei (1922-88). I am not trying to establish any
historical genetic relation between Barth and these scholars (such as to investigate who is inspired by whom), but solely to use them as dialogue and
discussion partners. The purpose of using these various — and very different — thinkers is both to open Barth's theology so that it can interact with
other ways of practicing theology, and to get some tools through which
Barth's theology can be criticized in a constructive way.

My way of arguing throughout the book can be compared with the
form of a helix. It is circular in the sense that some of the central terms will
be treated under different headings throughout the study. But it is linear in
the sense that each time it is done for the purpose of establishing a more
comprehensive interpretation of the complex structure of the *CD.* One
way to accomplish this is also to choose some "alternative" headings that
may illuminate the content and the structure of the *CD* without necessarily being read "off the wall" from a literal reading of the *CD.*

Thus, different thinkers who differ quite distinctively from Barth in
their overall methods and aims may function as perfect tools for a constructive reading of Barth. I am not bringing all these other scholars in

with the purpose of making a comparison between each individual thinker and Barth. Rather, I will use them as either an auger for digging into the *CD*'s deeper layers (for example, to investigate the structures hidden in the text), or as a satellite that in its orbit around its planet can help obtain a better overall view of the surface. Non-metaphorically, the use of these various thinkers serves both to improve a detailed analysis of specific themes and to help put the various matters into perspective.

If in the light of this study Barth appears to be a worthwhile dialogue partner for theology today, I have succeeded in my task. If the *CD* is instead written off as an impressive but nevertheless totally outdated approach to theology today, I have failed. This is said out of the frustrating experience of finding Barth's words confused with the "Word of God" (both by "disciples" and opponents), in the sense that you have to be either for it (i.e., accepting it all) or against it (i.e., rejecting it all). The truth-claim inherent in Barth's theology (as in any other theology) has hereby been confused with the truth-claim of God that it refers to.

Content

I have divided my study into three parts.

Part I, "Revelation," consists of an analysis of how Barth interprets and uses revelation. The main point is to investigate and explain the impact of the claim that God is both the subject and the object in the act of revelation. This double movement within the act of self-revelation belongs to what I have described as the objective aspect of revelation. But this double movement does not exclude or undermine the subjective aspect of revelation, which asks for the human being's participation.

The reality of God is given through God's own revelation. This revelation has taken place in the incarnation, and is witnessed in the Holy Scriptures. The revelation is given "only" in the form of the biblical text's witness to revelation. The biblical narrative is in itself the first communities' interpretation of the identity of Jesus Christ. The witness demands reinterpretation, which includes both the reception history of the Bible and the actual context in which the Bible is read/heard. Thus it is illegitimate to present Barth's theology of revelation as if it is an anti-hermeneutical theology, or as if revelation in itself provides an unsurpassable interpretative key through which the ambiguity of human experience is overcome.[5] Such interpretations would imply that revelation is synonymous with a direct access to the divine reality. If this had been the case, revelation would be a purely esoteric knowledge.

On the contrary, one consequence of the strong emphasis on revelation in Barth's dialectical theology is that revelation in itself entails a demand for an ongoing, non-static reinterpretation. I will argue that Barth's use of revelation takes into consideration the epistemological ambiguities that are reflected in modernity, including the crisis of representation. Thus, revelation cannot be owned or possessed by a human being. Revelation is dynamic and not static. The Bible is in continual need of being reinterpreted. This is both because of the situation of the reader (the quest for actuality) and the genre of the Bible as a text (the Bible read as a witness of revelation). To understand the Bible as the witness of revelation is to enter into a community of interpretation. If this act of interpretation is dismissed, the whole *kerygma* of the Bible is betrayed, since it is then read as being the literal words of God rather than a human (and thereby strictly limited) witness to God. Such a literal understanding of the Bible as the Word of God would lead to a rejection of the need for interpretation. From such a point of view interpretation would be judged as not only unnecessary but also as an expression of arrogance and blasphemy. (Who are you to question the Word of God?)[6]

Thus Barth's perception of revelation entails a sharp critique of biblicism. In fact, it is an acid critique of letting any specific method be onesidedly decisive for the result of interpretation. Barth's way of using revelation as a hermeneutic key presupposes that no particular method can be seen as *the* method through which Scripture should be read. If this were the case, the method would become more decisive than the biblical text itself. The method would no longer be a reading tool, the aim of which is to

___

5. The anti-hermeneutic strain can be found in both anti-modern and postmodern types of readings. Biblicism (a literal reading) relates to the former. Different types of literary criticism such as, for example, New Criticism and structuralism, relate to the latter.

6. Such an argument is in itself a prime example of what happens when the distinction between the Word of God and the words about God is either neglected or misinterpreted. Human beings take the Word of God into their own control. God thereby becomes an instrument in human beings' struggle for power. Of course, the rejection of the need for interpretation is itself an interpretation. But such rejection — in contrast to other interpretations — places a human being out of reach for entering into dialogue with other points of view.

help the reader interpret the text. Instead, the question of methodology would have turned into a strategy of conformity.

Revelation can only be said to be revealed when it has had an actual impact on the individual hearer. According to Barth, "acknowledgment" is the most adequate way to describe the human being's experience of revelation. With the term "acknowledgment" it is possible to describe how God can be both the subject and the object of revelation without excluding the category of human experience as such. The term "acknowledgment" makes it possible both to maintain the radical difference between God and the human being, and to evaluate the human being's experience of God positively (as something that does not have to be negated to obtain "theological value"). I will investigate Barth's use of the term "acknowledgment" with the help of a reading of both Hegel and Schleiermacher. My analysis will show that Barth's use of the term, when it relates to the encounter between God and the individual human being, is much closer to Schleiermacher's emphasis on "absolute dependence" than Hegel's perception of acknowledgment.

Further, a transformation of the self is included within the dialectic between the objective and the subjective aspect of revelation. This transformation of the self takes place through a call for participation. The section on participation serves to describe how the human being — through the revelation — is enabled to become a part of revelation. This includes an investigation of how Barth interrelates the justification and the sanctification of the human being. This section anticipates the importance of the Christological double movement: the humiliation of God and the exaltation of the human being (both of which have taken place in the incarnation of Jesus Christ).

Part II is titled "The Humanity of the Creature." Here I have chosen to focus on the relational character of the human being, and the relation between sin and nothingness. In both chapters I will pay attention to Barth's distinction between the phenomenon of man and the real man.

In Jesus Christ true humanity is revealed. Jesus was the one (and only) man who was able to fully live in and out of his relation to not only God but also to his fellow human beings. This does not, however, in itself disqualify any theological investigation of or interest in the phenomenon of man. It is, however, only in the light of the real man that the phenomenon of man can be seen as what it is: the phenomenon of man. Further, it is in the acknowledgment of this relation that the phenomenon of man can serve as an analogy to the real human being. Having clarified this, Barth can work out an analysis of the basic form of humanity, where he turns from the man Jesus to man in general. In his description of the basic form of humanity Barth is heavily influenced by the I-Thou philosophy of Martin Buber. I will demonstrate this by a reading of his lectures on anthropology in 1943/44, in which he gave a theological evaluation of Buber's book *I and Thou*. In the *CD* references to Buber are nearly absent. But one clearly sees the influence of the I-Thou philosophy in Barth's account of the essence of humanity, an analysis that has its strength in its phenomenological perceptiveness.

The differentiation between the phenomenon of man and the real man includes an investigation of the relation between revelation and sin. Barth's reversing of the Lutheran order between law and gospel to gospel and law implies that a human being can only realize that one is a sinner in and through the gospel (not by the law alone). Thus, the sin of the human being is both realized and overcome in one and the same movement. The distinction between the real man and the phenomenon of man should therefore be read in continuation of the themes worked out in Part I regarding the *participatio Christi*, in which I describe the relation between the justification and the sanctification of the human being.

Through my analysis of the relation between sin and nothingness it becomes clear why it is so vital for Barth both to emphasize the inevitable character of sin and to state that sin is neither the first nor the final word to be said about the human being. Not only sin but also nothingness is defeated in Jesus Christ. The human being is called to be the partner of God in the fight against nothingness. An adequate description of the reconciled humanity must take this aspect of the call into consideration. In the interrelation between incarnation and atonement the human being is revealed both in its *status corruptionis* and *status redemptionis*. A theological description of the human being is in its very center different from a non-theological description, since it takes its starting point in the theological claim of resurrection. Not death but resurrection is the basis for a theological anthropology.

Barth's theology is surely to be defined as a theology of revelation. But not much is said by this heading alone, since one could ask which Christian theology is *not* a theology of revelation in the sense that it places the Christ-event at its very core. What is specific for Barth is the way in which he combines the incarnation (God's becoming man) with the atonement (the human being's reconciliation with God). In Part III, "Christology and Atonement," I will investigate not only how this close relation is worked out, but also explore the dogmatic consequences of this close relation. The incarnation is more than just the neutral precondition for the saving act of Christ. Jesus did not first become Christ through his life, death, and resurrection. Jesus *is* Christ from the very beginning of his life. Barth's Christology is so far a *logos Christology,* from above. In Christ the eternal Word of God is incarnated. This statement requires — if it is to be strictly logical — a reference to a *logos* prior to the incarnation. Consequently, Barth operates with a distinction between the λόγος ἄσαρκος and the λόγος ἔνσαρκος. I will analyze this distinction under the heading, "The Chalcedonian Pattern." The other main theme under this heading is an investigation of how Barth uses the traditional teaching of the enhypostasis and anhypostasis.

The investigation of the relationship between the λόγος ἄσαρκος and λόγος ἔνσαρκος serves also to investigate how the *being of God* is perceived within Barth's theology. Are the acts of God a result of the essence of God, or is it rather the acts of God that constitute the essence of God? This question cannot be rejected as "a chicken and egg" problem. If it is the acts of God that constitute the being of God, the being of God can be described as dynamic and actualistic. This opens the possibility that God in Christ can enter into a mutual relationship with the human being. There would then be no necessary conflict between the being of God and the absorption of Jesus' experience of the absence of God within the being of God. In this case, the being of God is in fact constituted by the acts of God. God can change and still be God. Barth does not explore the full potential of this actualistic interpretation of the being of God, as he does not leave room for any change within the being of God. To make room for this, Barth would have had to change his perception of the Trinity from one subject with three modes of being, where the unity of the Trinitarian God is worked out within the framework of "a single thinking and willing I" to a perception of the Trinity, where the subjectivity of God is the result of the mutual relations between the three persons of the Trinity. The subjectivity of God would then be the result of the Trinitarian relations rather than their precondition.

The analysis of the relation between sin and nothingness in Part II should be kept in mind when I am interpreting the content of Barth's emphasis on God's wrath and punishment. This investigation follows my presentation of Barth's Christological reinterpretation of the teaching of the double outcome and a thorough analysis of Barth's heading in *CD* IV/1 §59,2: "The Judge Judged in Our Place."[7] It is not God but the human being who is in need of reconciliation. God does not have to overcome any obstacles within himself for the sake of being enabled to reconcile himself with the human being. The focus is on the eternal will of God to live in a covenant with the human being. I will not only investigate how the covenant is interpreted as the expression of God's basic and original will, but I also intend to take into account Barth's own reservations in relation to a classical Federal Theology.

My interpretation of Barth's teaching of the atonement is largely inspired by René Girard's analysis of the interrelation between violence and the sacred, especially his claim that Christianity — in opposition to other religions — disqualifies a religious legitimating of sacrifice. Sacrifice is revealed as an act of violence. In the death of Jesus Christ the sinful structure of the human being is revealed, which in Barth's theology is a revelation of the sinful nature of the human being. This analysis is right at the center of my constructive reading of Barth's teaching of the atonement. I am not claiming that Barth had read Girard or vice versa, or that there should be any historical genetic relation between the two. Yet I am stating that Girard can be used to reveal aspects of Barth's teaching of the atonement, enabling us to see the radical content of the atonement: that in and through Jesus Christ God reveals the human being as a sinner. In and through this revelation the human person is empowered to live in and out of the hope for the coming of the kingdom of God. The atonement is the act through which the human being is given a certain *telos,* whereby the human being is taken out of his or her own selfishness. According to Barth this selfishness can further be qualified as the wish to judge others for the sake of oneself, which Barth also describes as the sin *in nuce.* This is finally revealed on the cross, where the one who has the right to judge (Jesus Christ) lets himself be judged, without judging those who judge him. The lack of judgment is then in itself a judgment, which is fulfilled in the resurrection. Here the final rejection of the human being's rejection is revealed. In the resurrection God not only confirms that the proclamation of Jesus was his

---

7. See Karl Barth, *Church Dogmatics* IV/1 (Edinburgh: T. & T. Clark, 1956), p. 211 (hereafter cited as *CD* IV/1).

own proclamation (i.e., Jesus is the self-revelation of God), but he also judges human beings' judgment of Jesus. Thus the judgment of God cannot be limited to the cross.

Barth's teaching of the atonement is peculiar in the way that it relates the incarnation of Jesus Christ to the life, death, resurrection, and ascension of Jesus Christ. Each of these elements can only be understood when looked upon in relation to the others. The death of Jesus is empty if it is not viewed as the prolongation of his life. His life is without saving significance if it is not viewed in relation to his death and resurrection. The revelation of the content of his life finally takes place in the resurrection, in which it is revealed that Jesus is Christ. Together with the ascension the resurrection points forward to the final coming of the kingdom of God (the second coming of Christ); a coming that already has content through the life, death, and resurrection of Jesus Christ.

At this stage in the study, after an investigation of the content and the interrelation between revelation and the atonement in the *CD*, we should hopefully have gained an insight into what I define as the theological realism of the late theology of Barth. This realism is bound up with the dialectical movement between the objective and the subjective aspects of both atonement and revelation. The practical impact of this dialectic is that the human being has been freed to live in and out of the hope for universal salvation. The result of Barth's reinterpretation of the double outcome is that all human beings are united in God's judgment and salvation. No one can therefore take the standpoint of God and judge a fellow human being in the name of God. The only one who would be judged in that case is the one who judges.

Further Remarks

Barth writes his *CD* in a language that some modern readers might find offensive, as it is heavily gender-biased, i.e., patriarchal. For many reasons Barth has not been particularly popular among feminist or feminist-inspired theologians. However, I have chosen not to exercise any kind of censorship in my quotations from the *CD*. Instead, I ask readers to abstract from what they might consider gender-biased language. This appeal also includes my own writing wherever I have chosen to stay within the terminology used by Barth. The reason for this is that I find it would have been both artificial and restrictive to the flow of the language if I'd had to oper-ate with two "mother tongues" throughout this book. I have, for example, neither opposed nor revised Barth's theological vocabulary in ascribing masculine gender to God. In line with this argument I have not revised the quotes from the *CD*, when and where Barth uses "man" as a synonym for the human being.

However, it will appear that I explicitly criticize Barth where I find that for theological reasons he is deliberately patriarchal. Here I have his gender-biased interpretation of the I-Thou relationship in *CD* III/2 in mind.[8] Such an interpretation operates clearly within the conservative tra-dition that just as Christ is the head of the church, so is the man the head of the woman. I can assure the reader that this analogy is by no means popular in Scandinavia. The only (and lonely) subscribers to such a gender-biased hierarchy would be a few fundamentalists who have no un-derstanding of the historical character either of the Bible or of society. Barth should certainly not be placed within this group.

Finally, I am well aware that I am using the word "it" in an improper way, when I use "it" as a reference to the human being. Thus I am "invent-ing" a generic singular pronoun, which might seem rather odd for a native English reader. However, my aim is to avoid a constant shift between "he" and "she," when I refer to the human being. I hope that the reader will be able to read my use of "it," without every time blaming me for an incorrect use of the English language.

8. See Karl Barth, *Church Dogmatics* III/2 (Edinburgh: T. & T. Clark, 1960), pp. 285-324; hereafter cited as *CD* III/2.

PART I

REVELATION

I think every work of art should survive after all the labour bestowed on it, and survive as a sketch. To the last it must be something struck off at a first heat — this is the meaning of impressionism.

John Butler Yeats, letter 1906

God may speak to us through Russian Communism, a flute concerto, a blossoming shrub, or a dead dog. We do well to listen to him if he really does. But, unless we regard ourselves as the prophets and founders of a new church, we cannot say that we are commissioned to pass on what we have heard as independent proclamation. God may speak to us through a pagan or an atheist, and thus give us to understand that the boundary between the church and the secular world can still take at any time a different course from that which we think we discern. Yet this does not mean, unless we are prophets, that we ourselves have to proclaim the pagan or atheistic thing which we have heard.

Karl Barth, *CD* I/1

CHAPTER 2

Barth's Dialectical Theology of Revelation

God as the Subject and the Object of Revelation

It is not without reason that one of the slogans that has often been used to describe Barth's theology as a whole is "theology of revelation." The emphasis on revelation as God's self-disclosure has, since Barth's break with liberal theology, been one of the consistent themes throughout his entire work. God is, from Barth's point of view, not only the center but also the starting point of theology. God is both the subject and the object of revelation. Thus, revelation is the only way through which the human being can obtain any real knowledge of God. Barth's way of arguing here is truly circular, as it is only through God's own disclosure of himself in Jesus Christ that human beings become aware of the fact that they cannot receive any independent knowledge of God outside of this self-revelation. It is in the one and same revelation that the human being obtains knowledge of God and understands that it cannot receive this knowledge anywhere else. Or rather that it understands that the revelation of God in Jesus Christ has to be the touchstone for all human knowledge and experience of God.

But what does it actually mean that God is both the subject and the object of revelation? God is the subject (the revealer) as it is only God himself who can give a true and adequate account of the one and true God. All true knowledge about God derives from God. This is not only due to the epistemological restrictions of the human being (that the human being as finite is unable — through its own reason — to perceive the infinite), but it is also due to the ontological gap between God and the human being. There is no correlation between the being of God and the being of the human being that would enable the human being — through its own reason — to obtain knowledge of God.[1] God is the object (the revealed), as the content of revelation is God himself. What is revealed is how God is God in relation to the human being. And it is through this axis that the human being is enabled to see its true relation not only to God, but also to its fellow human beings and to the creation.

What is unusual in Barth's theological conception of revelation is not so much the strong prominence he gives to the revelation of God in Jesus Christ (a Christological approach to God), as it is the strong connection he establishes between the revelation of God in Jesus Christ and the election of the human being in Jesus Christ. In Barth's view, the incarnation reflects both Jesus Christ as the electing God and Jesus Christ as the elected human being. (I will elaborate on this point in Chapters 7 and 8.)[2]

The Qualitative Difference Between God and the Human Being

In his early writings Barth unremittingly stresses the qualitative difference between God and the human being. A frequently used quote that expresses this difference is from his speech in Elgersburg to the gathering of the "friends of the Christian World" in October 1922 where he states:

1. According to the logic of Barth, the human being is bound to end up with nothing more than an idealized projection of itself if it uses the method of correlation in its search for God. Barth is not even willing to grant the questions of the human being a positive preliminary function (a John-the-baptizer-function). The latter presupposes that a dialectic between the human being's questions and the answers of God to these questions is possible (cf. Paul Tillich's method of correlation). This would, again according to Barth, imply that God is reduced to the function of filling out the existential questions and gaps of human beings. Thus God is diminished to being a kind of guarantee for meaning in life. But God has hereby lost his power, as he has been turned into a principle of life. God is no longer the God who demands, no longer the God who judges, no longer the God who also entails wrath. Instead Barth claims that it is God who questions the human being.

2. Barth also expresses this connection in the relation between "God with us" and "we with God." See for example *CD* IV/1, pp. 3-22. A further way of expressing this connection is in the relation between the promise, "I will be your God," and the command, "Ye shall be my people." See for example *CD* IV/1, p. 47.

> As theologians, we *ought to speak* of God. We are, however, human and as such *cannot speak* of God. We should *recognize both* our ought and our cannot and by that recognition give God the glory.[3]

This is a very useful key to the whole authorship of Barth, as it very concisely states the dialectical dynamic between revelation and interpretation. These brief sentences imply not only that the object of theology is God, but also that the human being — in its capacity as human — is unable to talk adequately about God. This entails that when the human being actually does succeed in talking adequately about God, then this is grounded in God's ability to use human words as his words. The analogy between the description of God's being and the being of God is in this case established by an actual act of God. The difference between God and the human being is presented here as a necessary precondition for a real meeting between God and the human being. The stressing of the radical difference can in this way be said to have a positive aim even in the works of the early Barth.[4] Admittedly, it is generally said that Barth's early works express this negatively, but already in the early stages of Barth's writing a dialectical as well as an analogical element is included.

The distance between God and the human being cannot be overcome from the side of the human being, but only from the side of God. The distance between God and the human being is then at one and the same time preserved and overcome in the incarnation: preserved, since the incarnation (and not only the resurrection) is a miracle, which cannot be described adequately outside of the frame of a miracle; overcome, since God in the incarnation reveals both the true God and the true human being, true both in the sense of what the human being was intended to be (the partner of God) and in the sense that the human being is the fallen human being. God's election of the human being in Christ is decisive for a theological conception of reality.[5] The stressing of the ultimate difference be-

---

3. Here quoted from Bruce L. McCormack, *Karl Barth's Critically Realistic Dialectical Theology: Its Genesis and Development 1909-1936* (New York: Oxford University Press, 1995), p. 307; my emphasis.

4. The term "early Barth" covers here the theology of Barth from the second edition of *The Epistle to the Romans* (published in 1922) to the beginning of the *Church Dogmatics* (published in 1932).

5. Barth's conception of reality can be described with the terms "real" — "unreal." The real is love; the unreal is sin. Such a conception of reality differs from, for example, Rein-

tween God and the human being does not in itself necessarily include an ultimate distance between God and the human being.[6] This distinction, as we will see in Part III, becomes evident in the relation between atonement and Christology in *CD* IV.

Christ is the "eye" through which doctrines about both God and humanity not only can but *must* be explored and tested. From this perspective the difference between the early and late Barth can be described as a change from a merely formalistic account of revelation and its presuppositions to a stronger focus on its dogmatic content. The former stresses the presupposition that revelation, which is enacted due to God's free will, is the only way through which any contact between God and the human being can be established. The latter accentuates the Christological content of revelation, which is revealed in history. Thus, it is of fundamental importance to understand the issues raised by the early and late Barth in a dialectical interconnection.[7] If the Christological content is not elaborated on,

hold Niebuhr's conception of reality, which can be described with the terms: "real" — "ideal." The real is sin; the ideal is love. See George Hunsinger, *How to Read Karl Barth: The Shape of His Theology* (New York: Oxford University Press, 1991), pp. 38-39.

6. "He [God] is all this as the Creator, who has created the world as the reality distinct from Himself but willed and affirmed by Him and therefore as His world, as the world which belongs to Him, in relation to which He can be God and act as God in an absolute way and also a relative, in an infinite and also a finite, in an exalted and also a lowly, in an active and also a passive, in a transcendent and also an immanent, and finally, in a divine and also a human — indeed, in relation to which He Himself can become worldly, making His own both its form, the *forma servi*, and also its cause; and all without giving up His own form, the *forma Dei*, and His own glory, *but adopting the form and cause of man into the most perfect communion with His own, accepting solidarity with the world.* God can do this. And no limit is set to His ability to do it by the contradiction of the creature against Him" (*CD* IV/1, p. 187; my emphasis). In the *CD* the German sentence "indem er sich mit der Welt solidarisch macht" is translated with "accepting solidarity with the world." The English translation is here inaccurate, as it could give the false impression that God were forced (or at least reluctantly accepts) being a God in solidarity. And nothing could be more off the point. Barth repeats consistently throughout the *CD* that God shows solidarity with the world due to his own original free will. Due to God's original will there is therefore no schism between *forma Dei* and *forma servi*.

7. Bruce McCormack argues strongly against Hans Urs von Balthasar's thesis about a fundamental methodological shift from a dialectical to an analogical method in Barth's theology. Such a fundamental shift in methodology is, according to McCormack, incompatible with the inner dynamics of Barth's work. The later Barth's use of analogy is dialectical; the early Barth does not exclude analogical thinking. See McCormack, *Karl Barth's*

the early Barth can be misused as a forceful example of an intellectual approach to *theologia negativa,* where the dialectic between the reality of God and the human perception of this reality consists in a dialectic between affirmation and negation.

Similarly, the late Barth can be misinterpreted as a pre-modern thinker, if the conditions under which it is possible to operate with a theology of revelation after Kant are not made clear. The *CD,* with its heavy emphasis on the revelation in Christ, needs to be read in the light of the representation-crisis. The awareness of the limitation that is given within the human being's perception of reality (since the human being has no access to a reality outside of its own perception of it) is the philosophical background for the epistemological structure in both the commentary on *The Epistle to the Romans* and the *CD.* Again: the difference between the early and late Barth expresses a change in the theological accent. With the help of a highly expressionistic language the early Barth stresses the gap between God and the human being. The later Barth emphasizes in his Christology, especially in the teaching of the atonement in *CD* IV, how God, despite this gap, has revealed himself for human beings in the man Jesus from Nazareth.

Barth's theology of revelation not only opposes any kind of natural theology, in which it seems possible for the human being to establish rational arguments for the existence of God, or to deduce the essence of the being of God from the being of being. It also resists any kind of theology of revelation that takes its starting point either in the human being's ability to receive revelation or in the human being's actual experience of redemption (in which the effect of the revealed truth is confused with the truth itself). The human being cannot grasp the being of God in correlation with being in general, but it can instead receive a new understanding of its own being in the light of God's being, as revealed in God's self-revelation in Jesus Christ. God's primacy is solely revealed in God's words and acts *(deus dixit).*[8]

Critically Realistic Dialectical Theology, pp. 1-28, 313-14, 421-23, 437-41; Michael Beintker, *Die Dialektik in der "dialektischen Theologie" Karl Barths. Studien zur Entwicklung der Barthschen Theologie und zur Vorgeschichte der "Kirchlichen Dogmatik"* (München: Chr. Kaiser Verlag, 1987), pp. 245-85.

8. As is well known, Barth distinguishes between three different ways through which the Word of God can be heard as the Word of God: the word as preached, as written, and as revealed. See Karl Barth, *Church Dogmatics* I/1 (Edinburgh: T. & T. Clark, 1975), pp. 88-124; hereafter cited as *CD* I/1.

When the human being hears the Word of God in the form of Scripture or a sermon, when the human being acknowledges the acts of God in the human proclamation of God, it is God himself who makes use of the human words. When people hear the Word of God in the words of, for example, Paul, it is not Paul but God who speaks.[9] God can only be properly understood as an object when God — and not the human being — is seen as the primary subject.

Revelation as God's Free and Eternal Decision

Barth stresses again and again that God remains the one who has chosen to reveal himself for human beings in a human being. Prior to creation God had decided to disclose himself *in* the creation as a *part of* the creation. Still, this does not imply that God has limited himself to an immanent structure of history or that God had to enter history for the purpose of being the true God. The term "necessity" cannot be applied to God's entering into history. Barth opposes any understanding of God that might include the possibility of viewing God as the principle of history.

The reason why Barth so strongly wants to dissociate himself from Hegel is therefore twofold. *First,* the aim is to maintain the absolute and radical freedom of God. God does not need to do anything, but God can, in his mercy, decide (and God has actually decided!) to do something. God

---

9. The dialectic between the human words about God and God's ability to speak through human words is described in various ways: "Recollection of God's past revelation, discovery of the Canon, faith in the promise of the prophetic and apostolic word, or better, the self-imposing of the Bible in virtue of its content, and therefore the existence of real apostolic succession, is also an event, and is to be understood only as an *event. In this event the Bible is God's Word.* That is to say, in this event the human prophetic and apostolic word is a representative of God's Word in the same way as the word of the modern preacher is to be in the event of real proclamation: a human word which has God's commission to us behind it, a human word to which God has given Himself as object, a human word which is recognised and accepted by God as good, a human word in which God's own address to us is an event. The fact that God's own address becomes an event in the human word of the Bible is, however, God's affair and not ours" (*CD* I/1, p. 109; my emphasis); "The Bible is God's Word to the extent that God causes it to be His Word, to the extent that He speaks through it" (*CD* I/1, p. 109); "It does not become God's Word because we accord it faith but in the fact that it becomes revelation to us" (*CD* I/1, p. 110).

can therefore never become a sort of principle for human understanding in general, as one cannot systematize the freedom of God. Such systematization would not be able to grasp the radicality of God's grace. It would not be a free and "expensive" gift, but instead would turn into some kind of cheap grace. The disruptiveness of the radical grace would thereby be disrupted.[10] *Second*, in the *CD* Barth is much more inspired by Hegelian thought-structures than he himself either is able to see or is willing to admit.

An interesting — and alternative approach — to Barth's understanding of the relation between God and the world would be to analyze the way he mixes Hegelian and Kantian strains of thoughts in his dogmatic thinking. An example of the Hegelian input could, for example, be the following description of the relation between the history of God and the history of the world:

> We have already said that in this event [the incarnation] God allows the world and humanity to take part in the history of the *inner* life of His Godhead, in the movement in which from and to all eternity He is Father, Son and Holy Spirit, and therefore the one true God. But this participation of the world in the being of God implies necessarily His participation in the being of the world, and therefore that His being, His history, is *played out* as world-history and therefore under the affliction and peril of all world-history. (*CD* IV/1, p. 215; my emphasis)

But the necessity comes from within God himself, which again means that it is to be assigned to the eternal decision within God himself. Again, the radical free will of God is used as an attempt to avoid any final systematization of the relation between God and the world.

In Barth's theology the being of God is interpreted in continuation of a voluntaristic understanding. With his emphasis on God's self-revelation Barth manages to incorporate elements from modernity (the emphasis on God as an autonomous subject) with the tradition of a theological voluntarism where the will of God is prior and superior to reason. Barth's actualistic understanding of being might very well have its roots in this tradition.

Barth fiercely opposes any attempt to reinvent theology within the

---

10. See George Hunsinger, *Disruptive Grace: Studies in the Theology of Karl Barth* (Grand Rapids: Eerdmans, 2000), pp. 16-17, 276-78.

realm of metaphysics, as God cannot remain the one who seeks to be worshiped by mankind if mankind turns God into a hermeneutical principle through which the ultimate understanding of history can be achieved. Barth wants to keep the personhood of God as the correct metaphor through which God as the wholly other can be grasped in its otherness for the human mind. This metaphor enables Barth to stress the free will of God to its limit (or beyond?). Yahweh, God of Israel, decided of his own free will to be God for human beings. This decision was not necessary, as God would have remained God without a people, a land, or even a world (the creation).[11]

The human being can only fully grasp the content of the grace of God when it understands that the grace of God is rooted in nothing other than the free will of God.[12] In the relation between God and the human being there is only one fundamental modus: the modus of receiving. However, this modus does not as such leave out the demand for the human being's participation. Revelation of God includes the human being's self-involvement within this revelation. I will emphasize this aspect of self-involvement later. Let me simply state here that Barth rejects any non-personalized understanding of either God or the human being.

---

11. See for example *CD* I/1, pp. 139-40.

12. "Only when we are clear about this can we estimate what it means that God has actually, though not necessarily, created a world and us, that His love actually, though not necessarily, applies to us, that His Word has actually, though not necessarily, been spoken to us. The purposiveness we find in proclamation, the Bible and revelation is thus *a free and actual purposiveness by no means essential to God Himself.* We evaluate this purposiveness correctly only if we understand it as the reality of the love of the God *who does not need us* but *who does not will to be without us,* who has directed His regard specifically on us" (*CD* I/1, p. 140; partly my emphasis). The German underlining of the above sentence has not been reproduced in the English translation. The German text says: "Es ist also freie tatsächliche nicht Gott wesensnotwendige Absichtlichkeit, die uns in der Verkündigung, in der Bibel, in der Offenbarung begegnet." See Karl Barth, *Die Kirchliche Dogmatik* I/1 (Zollikon-Zürich: Evangelischer Verlag A.G., 1932), p. 144 (hereafter cited as *KD* I/1). A further quote that should be noted is: "God cannot be forced to give us a part in His divine being. . . . But where God is not bound and man has no claim, even more compelling is the will and plan and promise of God. It goes beyond, or rather it precedes His will and work as Creator. Therefore it has to be distinguished from it, as something prior, which precedes it" (*CD* IV/1, p. 9). The English translation is misleading here, as it translates the word *Verplichtung* (which relates to God's inner being) with "forced to" (which might or could relate to a power outside of God). See also *CD* IV/1, pp. 212-14.

CHAPTER 3

The Bible as the Witness of Revelation

The Bible as the Word of God

According to Barth the construction of an adequate methodology within the various sciences depends on the particular object of each individual science.[1] The object in theology is God, who then again — from the standpoint of a theology of revelation — is revealed to the human being as being the real subject of theology. Thus, knowledge about God can only be conceived as a mediated knowledge — given by God himself in revelation. And where does the human being first and foremost encounter God's self-

---

1. Theology differs from most other sciences by referring to an object, which turns out to be the real subject of its own object matter. Barth claims therefore that theology differs from any other science in at least two ways. *First,* its subject and object are the same (God). *Second,* both the primary subject and object (God) are ontologically different from the secondary subject and object (the human being). Barth gives, in accordance with these presuppositions, the following minimalist account for how theology understands itself as a science: "If theology allows itself to be called, and calls itself, a 'science,' in so doing it declares (1) that like all other so-called sciences it is a human concern with a definite object of knowledge, (2) that like all others it treads a definite and self-consistent path of knowledge, and (3) that like all others it must give an account of this path to itself and to all others who are capable of concern for this object and therefore of treading this path" (*CD* I/1, pp. 7-8). Barth expresses further on in the same chapter that "it [theology] cannot allow itself to be told by them [the other sciences] what this means concretely in its own case. As regards method, it has nothing to learn from them. It does not have to justify itself before them, least of all by submitting to the demands of a concept of science, which accidentally or not claims general validity" (*CD* I/1, p. 8).

revelation? In Scripture! However, this does not imply that the Bible should be read as the direct revelation of God on a word-for-word basis. Instead the Bible is the human witness of God's revelation. So, Scripture is the locus where the witness of Jesus as Christ is witnessed.

Through the claim that the Bible is the Word of God Barth manages to navigate between two characteristic *isms* of our time: relativism (the rejection of any absolute truth) and fundamentalism (a non-historical understanding of truth). The Bible is not divine speech in the sense that it is God's own eternal words to the human being. Such an essentialistic type of fundamentalism would, in its more "modern" versions, reduce any hermeneutic task to the pure act of translation. The precondition for such an essentialistic type of reading is that the eternal truth is revealed once and for all in the written text. It just needs to be translated into modern language to make sense today. Instead, one has to take note of the fact that the Bible from the very beginning is human words about God, limited and conditioned as such. Any other claim would confuse the revelation with the human witness of revelation.

> The Bible is a witness of revelation which is really given and really applies and is really received by us just because it is a written word, and in fact a word written by men like ourselves, which we can read and hear and understand as such. And it is as such that we must read and hear and understand it if this is to happen at all and there is to be any apprehension of revelation.[2]

> It [the Word of God] is there and always there as a sign, as a human and temporal word — and therefore also as a word which is conditioned and limited. It witnesses to God's revelation, but that does not mean that God's revelation is now before us in any kind of divine revealedness. The Bible is not a book of oracles; it is not an instrument of direct impartation. It is *genuine witness*. (*CD* I/2, p. 507; my emphasis)

Yet, this does not mean that the Bible is without authority, that the Bible is just a tale among other tales. The Bible contains an extra surplus due to its reference to the revelation of God. This surplus can only be qualified as a

---

2. Karl Barth, *Church Dogmatics* I/2 (Edinburgh: T. & T. Clark, 1956), pp. 463-64; hereafter cited as *CD* I/2.

claim of faith — but this claim is a claim that is not restricted to the Bible, let alone the realm of theology.

> But when we do take the humanity of the Bible quite seriously, we must also take quite definitely the fact that as a human word it does say something specific, that as a human word *it points away from itself,* that as a word *it points towards a fact, an object.* In this respect, too, it is a genuine human word. What human word is there which does not do the same? (*CD* I/2, p. 464; my emphasis)

God himself establishes the reference between the words of human beings and the Word of God. It is God who uses human words; it is God who enables human beings to hear the Word of God in human words about God.

> If what we hear in Holy Scripture is witness, a human expression of God's revelation, then from what we have already said, what we hear in the witness itself is *more* than witness, what we hear in the human expression is *more* than a human expression. What we hear is revelation, and therefore the very Word of God. (*CD* I/2, p. 473; my emphasis)

This does not in itself imply that God cannot reveal himself outside of Scripture, but it means that the content of the Christ-event, as witnessed to in Scripture, is the criterion for any other claim of revelation. If God could not reveal himself outside of Scripture, the freedom of God would have been reduced. Barth states for example that "God may speak to us through Russian Communism, a flute concerto, a blossoming shrub, or a dead dog. We do well to listen to him if He really does" (*CD* I/1, p. 55). But this does not mean that we as human beings can claim that freedom in and for ourselves: "But, unless we regard ourselves as the prophets and founders of a new Church, we cannot say that we are commissioned to pass on what we have heard as independent proclamation" (*CD* I/1, p. 55). The criterion for any claim of revelation will always be the Christ-event, as it is witnessed in Scripture. It is important here to note the dialectic between God's freedom in revelation and the limitation of the way in which the human being can refer to God's free revelation.[3] From the viewpoint of the human being,

---

3. I agree with Thies Gundlach, who states: "But this radical freedom of God is just radical freedom of God according to Barth, not freedom of the church and its way of

revelation is in a constant need of an ongoing revelation, as it must be revealed as what it is: a revelation.

To state the point as clearly as possible: from the perspective of the human being the only location of the revelation and the only criterion for the content of revelation is the story of God's interaction with the world — as it is witnessed to human beings by the human beings in the Old and the New Testament. God is, however, free to reveal himself when and where he wants to do this. But this must be understood from the perspective of the freedom of God — not from the perspective of the human being's ability to receive a revelation. In the latter case revelation would turn into what critics define as esoteric knowledge. In the thought of Barth all human beings are united in their inherent incapability of receiving revelation. This means that the human being can never possess revelation. Revelation is an ongoing act that is established as an encounter between God and the human being. A theology of revelation does therefore in itself contain an aspect of deconstruction.

Revelation is not a revelation of eternal truths or ideas independent of time, in any kind of Platonic sense, where the phenomenon is just a shadow of the real reality behind the phenomenon (the eternal ideas). Instead, the incarnation is a revelation of God in time, which in itself demands an ongoing interpretation of what the meaning and content of God's reality is. God is therefore not without time or purely above time. God has entered time, and since the time at which he did so the only way to recognize God as true God is through God's self-revelation in time. Not only the witness to the incarnation, but also the incarnation itself is contextual, as to a certain degree it is dependent on the time and culture in which it actually took place. For example, Barth not only assumes that Jesus of Nazareth can only be properly understood in and from his Jewish identity, but also that it is very essential for Christianity itself to realize that it has its origin in a Jewish community.[4]

---

speaking of God. . . . God's freedom to speak when- and wherever God wants to is not freedom for the church to speak of God when and where it wishes to do so. It is only limited freedom to speak of God in accordance with God having spoken in Jesus Christ and with the prospect of God speaking again in and through Jesus Christ." Thies Gundlach, *Selbstbegrenzung Gottes und die Autonomie des Menschen. Karl Barth's Kirchliche Dogmatik als Modernisierungsschritt evangelischer Theologie* (Frankfurt am Main: Peter Lang Verlag, 1992), p. 103 (trans. Michael Waltemathe).

4. Here Barth differs strongly from Schleiermacher's negative understanding of Ju-

To clarify: in the theology of Barth revelation is a hermeneutic key that does not give any direct and unmediated understanding of the eternal truth of God, but — due to its heavy emphasis on the incarnation — it requires instead an ongoing revelation and thereby an ongoing interpretation of the eternal truth of God. This interpretation has to take into account the historical context of the revelation as well as the actual surroundings in which it will now be revealed again (and thereby also interpreted).

As should already be clear, however, Barth is not willing to push the historical point to its ultimate conclusion: that God, due to God's entering into history, should have assigned himself to the limits of history (as they are defined in and by the view of historical criticism). The result would then have been that the historical-critical method would be the only legitimate way through which a scientifically adequate reading of the Bible could be obtained. Barth opts instead for a reading that does not itself subscribe either to historical criticism or to uncritical biblicism, i.e., reading the Bible as the Word of God. The human witness to revelation needs in itself to become a part of the revelation, so that it can be heard as what it is, a witness. Scripture becomes the *Holy* Scripture by being read in the light of its own intention, namely, to bear witness to the self-revelation of God in Jesus Christ.[5]

---

daism as being a pure pre-Christian phenomenon, the only function of which is to serve as the negative prehistory out of which Christianity arises. Judaism is hereby solely described as a negative contrast to Christianity. See Friedrich Schleiermacher, *The Christian Faith,* trans. H. R. Mackintosh (Edinburgh: T. & T. Clark, 1989), pp. 115, 133, 608-11. For an elaborated discussion of Barth's understanding of the relation between Christianity and Judaism see Eberhard Busch, *Unter dem Bogen des einen Bundes: Karl Barth und die Juden, 1933-1945* (Neukirchen-Vluyn: Neukirchener, 1996); Katherine Sonderegger, *That Jesus Christ Was Born a Jew: Karl Barth's "Doctrine of Israel"* (University Park, PA: Pennsylvania State University Press, 1993).

5. "The Bible, then, is not in itself and as such God's past revelation, just as Church proclamation is not in itself and as such the expected future revelation. The Bible, speaking to us and heard by us *as* God's Word, bears witness to *past* revelation" (*CD* I/1, p. 111; my emphasis); "Once again, the Bible is not in itself and as such God's past revelation. As it is God's Word it bears witness to God's past revelation, and it is God's past revelation in the form of attestation" (*CD* I/1, p. 111). The German text expresses the dialectic better than the English translation: "Nochmals: die Bibel ist nicht selbst und an sich Gottes geschehene Offenbarung, sondern indem sie Gottes Wort wird, *bezeugt* sie Gottes geschehene Offenbarung und *ist* sie Gottes geschehene Offenbarung in der Gestalt der Bezeugung" (*KD* I/1, 114; my emphasis).

Nicholas Wolterstorff has in his painstakingly concise and accurate analysis of Barth's use of the Word of God realized that Barth basically only operates with one way of divine speech: revelation. Wolterstorff himself finds this result astonishing, as Barth states in the *CD* that there is a "'threefold form' of the Word of God: the Word of God preached in the Church, the Word of God written in the Scripture, and the Word of God revealed in Jesus Christ."[6] But according to Wolterstorff's analysis the former two are only instruments through which the divine speech can be heard — they are not in themselves divine speech. From an external perspective Scripture and the proclamation of the church are united in bearing witness to the revelation. The aim of both Scripture and the church's proclamation is the same: to be a witness-of and witness-to the revelation. From an internal perspective, a distinction must be made between a primary witness (Scripture) and a secondary witness (the church's proclamation). The contemporary preacher is dependent on the first witness-of and witness-to the revelation. Wolterstorff's claim that Barth, in fact, only operates with one form of divine discourse is correct insofar as Barth very strongly stresses the difference between God's own word (the revelation in Jesus Christ) and human words about God's word. But God can, when and where he wants to, use human words as his own words. It is here that Wolterstorff's critique of Barth really starts. On the formal level Wolterstorff criticizes Barth for defining Scripture and the proclamation of the church as the Word of God, as within Barth's own theological theory it has nothing to do with divine speaking or discourse. It could rather, according to Wolterstorff, be defined as divine persuasion. However, what is really interesting here is the material level of Wolterstorff's critique. The real reason why he is so uneasy with Barth's use of the Word of God is that Barth's perception of the Word of God makes it impossible to establish any direct identity between Scripture and the Word of God. Barth is strictly modern in the sense that throughout his authorship he maintains a sharp distinction between God's Word and human words about God. The result of this, viewed from the perspective of the human being, is that no human being can claim to speak the direct Word of God. If this were the case, the border between the revealer (God) and the receiver of the revelation (the human being) would be transformed into an internal distinction between "medi-

---

6. See Nicholas Wolterstorff, *Divine Discourse: Philosophical Reflections on the Claim That God Speaks* (Cambridge: Cambridge University Press, 1995), p. 63.

ums" and "non-mediums" (a border between the one who has received the revelation and all the others — who have not — would hereby have been established). The revelation would then be turned into a human instrument of power. If a human being actually speaks the Word of God, this is due to the act of God and not the act of the human being. Further, the human being cannot count on the fact that this act will take place (as it is not subject of this act). God is always the subject of his own speech *(deus dixit)*. Barth's position entails, as we know, that God is not even restricted to Scripture.

It seems to me that Wolterstorff — in opposition to Barth — wants to establish a more "secure" connection between Scripture and God's own talk, so that Scripture really can be interpreted as being God's own talk. He therefore opposes the idea that human words cannot really be God's words, except when God makes it in the actual speech act. According to Wolterstorff, divine discourse can take place through human discourse; it is not imperative that it be transformed. This is different from Barth, who states that Scripture can be used of God, so that it becomes the Word of God, but in itself it is fallible human words about God (see for example *CD* I/1, pp. 109-10).[7]

In his use of Scripture in the *CD* Barth demonstrates a high appreciation of Scripture's liturgical function, both at the time of origin and now. That Jesus is Christ is the basis of the self-understanding of the New Testament writers. According to this view, the New Testament can be described as a witness to the proclamation of the first witnesses. It is in this sense that Scripture can be described as the Word of God. Any reading of the Bible must therefore take the Bible's own intention into consideration.

It is from this point of view that Barth's ambivalent acceptance of the historical-critical method should be taken into consideration.[8] Barth criticizes a one-sided use of the historical-critical method, as, from his point of view, this is closer to an intellectual apologetic than a radical exegesis. The problem with the historical-critical method is that it is in danger of reduc-

---

7. For a further insight into this discussion see Wolterstorff, *Divine Discourse*, pp. 63-74.

8. Barth explicitly points out that he acknowledges the historical-critical method as one method among others. What he opposes is a rigid use of it as *the* method. See *CD* I/2, pp. 464 and 494. It should, though, be noted here that Barth, despite his own affirmation of the historical-critical method, very seldom uses it constructively in the exegetical paragraphs of the *CD*.

ing interpretation to a search for historical facts.[9] The Bible is then read solely as a book of historical sources. Thus, the question of truth is equated with the question of historical authenticity (the main question could then for example be an investigation of authentic Jesus words). The emphasis is thereby not so much on the attempt to interpret Scripture as the human witness of God's revelation, as it is on the search for historical facts. The aim of reading could thereby be described as a search for a text behind the text.

In Barth's perspective the Bible is in that sense in danger of becoming an unhistorical historical textbook, which takes into account neither the purpose of the writer(s) nor the actual situation of the reader(s) in the search for the Word of God today.

> Theology at least, even and especially historical theology, which applies itself particularly to the biblical texts, ought to have (let us say it at once) the tact and taste, in face of the linking of form and content in those texts of which it must still be aware, to resist this temptation, to leave the curious question of what is perhaps behind the texts and to turn with all the more attentiveness, accuracy and love to the texts as such. (*CD* I/2, pp. 493-94)

Thus, Barth can be said to anticipate parts of literary criticism's critique of the historical-critical method, which in its search for authentic textual traits neglects the compositional unity of the text. Especially from the *CD* onward Barth emphasizes the narrative structure not only of the Bible but also of the dogmatic attempt to clarify the content of Christianity as it is described in the Bible.[10]

9. See *CD* I/2, pp. 492-94.

10. For example, Hans Frei, David Ford (1948-), and David Kelsey have exploited this theme. See David Ford, *Barth and God's Story: Biblical Narrative and the Theological Method of Karl Barth in the Church Dogmatics* (Frankfurt am Main: Peter Lang Verlag, 1981); David Kelsey, *The Uses of Scripture in Recent Theology* (Philadelphia: Fortress Press, 1975); Hans W. Frei, *Types of Christian Theology*, ed. George Hunsinger and William C. Placher (New Haven: Yale University Press, 1992). Hans Frei is, as far as I know, the first who consistently reads Barth's *CD* from this narrative perspective, whereby he has succeeded in changing the whole ground for the Barth discussion in America. Frei elaborates this theme much more than Barth does, as he takes the methods of literary criticism, as it is worked out and used on its own terms, into account. A good example of Frei's emphasis on the narration can be found in his analysis of the resurrection in his Jesus book. See

A Two-Way Reading of Scripture

The next question that arises is: Can the theological quest for the meaning of the text (an interpretation that presupposes the Bible is the witness of the Word of God) be reduced to a matter of retelling the same story, or does the interpretation need to take the historical gap between the now (the situation of the actual reader) and the then (the incarnation as it is witnessed in the text) into account in a more complex way? My concern here is how Barth's understanding of the Bible as the Word of God determines his hermeneutics. (This includes a critique of a pure narrative interpretation of Barth's exegesis.) My considerations can be expressed in the following seven points:

(1) The only place where the human being can refer to a witness of the revelation of God is Scripture (the sacred text of the church).

(2) Scripture is understood as a document that refers to something other than itself, namely God.

(3) The way in which Scripture gives witness to the witnesses of God is highly influenced by its concrete historical and cultural settings.

(4) The way the reader reads the text is highly influenced by the reader's embeddedness in history and culture.

(5) The meaning of the text is therefore not given once and for all.

(6) The meaning of the text can only be found in the dialectic between text and reader, reader and text.

(7) The search for the meaning of the text is a search for the actual *kerygma*, which can only arise in an awareness of the dialectic between the reader, the reader's actual context, the text read within this context, and the original context of the text (as far as this context can be reconstructed).

The question that I want to raise here is whether Barth's use of revelation as the hermeneutic key takes these concerns into consideration, and if so, how? It is obvious that Barth's way of interpreting Scripture without reservations entails the first three points, but at first glance it is not so obvious

---

Hans W. Frei, *The Identity of Jesus Christ: The Hermeneutical Bases of Dogmatic Theology* (Philadelphia: Fortress Press, 1975). See also David E. Demson, *Hans Frei and Karl Barth: Different Ways of Reading Scripture* (Grand Rapids: Eerdmans, 1997).

that he would accept the other statements as valid considerations for a theological hermeneutics.

Certainly Barth cannot be read as a traditional biblicist, since he stresses that the Bible cannot be claimed to be more than a human witness to the Word of God. The Bible can therefore never be interpreted as God's literally spoken word. The Bible is on the one hand not identical with revelation itself, as it is only a human witness of revelation. On the other hand the Bible is united with revelation insofar as revelation is the object and content of the human witness.

> If we want to think of the Bible as a real witness of divine revelation, then clearly we have to keep two things constantly before us and give them their due weight: the *limitation* and the positive element, its *distinctiveness* from revelation, in so far as it is only a human word about it, and its unity with it, in so far as revelation is the *basis, object* and *content* of this word. (*CD* I/2, p. 463; my emphasis)

From internal theological reasons a biblicistic approach to the reading of Scripture is to be judged as false, as it simply confuses the incarnation of God in Christ with the Bible's witness to the incarnation.

> Why and in what respect does the biblical witness have authority? Because and in the fact that he claims no authority for himself, that his witness amounts to letting that other itself be its own authority. We thus do the Bible poor and unwelcome honour if we equate it directly with this other, with revelation itself. (*CD* I/1, p. 112)[11]

Any hermeneutics that does not take the relativity (which is not to be equated with relativism) of the Bible into account at its very center is at best reducing interpretation to a question of how it is possible to communicate eternal truth (as it is given in the Bible) to the "modern" reader. Such a reduced perspective on the aim and content of a theological herme-

---

11. The German version expresses the dialectic between the witness and the otherness of what is witnessed better: "Warum und worin hat der biblische Zeuge Autorität? Eben darum und darin, daß er gar keine Autorität für sich selbst in Anspruch nimmt, daß sein Bezeugen darin aufgeht, jenes Andere selbst und durch sich selbst Autorität sein zu lassen. Man tut also der Bibel eine schlechte und ihr selbst unwillkommene Ehre an, wenn man sie mit diesem Anderen, mit der Offenbarung selbst direkt identifiziert" (*KD* I/1, p. 115). See also *CD* I/2, p. 513.

neutics will inevitably find itself being occupied with an attempt to reinforce the tradition, and can be defined as a one-way hermeneutics. It is characteristic for a one-way hermeneutics that the meaning of the Bible is sought solely within the universe of the Bible itself, as there is no questioning of the biblical universe from the reality outside of the Bible.[12]

I find that in his perception of the Bible as a written witness of the revelation Barth leaves space for a two-way reading of the text, in which the interpretation of the gospel in the Bible is determined not only by the Bible itself but also by the actual situation in which the reader tries to understand the Bible as the living Word of God. Barth states, for example, that "Exegesis is always a combination of taking and giving, of reading out and reading in" (*CD* I/1, p. 106). The Bible cannot be understood as the Word of God without an interpretation that takes the relativity of the Bible itself into account. This relativity is not solely given by the acceptance of the Bible as being no more (and in the case of Barth's hermeneutics surely no less) than the human witness of God's interaction with the world, but also by the acceptance of the importance of the reader's own situation and role in the hermeneutic process. This implies not only that any interpretation of the Bible must accept itself as what it truly is — an interpretation, but also that the Bible only can be understood on its own premises when it is read from a perspective of faith, which is not the same as to abandon the limitedness and contextual embeddedness of the human witness of the revelation (then and now).

The biblical text is therefore given a certain authority in the theology of Barth, as it differs from all other texts by being the Word of God (as it is witnessed in the human witness). This authority is not, however, based on the text itself, nor is it based on the early church's decision to let this particular collection of books be its sacred texts.[13] Such an understanding

12. The narrative reading can therefore also — from this point of view — be evaluated as a one-way hermeneutics, well knowing that it itself would not operate with any kind of an external, non-narrated truth.

13. Barth does not deny the historical fortuitousness character of the actual collection of the canon. He expresses it for example in the following lapidary way: "Sie ist Kanon, weil sie sich als solcher der Kirche imponiert hat und immer wieder imponiert" (*KD* I/1, p. 110). The English translation blurs the point, saying: "It is the Canon because it imposed itself upon the Church as such, and continually does so" (*CD* I/1, p. 107). For a further exploration of this argument see Gundlach, *Selbstbegrenzung Gottes und die Autonomie des Menschen*, p. 106.

would reverse the relation between the church and Scripture, as the church then would have acquired authority over its own scripture, since the authority of Scripture subsequently would be grounded in the decision of the church. Instead, the Bible is the Word of God due to the agency of God.

> The Bible is God's Word to the extent that God causes it to be His Word, to the extent that He speaks through it. In this second equation no less than the first (namely, that Church proclamation is God's Word) we cannot abstract from the free action of God in and by which He causes it to be true to us and for us here and now that the biblical word of man is His own Word. The statement that the Bible is God's Word is *a confession of faith*, a statement of the faith *which hears God Himself speak through the biblical word of man*. (*CD* I/1, pp. 109-10; my emphasis)

From one perspective the Bible is a text like any other text, for which reason no specific "tools" can be given for how to read it. But from another perspective the Bible is perceived as a special book, due to what it bears witness to, which implies certain hermeneutic considerations. To obtain the full potential of these two perspectives, they need to be seen as dialectically related. (The focus of both these points is retained through the inner tensions between them.)

The two-way dialectic, which is entailed in Barth's understanding of revelation as a hermeneutic key for Christian theology, has often been neglected by both critics and followers, as both parties have tended to understand his reading solely from an intra-textual perspective. The resulting relativity has then been limited to a question of the adequacy of the translation of the original message. A theology of revelation, as it is developed in the perspective of Barth, does not give any credit to a static theology where all answers are given independent of and prior to the actual interpretation of what theology, based on the written witness in the Bible, entails. The Bible is not only able to enlighten the reader (and the world the reader lives in), but the reader (and the world that the reader participates in) is also — through the process of interpretation — able to enlighten the Bible.

It is common to stress Barth's opposition to a general hermeneutics — especially his sharp critique of Bultmann's use of Heidegger's *Vorver-*

ständnis. This critique has, so to speak, reduplicated itself, in that it has often been used as the negative *Vorverständnis* through which Barthians have either rejected engaging in serious hermeneutic considerations or non-Barthians have rejected the plausibility of Barth's theological project as such, due to its lack of a general hermeneutics. The typical point of view that Barth's theology views hermeneutics unfavorably has often been described with the help of some detached phrases from the "Barthian" vocabulary.

To really understand the questions that are raised by the text for the human being, however, it is necessary to understand the context of the reader. The interconnection between the reader of the text and the text itself is therefore not determined only by the text or by the reader. The historical implications of the text can therefore be summarized in the following two sentences. *First,* the questions raised by the text cannot be fully explored without an understanding of the actual context in which the text — at its time of composition — raises these. *Second,* the full potential of the text can only be grasped when it is interpreted in the actual world in which the reader is a participant. The context in which the Bible is read is thereby seen as a determining factor in the attempt to interpret the Bible as the living Word of God.

This implies that Barth operates with some kind of theological *Vorverständnis* despite his strongly and often-repeated aversion to Bultmann and Heidegger — a *Vorverständnis* that in his case is expressed in the consistent claim that the Bible is the Word of God then and now.[14] The Word of God cannot be read straight off the wall, but demands an ongoing interpretation — an interpretation that in the case of Barth consists in a reading established by a given center and a periphery, a center defined in Barth's hermeneutics as the saving act of God in Christ.[15] By the help of this center the reader tries to get some kind of univocal message out of the plurality of voices of which the Bible consists. Barth claims, furthermore, that this center is not given by him, but by the text itself, as he reads the

14. A *Vorverständnis* that in content is radically different from Heidegger's and Bultmann's use of the term, as in their work it can be described with the help of a phenomenological analysis of the human being's being. Bultmann uses this as a specific theological tool, as a description of the being's being "only" describes how the human being is, not how it should or could be.

15. Barth shares here a common feature with Luther, whose hermeneutic key was the question: "Does the text aim at Christ?"

text in accordance with its own intention: to be a witness of God's incarnation and saving act in Christ.

The radicality of Barth's theological hermeneutics can be seen in the way in which he is not willing to subordinate his way of doing theology to any general hermeneutics. He wants instead to give all the various methods free rein, which in his logic means that they are free as long as they share the basic view that the Bible is the Word of God, and that the common purpose for all theology can be found in its ongoing attempt to clarify the actual content of the Word of God: the *deus dixit,* a disclosure that, when it happens, happens through God's own revelation of the revelation. But if this should not be restricted to a category of divine persuasion, the historicity of not only human beings but also God must be taken into account. At the level of hermeneutics this implies that not only does the Bible enlighten the reader, but the reader might also enlighten the Bible. Said as simply as possible: in writing a sermon one should read not only the Bible but also the daily newspaper.

CHAPTER 4

Objective and Subjective Aspects of Revelation

Revelation does not have to do with knowledge alone, even though revelation contains a fundamental knowledge of the divine and the human being that the human being can only receive from outside of him- or herself. Revelation encounters the whole human being (including, for example, knowing, feeling, and acting). Revelation cannot be reduced to either abstract knowledge (which is totally independent of the individual human being) or to the individual's experience of revelation. On the one hand the revealed reality is a reality that encompasses each and every one whether or not they understand themselves in the light of the revelation or not. But, on the other hand, revelation must not be interpreted as a purely objective reality that does not have any fundamental consequence for the individual subject. A dichotomy between revelation perceived as an objective or subjective reality is simply false, according to Barth.

In this chapter I will focus on the subjective aspect of revelation in the *CD*. The reason for this is not only that it has been more or less neglected in interpretations of the *CD*, but also because I find it a suitable way to establish the ground for dialogue between Barth's theology of revelation and other approaches, both contemporary with Barth and later.

There is no doubt that Barth starts with the objective reality (revelation as a divine reality), as it is God who is the primary subject in the relation between God and the human being. But the objective perception of reality cannot rule out the subjective aspect. Barth emphasizes strongly that revelation has only been perceived as what it is (the revelation) when it breaks through the human being's self-understanding. This breakthrough can also be described as the demand for participation in the on-going Christ-event. In the language of the early Barth, this means that the gospel contains a "claim" on each individual human existence. In the ter-minology of the late Barth it is better described as the relation between *teilhaben* and *teilnehmen*. The human being receives a *telos* from outside of itself. The human being is called to be the partner of God, which means that the human being is called to take an active part in the kingdom of God.[1]

The objective and the subjective understanding of revelation must not be seen as two exclusive alternatives. They are, instead, as I am about to demonstrate, to be viewed as two moments in one and the same movement.

The Objective Aspects of Revelation

Revelation as Divine Reality

Revelation escapes any final and fully exhaustive definition, as such a defi-nition would destroy what it tries to describe: the mystery of God. The hu-man being will never be able to fully grasp the content of God. Even in reve-lation God remains the wholly other, as it is God himself who is the subject of the human being's knowledge of God.[2] Thus revelation cannot overcome the dialectic between God's veiling and unveiling.[3] Revelation is a divine re-

---

1. Wolf Krötke emphasizes this active aspect of God's election of the human being as his covenant-partner. See Wolf Krötke, "Gott und Mensch als Partner. Zur Bedeutung einer zentralen Kategorie in Karl Barth's Kirchlicher Dogmatik," *Zeitschrift für Theologie und Kirche* 6 (1986): 166-70.

2. God maintains an excess in his revelation. God is never fully revealed (in the sense of being fully accessible to the human being's reason), as he remains a free subject. See Dieter Schellong, "Barth Lesen," in *Einwürfe 3. Karl Barth: Der Störenfried?* ed. Friedrich-Wilhelm Marquardt, Dieter Schellong, and Michael Weinrich (München: Chr. Kaiser Verlag, 1986), pp. 42-43. Bent Flemming Nielsen notes that God does not lose his autono-mous subject — not even when he objectifies himself in the revelation. Bent Flemming Nielsen's point is that it is the human being — and not God — who is *redefined* [*neu bestimmt*] in the self-revelation. See Bent Flemming Nielsen, *Die Rationalität der Offenbarungstheologie. Die Struktur des Theologieverständnisses von Karl Barth* (Aarhus: Aarhus University Press, 1988), pp. 208-10.

3. Barth stresses this dialectic between God's veiling and unveiling throughout his entire authorship. For a description of the dialectic, as it is enfolded in the earlier writ-

ality, not a human possibility. God establishes the reality that is disclosed within and through revelation. This implies that the human being's possibility of hearing revelation is included in revelation itself.[4] Consequently, revelation cannot be described and analyzed adequately within the realm of perception-analysis. In the following I intend to demonstrate how revelation in Barth's theology is interconnected with creation, election, and atonement. They all are united by their inherent reference to the will of God. This reference can only be established in and through revelation.

Revelation is not a pure, formal structure serving to describe the absolute distance between God and the human being. The primary function of revelation is not to disclose what the human being *cannot* say about God. In the *CD* (as in *The Epistle to the Romans*) God remains the wholly other, but here it becomes clear that the wholly other is defined positively (in terms of its own independent content) and not negatively (in terms of what it is not). The latter approach is in itself an inconsistent way to avoid an anthropomorphically structured theology, as it makes itself fully dependent on what it negates. Revelation is, in other words, not primarily a way through which the absence of God is outlined. On the contrary its primary aim is to describe the presence of God as it is disclosed in God's self-revelation in Christ.

Revelation is concrete disclosure of God's own self as a self, which, due to the will of God, exists in relation to the human being. A description of

---

ings, see Bruce McCormack, *Karl Barth's Critically Realistic Dialectical Theology: Its Genesis and Development 1909-1936* (Oxford: Oxford University Press, 1995), pp. 17-18, 248-49, 327-28, 352-53, 423-24. I find that the anthropocentric correlate to the dialectic between God's veiling and unveiling (the theocentric precondition) is to be found in the human being's inability to talk adequately about revelation. Revelation is therefore in constant need of being revealed to the human being. This means from the anthropocentric perspective that the human being's attempt to understand the content of revelation never can escape the general ambiguity under which any human experience takes place (I will explore this point later in this chapter).

4. Barth's accentuation of God as the real and original subject in revelation correlates with his emphasis on the Reformation's stressing of salvation by grace alone, which at one and the same time is a mystery (how could it happen?) and a miracle (it did happen!). For Barth not only salvation (objective soteriology) but also the knowledge of salvation (subjective soteriology) is happening by grace through faith alone. For a further elaboration of the connection between revelation, the free will of God, and justification by grace alone see Thies Gundlach, *Selbstbegrenzung Gottes und die Autonomie des Menschen. Karl Barth's Kirchliche Dogmatik als Modernisierungsschritt evangelischer Theologie* (Frankfurt am Main: Peter Lang Verlag, 1992), pp. 111-16.

God's own self must therefore be a description that not only includes a description of the self's internal self-relation (the self's relation to itself — in the case of God: the immanent Trinity) but also the self's external relation to a self differentiated from itself (in the case of God: the economic Trinity).[5] The revelation in Jesus Christ discloses an inner connection between God's own inner being and God's being for us. This connection between God's own inner being and God's being for us is established by the sovereign will of God.[6] God wants to be the God who is not only for us but also with us and among us. The will of God is the constitutive element in the relation between God and the human being — a relation that is founded in God's self-determination prior to both creation and atonement. The relation between creation and atonement is not to be viewed chronologically, according to the order of appearance. It should rather be analyzed from the perspective of the eternal will of God.

> It [the will and plan and promise of God] goes beyond, or rather it precedes His will and work as Creator. Therefore it has to be distinguished from it, as something prior, which precedes it. The ordaining of salvation for man and of man for salvation is *the original and basic will of God, the ground and purpose of His will as Creator.* . . . A further point which we must now make in describing the event indicated by the "God with us" is this. The "God with us" has *nothing to do with chance.* As a redemptive happening it means the revelation and confirmation of the most primitive relationship between God and man, that which was freely determined in eternity by God Himself before there was any created being. (*CD* IV/1, pp. 9-10; my emphasis)

5. Other theologians, for example Dietrich Bonhoeffer, Jürgen Moltmann, and Eberhard Jüngel, stress this point even more strongly than Barth, as they claim that the economic and the immanent Trinity must be identical.

6. Already in 1929, Dietrich Bonhoeffer criticized the early Barth for creating a schism between God's free will and God's self-established relation to the human being. Bonhoeffer claimed that the human being as a result always might fear that God will withdraw himself from the world in anger and disappointment. See Dietrich Bonhoeffer, *Act and Being: Transcendental Philosophy and Ontology in Systematic Theology,* ed. Hans-Richard Reuter and Wayne Whitson Floyd (Minneapolis: Fortress Press, 1996), pp. 90-91. See also Michael Beintker, "Kontingenz und Gegenständlichkeit. Zu Bonhoeffers Barth-Kritik in 'Akt und Sein,'" in *Die Aktualität der Theologie Dietrich Bonhoeffers,* ed. Norbert Müller (Halle: Martin-Luther-Universität Halle-Wittenberg, 1985), pp. 29-54.

Barth stresses repeatedly that the atonement is a primary expression of the will of God and not a secondary reaction to what turns out to be a "lack" in the creation. If the latter were the case, God's saving act in Christ would not be a manifestation of God's own radical free will, but would instead be an expression of a reaction imposed on God by circumstances (a lack in the creation). Thus, the creation is not logically prior to the atonement in the thought of Barth, as they both refer to the original will of God before creation.

Revelation and Self-Limitation

Creation and atonement are not only united in the sense that they both must be interpreted as an expression of the free will of God. God's own will to self-limitation is also inherent in both the creation and the atonement. This self-limitation is expressed most clearly in the election of Jesus Christ. Jesus Christ is at one and the same time the electing God and the elected human being.[7] A perception of God that is in conflict with God's own self-revelation (and self-limitation) in Jesus Christ is therefore not a picture of the Christian God. It is instead a man-made idol. Or to phrase it in other terms: *deus absconditus* cannot be understood apart from *deus revelatus*, which in the theology of Barth is identical with *deus incarnatus*.[8]

7. See also Chapters 5, 7, and 8; Bruce L. McCormack, "Grace and Being: The Role of God's Gracious Election in Karl Barth's Theological Ontology," in *The Cambridge Companion to Karl Barth*, ed. John Webster (Cambridge: Cambridge University Press, 2000), pp. 92-110; Walter Kreck, *Grundentscheidungen in Karl Barths Dogmatik. Zur Diskussion seines Verständnisses von Offenbarung und Erwählung* (Neukirchen-Vluyn: Neukirchener Verlag, 1978), pp. 193-201.

8. I am here following Gundlach's description of election as self-limitation; see Gundlach, *Selbstbegrenzung Gottes und die Autonomie des Menschen*, pp. 231-63. Gundlach concludes that Barth by the *rejection* of a hidden God, who is potentially radically different from the revealed God in Jesus Christ, has characterized God in a way that adapts to the rationalism of the Enlightenment. Gundlach finds that Barth hereby can be read in continuation of liberal theology, a point that Hans Urs von Balthasar agrees with — only with the difference that he, unlike Gundlach, sees this as a major problem within Barth's perception of the atonement (and the picture of God that is given within this teaching of the atonement). Barth, according to Balthasar, turns "the 'merciful God of the bible into the innocuous father' of Harnack." See Gundlach, *Selbstbegrenzung Gottes und die Autonomie des Menschen*, p. 239, and Hans Urs von Balthasar, *The Theology of Karl Barth*

The self-limitation in election implies that God can only be known through the witness of the life, death, and resurrection of Jesus Christ. A "God in general" does not exist.[9] This implies that the God-predicates, such as for example absoluteness, omnipotence, and sovereignty, have to be read in the light of this witness. This insight is expressed, for example, in the following two passages:

> the true God is the One whose freedom and love have nothing to do with abstract absoluteness or naked sovereignty, but who in His love and freedom has determined and limited himself to be God in particular and not in general, and only as such to be omnipotent and sovereign and the possessor of all other perfections. (*CD* II/2, p. 49)

> In a free act of determination God has ordained concerning Himself; He has determined Himself. Without any obligation, God has put Himself under an obligation to man, willing that that should be so which according to Jn. I$^{1-2}$ actually is so. It is grace that it is so, and it is grace that God willed it to be so. (*CD* II/2, p. 101)

A divine reality is established in the incarnation that reveals the inner connection between the will and acts of God. Revelation of the revelation (the subjective dimension of revelation) is not identical with the revelation (the objective dimension of revelation), but it lives out of the inherent reference to the revelation as a divine reality.[10]

(New York: Anchor Books, 1972), p. 186. See also Volker Stümke, "Eschatologische Differenz in Gott? Zum Verhältnis von Barmherzigkeit und Gerechtigkeit Gottes bei Karl Barth und Friedrich-Wilhelm Marquardt," in *Wendung nach Jerusalem. Friedrich-Wilhelm Marquardts Theologie im Gespräch*, ed. Hanna Lehming, Joachim Liß-Walther, Matthias Loerbroks, and Rien van der Vegt (München: Chr. Kaiser Gütersloher Verlagshaus, 1999), pp. 373-74.

9. See for example Karl Barth, *Church Dogmatics* II/2 (Edinburgh: T. & T. Clark, 1957), p. 45: "But we must also assert that we do not exhaustively define or describe God, when we identify Him with irresistible omnipotence. Indeed, if we make this identification *in abstracto*, we do not define or describe God at all. Irresistible omnipotence cannot be made the beginning and end of the being of God." References to this book hereafter cited as *CD* II/2.

10. Bruce McCormack claims that Barth's theology of revelation is a critically realistic dialectical thinking, where revelation can be grasped adequately only if it includes an external reference to a reality outside a revelation of the revelation. See McCormack, *Karl Barth's Critically Realistic Dialectical Theology*, pp. 67, 129-30, 464-67.

The acts of God are different from any human acts due to the fact that there is no valid distinction between God's intention in an act and the actual consequences of the very same act. Thus it is not possible to maintain a distinction between God's wish to save human beings and God's actual saving act in Christ. This does not, however, establish any kind of monistic identity between creation and salvation, where salvation is identical with or an irreducible part of creation. Neither does it create a dualistic schism between creation and salvation. Salvation and creation are instead united in the will of God, which the human being only has access to through revelation.

It is therefore only possible to reconstruct the relation between God the Creator and God the Redeemer through God's own self-revealing and saving act in Christ. The creation can therefore, despite its chronological preference, not be taken as the starting point for a theological attempt to describe either God or the creation. The interaction between God the Creator and creation as created by God can therefore only be understood from a Christological point of view. But, this does not lead to Christo-monism. The strong accentuation of the connection established between God the Redeemer and God the Creator in God's own free will, prior to the atonement as well as the creation, is an argument against such a charge of Christo-monism.

In conclusion: in the passage above we have seen that revelation takes place as a divinely established reality. The precondition for the human being's understanding of revelation can therefore not be grounded in the human being's ability to receive it. To acknowledge the revelation in Jesus Christ as the theological starting point involves an acknowledgment of not only God's supremacy but also God's secrecy — in short, the dialectic between God's veiling and unveiling. This secrecy is far from mysticism, as the content is given in and with revelation. The theology of revelation enables the human being to speak rationally about the irrational, without letting the irrational become rational. Further, we have seen how both the creation and the atonement are rooted in the eternal will of God, so that the chronological order between the two is displaced by an order determined by content. The being of God for us and the being of God in and for himself is thus strictly connected. The latter serves as the logical precondition for the former, which is included both in the act of creation and in the act of atonement.

The Subjective Aspect of Revelation

Barth distinguishes sharply between the experience and the object that is experienced in the experience. From a theological perspective (where the object experienced is God) this implies that a sharp distinction must be made not only between the revealer (God, who reveals himself in revelation) and revelation (where God is revealed as God for human beings), but also between the revelation and the human perception of it. But this is not the same as to say that experience as such is dismissed, as a legitimate theological category. Rather, the question is which status the human experience of revelation should have.

Here the difference between a theology of revelation and a theology of creation becomes clear, as the former gives experience a derived status, whereas the latter gives it a more fundamental status. In the theology of creation the experience of God is viewed as the most fundamental experience of all. It is not only prior to but also deeper than all other experiences. The human being is from this point of view seen as a *homo religiosus,* where the religious experience — and thus also the experience of God — deals with the fundamental questions in life. Thus human talk about God must have its starting point in the human experience of God (a line of theology often combined with a critique of Kant's epistemology).

Barth does not share this belief in the possibility of a pure human experience (prior to reason) that conquers the gap between the object and the subject, and cannot therefore accept that the human experience of God can be the platform for human God-talk. This said, Barth does not neglect the human experience of God, as long as its precondition is that the experience happens due to the agency of God.[11] In fact the revelation must have an actual impact on the individual human being. If not, the revelation has not been revealed as such. The question that follows is, then, how does Barth give language to this impact — both philosophical and theological?

11. Cf. Trevor Hart, who states: "Christian faith and speech are essentially response and not essentially source. God produces faith, and not vice versa. It is this concern which lies behind Barth's relentless appeal to the category of revelation and his particular way of interpreting what is involved in revelation." This does not in itself exclude that the human being's experience of revelation can be granted a theological validity. It relocates "only" the place and the role of that experience, as it belongs within the realm of response and not within the realm of source. See Trevor Hart, *Regarding Karl Barth: Toward a Reading of His Theology* (Downers Grove, IL: InterVarsity Press, 1999), pp. 8-9.

The Eschatological Reference

The question concerning the theological status of revelation can neither be resolved from an analysis of the experience of revelation (due to the ambiguity contained within it), nor from a description of the general criteria that enable the human being to experience revelation. According to Barth the latter approach fails by seeking to understand revelation from the recipient's point of view.[12] The human being's ability to hear would then determine the content of what potentially could be said (and heard). Such a focus on the human being's precondition for hearing the revelation will, again according to Barth, dismiss the central point of the Reformers: justification by faith alone.[13] If the human being is justified solely by the grace of God, it makes no sense to determine any general precondition for the human being that would enable it in one way or the other to receive justification (even if it may still be claimed to be enacted by grace alone). Following Barth's line of thought, the effect of such a search would, willy-nilly, undermine the very point that salvation of the human being is embedded in God's own sovereign will and act (the election of the human being in Christ).

Another reason why Barth is skeptical toward an investigation of the human being's ability to hear the Word of God is that the human being is a fallen being.[14] The distinction between *status integritatis* and *status corruptionis* goes beyond the philosophical distinction between God as infinite and unlimited and the human being as finite and limited. Due to the fallenness of the human being only God can make himself known for the human being.

> The saying *finitum non capax infiniti* cannot really prove what has to be proved at this point. If the real experience of the man addressed by God's Word is against this saying, then the saying must go, as every philosophical statement in theology that is in contradiction with this experience must go. As a philosophical saying it

---

12. See for example *CD* I/1, p. 29.

13. I find, however, that Barth hereby confuses questions of hermeneutics with questions of soteriology — which is the theological reasoning behind his quite rigid and unpleasant critique of Emil Brunner in the article "Nein! Antwort an Emil Brunner" from 1934. For a further elaboration of the relation between Barth and Brunner see Chapter 6.

14. See *CD* I/1, p. 131.

does not interest us in the slightest. We do not say *finitum* but *homo peccator non capax,* and we do not continue *infiniti* but *verbi Domini.* The real experience of the man addressed by God's Word is the very thing that decides and proves that what makes it possible lies beyond itself. (*CD* I/1, pp. 220-21)

For both soteriological and harmatological reasons Barth refuses Brunner's emphasis on the necessity of an *Anknüpfungspunkt.*[15] Thus, the ongoing revelation of the revelation cannot be dependent on any general capacity in the human being — let it be created by God or not.[16] When the human being hears the Word of God, it is due to a miracle enacted by God.[17] Hence, the essence of the revelation is not to be found in the human being's perception of revelation (as this perception is as ambivalent as any other human perceptions), but in the inherent reference to the subject behind revelation in revelation.

In revelation the human being is encountered by an eschatological reality; something really new has happened. Revelation cannot be reduced to a better understanding of what is already immanent in the structure of the being itself. Consequently, revelation cannot be adequately described as a mode of being that, one way or another, actualizes what is already there (immanent in the human being's being). From this perspective the new being would be nothing more than a potentialization of the being itself. Such an understanding of the being's being will unavoidably have death (the finality of being) as its own final limit. The new being would in that case be understood in terms of a human reconciliation with death as the unavoidable end of life (a reconciliation that enables the human being to see death as a gift). The power of death would then not really have been broken. Resurrection would then have been nothing more than a metaphor for an "internal" overcoming of death (which is given within the limits of the being itself). Heidegger's definition of *Dasein* as a *Sein zum Tode* comes to mind here.[18]

---

15. See *CD* I/1, pp. 238-40.

16. See *CD* I/1, pp. 236-37.

17. See *CD* I/1, p. 241.

18. Bonhoeffer has stated a similar point of critique — see for example Dietrich Bonhoeffer, "Antrittsvorlesung: Die Frage nach dem Menschen in der gegenwärtigen Philosophie und Theologie," in *Barcelona, Berlin, Amerika 1928-1931,* ed. Reinhart Staats, Hans Christoph von Hase, Holger Roggelin, and Maathias Wünsche (München: Chr. Kaiser Verlag, 1991), pp. 363-64; *Act and Being,* pp. 59-76.

An understanding of revelation that does not take its origin in the free will of God will not be capable of describing the actual power and impact of revelation. The consequence would be that the condition for an actual event (revelation rooted in the will of God), the actual event (revelation), and the actual experience of the event (the revelation revealed as revelation to the recipient of revelation) are confused. Instead, the adequate modus through which the human being's experience of revelation can be theologically described, without making such a confusion of its cause and consequence, is acknowledgment.

I have until now focused on the limits of the experience as a theological category. But before I turn to a more positive elaboration of the experience as a theological category within Barth's theology (which will be established through an analysis of Barth's use of the term "acknowledgment"), I will first investigate the already-mentioned ambiguity, which is an inevitable part of the human being's perception of revelation.

The Ambiguity of the Experience of Revelation

The human being's use of and references to revelation must always be both open-ended and self-critical.[19] The human being can never own or possess the final and ultimate truth, as the human being's experience of revelation is as ambiguous as any other human experience.

> In §5 we spoke of the secularity of the Word of God, i.e., of the fact that it comes to us in a form which also means its *concealment*. Experience of God's Word, then, must also consist in the fact that we receive it in this form and this concealment, in this *twofold indirectness*. Our very acceptance of the Word, which will be especially important later, will participate in this twofold indirectness. It, too, will have a *secular* form, the form of all kinds of human acts, and this form will be its concealment, its ambivalence. Apart from this ambivalence, which is deeply rooted in the very nature of the mat-

---

19. Dieter Schellong emphasizes the process character of theological thinking. Barth's emphasis on revelation is not to be equated with a final human knowledge of God. In fact Barth continually deconstructs his own positions, so that the reader is set free to participate in this process. Barth's theology is not a system in the sense that it attempts to give any final methods or answers. See for example Schellong, *Barth Lesen*, pp. 39-46.

ter, there is no experience of God's Word. It will always consist also
in respect for, and acknowledgment of, the *mystery* of this Word.
(*CD* I/1, p. 207; my emphasis)

Thus revelation cannot be used as an argument for any kind of religious
fanaticism. On the contrary, it is a protection against it. In other words, the
emphasis on revelation functions as a protection against a literal reading
of the Bible, which is one of the necessary preconditions for a fundamen-
talist reading.

In Chapter 3 I have argued that Barth operates with a two-way type of
reading. He is hereby able to combine a narrative understanding of the text
with a more hermeneutical type of reading, where it is the interaction between the universe of the reader and the text that is in focus (the text is
here talking *into* a universe, not creating one). The latter point is rooted in
the theological claim that the text can only remain to be a witness of God's
self-revelation if it is read in relation to the "daily" situation of the reader.
This aspect of Barth's reading strategy should be seen in relation to his emphasis on the need for an ongoing revelation of revelation. If this
actualistic element is ignored, revelation will inevitably turn into a kind of
esoteric language — or to phrase it as clearly as possible: to "ecclesiastical
rigmarole."

However, from the perspective of Barth, a general hermeneutics cannot be fully exhaustive because only God can reveal revelation as revelation.[20] If one really does hear the Word of God in the words about God,
God himself is the informer.

20. Barth expresses this point in his own subtle way when he rejects a specific kind of
biblical hermeneutics. But he uses this rejection to state that the general rule for hermeneutics must be found in the Bible interpreted as the witness to revelation. One must read
a text according to its own intention. And, as regards the Bible, this intention — or plot
— can first be truly perceived when it is revealed to the human being, as what it is: a revelation. "There is no such thing as a special biblical hermeneutics. But we have to learn that
hermeneutics which is alone and generally valid by means of the Bible as the witness of
revelation. We therefore arrive at the suggested rule, not from a general anthropology, but
from the Bible, and obviously, as the rule which is alone and generally valid, we must apply it first to the Bible" (*CD* I/2, p. 466). The German text is more precise here: "Es gibt
keine besondere biblische Hermeneutik. Aber gerade die allgemein und allein gültige
Hermeneutik müßte an Hand der Bibel als Offenbarungszeugnis gelernt werden. Wir
kommen also mit der angegebenen Regel nicht von einer allgemeinen Anthropologie,
sondern von der Bibel her, um sie als die allgemein und allein gültige Regel nun selbst-

God and His Word are not given to us in the same way as natural and historical entities. What God and His Word are, we can never establish by looking back and therewith by anticipating. This is something God Himself must constantly tell us afresh. *But there is no human knowing that corresponds to this divine telling.* (*CD* I/1, p. 132; my emphasis)

In itself the text cannot convince the reader of its truth-claims. In itself the text cannot convince the reader of its reference to and relevance for something outside of the text. Thus the text is in need of a reference from what it itself refers to.

It is only by revelation that revelation can be spoken in the Bible and that it can be heard as the real substance of the Bible. If it is to be witness at all, and to be apprehended as such, the biblical witness must itself be attested by what it attests. (*CD* I/2, p. 469)

The question now is whether this emphasis on revelation turns into some kind of esoteric reading, in which revelation can be used as a kind of trump card, the last and final, invincible argument. The answer to this is, No. The human being can never be in control of or possess revelation, nor can it fully capture revelation, as revelation itself makes such a "captivity" impossible.[21] This is not only due to the difference between God and the human being, but also to the open-endedness of revelation. To do theology is always to begin with the beginning.[22] This is connected with the under-

---

verständlich auch und erst recht auf die Bibel anzuwenden." See Karl Barth, *Die Kirchliche Dogmatik* I/2 (Zollikon-Zürich: Evangelischer Verlag Zürich, 1938), p. 515; hereafter cited as *KD* I/2.

21. Bonhoeffer's critique, "Take it or leave it" *(friß Vogel oder stirb),* is not very successfully viewed from this perspective, as it does not take the dynamic and "communitarian" aspect of revelation into account. See Dietrich Bonhoeffer, *Widerstand und Ergebung. Briefe und Aufzeichnungen aus der Haft,* ed. Christian Gremmels, Eberhard Bethge, Renate Bethge, and Ilse Tödt (Gütersloh: Chr. Kaiser/Gütersloher Verlagshaus, 1998), p. 312.

22. From this perspective William Stacy Johnson sees some similarities among Barth, Emmanuel Levinas, and Paul Ricoeur in their respective use of open-endedness as a decisive factor for the whole understanding of what theology and philosophy are about and how theology and philosophy can be done. See William Stacy Johnson, *The Mystery of God: Karl Barth and the Postmodern Foundations of Theology* (Louisville: Westminster/John Knox Press, 1997), pp. 153 and 187.

standing of the task of a theological hermeneutics as not so much the task of reproducing the meaning of the text, but of reinterpreting the text in the actual situation of the reader. "Hence, dogmatics as such does not ask what the apostles and prophets said but what we must say on the basis of the apostles and prophets" (*CD* I/1, p. 16).

In the case of Barth, this is very clearly seen in his radical contextual understanding of Christian ethics.[23] Again, theological hermeneutics cannot claim to be neutral in its starting point. To read the Scripture is according to Barth not solely a question of understanding the text on its own premises *(explicatio)*, nor is it a question of too quickly wanting to find direct directions in the text for today's living *(applicatio)*. A goodhearted wish for direct application would lead straight into a naïve and biblicist reading. Instead a meditation *(meditatio)* has to take place, which takes place in a dialectic between *explicatio* and *applicatio*.[24]

My main point here is to stress that a theology of revelation, as it is worked out in the *CD*, does not neglect the general feeling of ambiguity that can be claimed for all human experiences. Revelation does not contain a kind of surplus that in itself should be able to overrule this general ambiguity in the human being's experience of revelation. Such an overcoming can only be eschatological. Thus, the Word of God must, prior to the final redemption, always be given in a form that not only allows but also includes ambiguity.

> The veil is thick. We do not have the Word of God otherwise than in the mystery of its secularity. (*CD* I/1, p. 165)

> The speech of God is and remains the mystery of God supremely in its secularity. When God speaks to man, this event never demarcates itself from other events in such a way that it might not be interpreted at once as part of these other events. (*CD* I/1, p. 165)

---

23. I agree with William Stacy Johnson, who states that: "Barth's ethic is radically contextual: one can know the will of God only in the very act of obedience in a given situation" (*The Mystery of God*, p. 154).

24. See also Johnson, *The Mystery of God*, p. 190. Barth, however, uses the terms in a more restricted sense than Johnson and I. The relation between the *explicatio, applicatio,* and *mediatio* is for Barth a way to express the relation between exegetical, practical, and dogmatic theology. See *CD* I/2, pp. 766-75.

The ambiguity that is given within the reception of the Word of God not only consists in the equivocacy of perception. No act of God can be performed in such a way that it is impossible to reject. From the perspective of the human being, revelation can never be more than a claim, a loaded interpretation. One of the characteristics of revelation, then, is that it allows space for a non-revelationary interpretation of revelation. Thus Barth's theology of revelation is a theology that in itself discredits any kind of biblicist interpretations of revelation, as it rejects a rejection of an ambiguous understanding of revelation. A biblicist understanding of the Word of God is not only doomed as inhuman but also as ungodly, as it does not take seriously into account the difference between God and the human being. Thus an essential part of revelation consists in the fact that it hands itself over to possible misperceptions. It belongs to the concept of revelation itself that revelation can always be rendered as non-revelation.

> As Christ became true man and remains true man to all eternity, real proclamation becomes an event *on the level of all other human events*. It can be seen and heard on this level, and its being seen and heard thus is no mere appearance but must take place in full essentiality. Without the ambivalence, the liability to misunderstanding and the vulnerability with which this takes place, with which it is itself one event among many others, it could not be real proclamation. (*CD* I/1, p. 94; my emphasis)

To summarize: the ambiguity is not only rooted in the ultimate difference between God and the human being, but also in the claim that God became a human being (the incarnation). This radical claim also implies that it is impossible to understand the full depth of revelation without a revelation of the revelation. That Jesus is Christ is not a self-evident fact, but an interpretation that, according to its own logic, must be revealed from the outside. But that revelation is in an ongoing demand for revelation further implies that revelation is only revelation as long as it also allows room not only for faith but also for doubts. For internal theological reasons revelation resists a final and ultimate interpretation. It is evident that Barth's theology of revelation cannot be evaluated as being either pre-modern or neo-orthodox. It is rather to be defined as a late-modern attempt to talk about God, without overruling the human being's situation in which this God-talk takes place. Barth's dialectical theology of revelation enables the human being to keep the distinction between God and human concepts of God, without having to escape into mysticism or silence. Revelation refers to an external reality that, on the one hand, cannot be fully grasped/encountered within the limits of language, but, on the other hand, can only be provisionally understood and explained in and through the limits of language. Theology is not irrational; it is rather rational talk about the irrational.[25]

Acknowledgment

In order to understand Barth's emphasis on revelation, and the impact this has on the understanding of the human being's experience of revelation, it is necessary to see the strong and close connection that exists between experiencing the Word of God and obtaining knowledge of the Word of God. The one cannot be fully understood without the other. Knowledge of the Word of God without experience of the Word of God is, on the one hand, empty abstraction. On the other hand, experience of the Word of God without a rational reflection on the content of this experience is abstract feeling. The problem is that neither the pure knowledge (knowledge without experience) nor the pure experience (experience without knowledge) has any necessary relation to the incarnated God, the God who once entered into history as a part of history. In the terminology of Barth experience and knowledge is another way to claim the connection between the *illic et tunc* and the *hic et nunc*. The God who is present is the God who has always been present and always will be present. The God who came is the God who is now and who will come again. The function of the experience of the Word of God is thereby to give an account of the Word of God's impact on the individual human person.

The God-experience relates to the whole human being, and not to a particular part of the human person. Experience cannot only consist of many elements, but can also relate to various aspects of the human being's being (such as, for example, will, consciousness, feeling, etc.). What is important here is to see how Barth tries to demonstrate that the Word of God

---

25. A point made strongly by Bent Flemming Nielsen. See Nielsen, *Die Rationalität der Offenbarungstheologie*, p. 11.

has to do with the human being's self-determination. The human being is affected by the Word of God in such a way that this word determines the way the human being defines itself. Thus, it is not only implied that the human being is a relational being (where self-determination takes place through a revelation coming from the outside), but also that there exists a dialectical relation between the Word of God coming from the outside and an internalization of this word in the human person. This internalization takes place through the human being's experience of the Word of God as the Word of God.

It is therefore not Barth's aim to exclude experience as a valid theological category. It is rather his aim to establish the right framework for a positive theological evaluation of the experience.[26] Experience is not only a legitimate but also an important theological category, as it expresses the actual impact and power that the Word of God has on the individual human being. Theology can thereby never be reduced to a purely theoretical system that does not include within itself a reference to the actual life of the individual human being.

---

26. I agree with Gundlach, who states that the peculiarity of the experience of the Word of God consists in its reference to the Word of God. Gundlach emphasizes the ambiguity of the experience of the Word of God and demonstrates hereby that the experience of the Word of God contains the same kind of ambiguity as any other experience. But Gundlach is unable to go beyond this negative statement, and cannot give a more nuanced account of how the Word of God can be experienced as the Word of God, when the actual experience in itself is just as ambivalent as any other experience. Jüngel has tried to account for this in his doubling of the experience: the experience of the experience. Jüngel wishes hereby at one and the same time to stress the peculiarity of the experience of the Word of God, and to stress that this experience can only take form as an experience of our experiences. That the experience is different due to the content of it (God) does not mean that it can be without relation to any of our other experiences. Jüngel tries to demonstrate the connection between the human being's experience of the Word of God and any other experiences positively, where Gundlach instead tries to demonstrate this connection negatively (in an affirmation of the ambiguity that is included in all human experiences). The problem with Gundlach's one-sided approach is that it cannot take into account the relation between the externality of the Word of God and the internalization of it — which happens in the human being's experience of it. The self-determination of the human being is actually changed in hearing the Word of God. The human being has been affected. This is — from the viewpoint of the human being — experienced as an experience. For a further elaboration of Gundlach's point, see Gundlach, *Selbstbegrenzung Gottes und die Autonomie des Menschen*, p. 138.

Experience differs from event in the sense that experience relates to the human being's self-understanding. Experience relates to the depth of the human self. To experience is to understand oneself in the light of what is experienced. The criterion for whether the actual experience can be claimed to be an experience of the Word of God is given prior to the very same experience, namely in the Word of God as it is revealed in Jesus Christ. Thus the internalization of the human experience of the Word of God is derived from its Christological content. The dialectic between the external and the internal function of the human being's experience of the Word of God can according to Barth be described in one term: "acknowledgment."[27] In *CD* I/1, pp. 205-9, Barth defines "acknowledgment" in nine points, which I will summarize in the following:

(1) Acknowledging the Word of God includes an emphasis on the aspect of knowledge. The Word of God is a speech act, whereby an interpersonal communication takes place. Barth emphasizes the human *ratio* as the addressee of the Word of God. The *ratio* is not only to be understood in terms of human intellect, but human intellect nevertheless has an important role in the human being's way of not only experiencing but also understanding the actual experience of the Word of God.
(2) The term "acknowledgment" implies that an interpersonal relation is at stake when a human being experiences the Word of God. The Word of God determines the existence of the human being.
(3) The term "acknowledgment" entails, when it concerns the relation between God and the human being, a clear asymmetry between the two individual subjects. The content of this relation is set by the one who is acknowledged. The human acknowledgment consists then not only in

27. "To summarise, human existence means human self-determination. If experience of God's Word involves the determination of human existence and hence also of human self-determination by the Word of God, then by self-determination we are to understand the exercise of all the faculties in whose exercise man is man without basic emphasis upon and also without basic repudiation of any specific human possibility. . . . This settled, we push on a step further to the question in what the experience of God's Word, i.e., the determination of the whole self-determining man by God's Word, might then consist. To this question, which is so crucial for the whole problem of this section, an answer is given in the introductory thesis when it speaks of *acknowledgment*. I am aware of no word relatively so appropriate as this one to the nature of the Word of God whose determinative operation is our present concern" (*CD* I/1, pp. 204-5; my emphasis).

an acknowledgment of the other person (God) as an individual and independent person, but consists also in an acknowledgment of the asymmetry of power that is a part of this relation. Acknowledgment contains also an inherent truth-claim. Barth describes the theological content of this as an affirmation of the content of the Word of God. The short version of this content is: "God with us."

(4) Acknowledgment is an acknowledgment of the presence of God. To hear the Word of God is to believe in the presence of God — a presence that surpasses an act of historical recollection, as God is the subject of the human being's experience of God-presence. *Illic et tunc* becomes *hic et nunc*.

(5) The Word of God has power. The content of the power that is entailed in the Word of God is the truth, promise, judgment, and blessing of God. The existence of the human being is changed through this power, as the power of God brings the human being "into conformity with itself." The human being's status as a sinner under God's judgment and blessing is made explicit. This structure is seen as a necessary component of the human being's self-understanding and self-determination. This includes the whole human being — not only the intellect, but also feeling, will, and consciousness.

(6) The Word of God to the human being is primarily established through the "act of divine freedom and choice" (*CD* I/1, p. 206). But the Word of God is only heard as such when it includes a human reply to the Word of God. The experience of the Word of God contains an act of decision from both the side of God and the side of the human being. The adequate answer to the Word of God is obedience; the non-adequate answer disobedience.

(7) To acknowledge the Word of God is to acknowledge the indirect character of the Word of God. The human being must participate in this indirectness. The twofold indirectness is partly based on God's hiddenness in revelation, and partly based on the human being's inability to possess the Word of God. Not to respect the twofold indirectness is to confuse the sayer with the hearer of the word.

(8) To acknowledge the twofold indirectness of the Word of God is to acknowledge the mystery of the Word of God. The actual experience of the Word of God can never be fully grasped by the human person. The human being is never — by the help of the experience of the Word of God — able to fully grasp God. The Word of God encounters the hu-

man person both in its veiled and its unveiled reform. The Word of God is in itself an act of God.

(9) The locus of the true human being's self-determination is the act of acknowledgment. The experience of the presence of God is hereby located in such a way that it not only comes from the outside, to the human being, but also — as this particular movement from the outside — causes an internalization of this movement within the human being. This not only implies that the self (the human self) first becomes the real self in the meeting of another self (the divine self), but it also means that this other self (the divine self) has the authority and power of the new self coming to itself. The human self has hereby become part of a determination that exceeds its own self-determination, but without which its own true self-determination cannot take place.

> He [man] submits to the authority of the other. This is not in contradiction with the concept of self-determination but it does mean that the self-determination of man as such takes place at a specific point in a specific context. It has found its beginning and its basis in another higher determination. In the act of acknowledgment, the life of man, without ceasing to be the self-determining life of this man, has now its centre, its whence, the meaning of its attitude, and the criterion whether this attitude really has the corresponding meaning — it has all this outside itself, in the thing or person acknowledged. So far as it has all this, it has it from the thing or person acknowledged. Thus acknowledgment as an attitude is in every respect the act of this man and yet from the standpoint of the meaning of the attitude it is not at all his act but a determination that has come upon him from the thing or person acknowledged by him and compelling his acknowledgment. (*CD* I/1, pp. 207-8)

Acknowledgment covers both the sovereignty of the Word of God and the human being's acceptance of and involvement in the Word of God. The Word of God does not leave the human being untouched or unchanged. The external word has an impact on the human being's existence when it is heard as what it is, the Word of God. But it does not change the existence of the human being in such a way that the human being can refer to this change as some kind of a theologically fixed point. The actual impact of the Word of God cannot be used as an argument for the existence of God;

neither can it be used as a basis from which the actual content of the Word of God can be derived.[28] If this were the case, the experience would, according to Barth's logic, be valued as a primary instead of a secondary source. The difference between the Word of God and the human words about the Word of God would thereby be eliminated. Experience would in this way be granted a status that it cannot have, as it would be seen as a "cleaner" expression of the Word of God than it possibly can be. This would, on a practical level, open up a possible personal misuse of the religious experience, where those who had strong religious experiences would be able to (mis)use these experiences as an argument for their interpretation of the Word of God (a term they of course would never use, as the term "interpretation" in itself accepts the relativity of the experience). The particular experience of the Word of God would then either turn out to be a stronger argument than the Word of God itself, or it would become identical with the Word of God. A distinction between source and derivation would hereby be dismissed. This means on the theoretical level that Barth rejects any possibility of having an impact that could be understood independently of its own reference to the Word of God. If this were not the case, the change in the human being that is given within the experience of the Word of God would become a change that the human being could in some way or other possess. Instead the change is a change that is in an ongoing need of change. This is not just to be seen as a play on words, but refers to the central point that the change is in never-ending need of being corrected, and thus renewed. The change is nothing in itself, but it is everything seen in connection with its external reference: the Word of God, which has this power to change. Barth therefore rejects the view that any investigation of the Word of God can begin with the believing ego. There is no neutral ground upon which a non-dialectical understanding of the ex-

---

28. That is, the experience can never become some kind of "extra," which the pious human person can use as an argument for the existence of God/the reality of God. Barth defines such a pious use of the experience as a type of indirect Christian Cartesianism. The problem with this is that the human being, after receiving the Word of God, thinks it now possess this word in such a way that it in itself can serve as a reference. See *CD* I/1, pp. 213-14.

Gundlach emphasizes that Barth's rejection of the experience as a theological starting point aims to reduce any theological overdetermination of the actual individual God-experience. The religious experiences are then "allowed" to entail the same kind of ambiguity as any other experiences. See Gundlach, *Selbstbegrenzung Gottes und die Autonomie des Menschen*, pp. 126-28.

ternal and the internal, the Word of God and the human being's experience of the Word of God, can be situated.[29]

To summarize: Barth evaluates the term "acknowledgment" as being
the most adequate description of the human being's experience of the
presence of God (a presence that is included in the actual human experience of the Word of God) due to the fact that it at one and the same time
accepts the human being's God-experience as an essential part of the
Christian faith and qualifies it in a way through which a theocentric approach to theology is maintained. The experience is then given a dogmatic
frame as it is placed within a non-experiential approach to theology. The
source for the human being's self-understanding is thereby — from a
theological perspective — placed in God. From the perspective of the human being this means that true human being can only be understood
when its center is withdrawn from itself to another self (the divine self).
This self is not just another self, but God. It is not possible to stand on neutral ground, describing what it means to understand yourself in and from
the relation to God and further to compare it with a non-religious point of
view. Knowledge about God is not a neutral knowledge (purified from
God-experiences), but it is a self-involving knowledge that can only be
fully explored from a participating subject.

Before entering into the question of participation, I want to make a further
remark on Barth's use of the term "acknowledgment." As already quoted,
Barth says that "I am aware of no word relatively so appropriate as this one
['acknowledgment'] to the nature of the Word of God whose *determinative
operation* is our present concern" (*CD* I/1, p. 205; my emphasis). With this
remark Barth not only stresses the asymmetry between God and the human being, but also allows space for a dialectic between the self-

---

29. See *CD* I/1, p. 210. Barth enters here into discussion with especially Schaeder (1861-
1936) and Wobbermin (1869-1943), whose theology Barth describes as indirect Cartesianism or as the Cartesianism of the believing Christian. God-consciousness is here turned
into some kind of human ability. The human being owns or possesses its own *religious
habitus,* through which the ability to hear and experience the Word of God has become a
possibility of the human being instead of a possibility of God. The power dynamic between the external Word of God and the human being's internalizing of this word has
thereby changed radically. The internalized experience of the Word of God has in this way
become the criterion and standard not only for how to talk adequately about the Word of
God, but also for the actual content of the Word of God.

determination of God and the self-determination of the human being. But is this word really so appropriate for demonstrating the dialectic between the self-determination of God and the human being's self-determination as Barth claims?

The word "acknowledgment" has a long history, and since Hegel it has been understood in quite a different way from that in which Barth uses it.

For Barth it makes sense to use the word "acknowledgment" in a relationship in which there is a very clear and unilateral power structure between the two individual subjects. The one subject (God) gives orders; the other subject (the human being) obeys or disobeys. The one is the master; the other is the slave or the servant. For Hegel, however, any kind of real acknowledgment cannot consist in a unilateral relationship, where one is master and the other is slave.[30] The reason for this is that real acknowledgment can only take place between two individual, free, and autonomous subjects.[31] The acknowledgment from another subject can be evaluated as a real acknowledgment only when the subject who acknowledges another subject is free and autonomous in relation to the other subject. The wish to obtain acknowledgment from another subject thus contains in itself an acknowledgment of the other subject as free and autonomous.[32] If this is not

---

30. With the term "real acknowledgment" I want to describe the normative status of the term "acknowledgment," which means acknowledgment in its most pure form. My interpretation of Hegel's use of the term "acknowledgment" is based on Arne Grøn's constructive reading of Hegel. Grøn himself notices that at some points he might go beyond Hegel's own use of the term "acknowledgment." This enables Grøn to criticize Hegel with the help of Hegel, as his constructive reading is based on the preconditions and the consequences of Hegel's own description of the term "acknowledgment" in the section about "Selbstständigkeit und Unselbstständigkeit des Selbstbewußtseyns; Herrschafft und Knechtschafft" in *Phänomenologie des Geistes*. See Arne Grøn, "Anerkendelsens dialektik og begreb" [The dialectic and perception of acknowledgment], in *Teologi og Modernitet*, ed. Peter Thyssen and Anders Moe Rasmussen (Aarhus: Aarhus University Press, 1997), pp. 50-65; G. W. F. Hegel, *The Phenomenology of Mind,* 2nd ed., trans. J. B. Baillie (New York: Humanities Press, 1971), pp. 228-40.

31. "The process then is absolutely the double process of both self-consciousnesses. Each sees the other do the same as itself; each itself does what it demands on the part of the other, and for that reason does what it does, only so far as the other does the same. Action from one side only would be useless, because what is to happen can only be brought about by means of both." Hegel, *The Phenomenology of Mind,* p. 230.

32. "*Consciousness* finds that it immediately is and is not another consciousness, as also that this other is for itself only when it cancels itself as existing for itself, and has self-

the case, the acknowledgment by the other subject is worth nothing, since it has been obtained under circumstances where it cannot be evaluated as real. The master can therefore never obtain a real acknowledgment from the slave, as the slave is not granted the status of being a free and autonomous person. If the slave were granted this status, he or she would no longer be a slave.

According to Arne Grøn, Hegel's theory of acknowledgment entails a demand for a structure of two individual and autonomous subjects who relate to each other in a non-unilateral way.[33] This implies that there is no clear one-sided power structure between the two. The relation is therefore a relation between two self-reflecting selves who do not receive their real self in the meeting, but who are constituted as a self before the meeting with the other self. Nevertheless, the human self is in an ongoing search for a confirmation from another human self. The meeting between an I and a Thou, which takes place as an acknowledgment between two individual selves, is still important for the individual self's self-understanding, but this meeting does not as such constitute the human self as a self.[34]

The need for acknowledgment is given within the individual human self prior to any meeting and therefore also prior to an actual obtaining of acknowledgment from another human self. If not, the striving for acknowledgment would first have been actualized by its first actual occurrence. Hegel is in this way able to establish a synthesis between the independence of the individual human self, the necessity of this independence, and the dialectic between the self-sufficiency of the human self and the interdependence that exists in the relation between two individual self-sufficient selves. Real freedom is, according to Hegel, a freedom in relation, which is established through the mutual act of acknowledgment.

I therefore conclude that Barth's use of the term "acknowledgment" is distinctly different from Hegel's. As seen, acknowledgment is in Barth's universe a term that in itself contains an acceptance of an asymmetrical structure between two selves. It is not a description of the relation between

---

existence only in the self-existence of the other. Each is the mediating term to the other, through which each mediates and unites itself with itself; and each is to itself and to the other an immediate self-existing reality, which, at the same time, exists thus for itself only through this mediation. They recognize themselves as mutually recognizing one another." Hegel, *The Phenomenology of Mind,* p. 231.

33. See Grøn, *Anerkendelsens dialektik og begreb,* pp. 53-54.
34. See Grøn, *Anerkendelsens dialektik og begreb,* p. 54.

two inherently self-sufficient selves, but it is a description of a relation that from the perspective of the weaker part (the human being) is necessary for establishing a true self (a self in relation to God), and which from the perspective of the stronger part, God, is pure grace.

The difference between Barth and Hegel thus becomes evident. From Hegel's perspective, Barth's structure of acknowledgment could be criticized as a master-slave relation, in which either the master-slave relation would have to be destroyed from within, so that a real acknowledgment could take place, or the master-slave relation would have to be preserved, with the consequence that no real acknowledgment could take place. Barth's understanding of acknowledgment is strictly theological (where Hegel's is strictly philosophical) and it has a theocentric (instead of an anthropocentric) starting point. Barth's use of acknowledgment as a theological category contains a clear power structure, with a clear asymmetry within the two selves, where Hegel operates with a symmetrical relation between two independent self-sufficient selves. The human self in the philosophy of Hegel is confirmed as what it is already before the relation (a self-sufficient self). However, this confirmation is necessary in order to obtain real freedom. Barth, on the contrary, states that the human self has been disrupted in its illusion of being a self-sufficient self in the act of acknowledgment. In Barth's view only God can be said to be self-sufficient. This illusion is broken in the encounter between God and the human being. The revelation is the necessary medium through which the human being is enabled to see itself as what it really is — a human being dependent on God. This self-awareness can only come about when the center for self-awareness has been changed. God, and not the human being, is the center of the human self.

Hegel and Barth's use of the term "acknowledgment" has proved to be distinctly different, as their evaluation of the human being's quest for autonomy is radically different. To explore and deepen the way Barth uses the term "acknowledgment," it is instead more helpful to go to Schleiermacher's understanding and use of the human being's feeling of absolute dependence.[35] To demonstrate this, I will reconstruct the strain of thought

---

35. In my analysis of Schleiermacher I am indebted to Professor Bruce L. McCormack and his course on "The Christian Faith" at Princeton Theological Seminary in the spring of 1999.

in Schleiermacher's use of the term "absolute dependence" in the following seven points:

(1) It is not possible for the human self to be absolutely free in relation to any given object. Neither is it possible for the human self to be absolutely dependent on any given object.

(2) This is due to the fact that there will always exist some kind of mutuality between the human self and the given object.[36]

(3) The human self cannot understand itself as being absolutely free, as the freedom of the human self is always a freedom in relation to a given object. The precondition for this understanding of the human self is that the human self always strives in the direction of a given object, whereby it is enabled to realize its freedom. Thus, due to the precondition stated in point 2, the given object can always interact with the subject (the human self) in such a way that the human self is influenced by this interaction. Potentially, the object can always have an impact on the human self, for which reason the human self cannot be characterized as absolutely free.[37]

(4) It is not possible for the human self to be absolutely dependent on a given object.[38] This is due not only to the above-mentioned reference to mutuality (that the human being actually might influence the object — whereby it cannot be claimed to be fully dependent), but also to the fact that the self of the human being can be affected by its own doing and knowing. The feeling of absolute dependence is therefore not possible, as the self of the human being becomes impulses from its own doing and knowing that cannot avoid disturbing this one-stringed feeling of dependence.[39]

---

36. Cf. Friedrich Schleiermacher, *The Christian Faith*, trans. H. R. Mackintosh (Edinburgh: T. & T. Clark, 1989), p. 15.

37. Cf. Schleiermacher, *The Christian Faith*, p. 15.

38. Cf. Schleiermacher, *The Christian Faith*, p. 16.

39. The precondition for this argument is Schleiermacher's distinction among feeling, doing, and knowing. This distinction must be seen in connection with the human self. Doing has to do with a passing-beyond-the-self (*Aussichheraustreten*), feeling has to do with an abiding-in-the-self (*Insichbleiben*), and knowing has to do with both. Feeling is thereby the locus, if you want to describe an ability in the self, that does not in itself contain a striving for an object outside of the self. So feeling is the category Schleiermacher uses when he wants to describe an affection of the self from outside of the self.

(5) Taking points 1 to 4 into account, the origin (the whence) of the human being's feeling of absolute dependence cannot be an object among other objects (as such a feeling could not be absolute).[40] The whence from where the feeling of absolute dependence derives is God. The feeling of the absolute dependence is a feeling of self-consciousness that incorporates the God-consciousness in the self-consciousness.[41] To be in relation to God is different from being in relation to any other object. The reason for this is that God neither is nor can be an object among other objects without ceasing to be God.

(6) The feeling of absolute dependence is a feeling initiated by God. From the perspective of the human being, God-consciousness, which is enclosed in self-consciousness, is established through an encounter between the human being and an Other. Thus the elements of receptivity are primary to the elements of activity in the human being's self-consciousness.[42]

(7) Consequently, the human being's consciousness of being absolutely dependent is a reflection of the human being's consciousness of being in relation to God.

To conclude: Barth's understanding and use of the term "acknowledgment" is much closer to Schleiermacher's than to Hegel's. Barth does not use the term "acknowledgment" in order to advocate human autonomy. It is only God who is an autonomous subject. Neither in the case of Barth nor of Schleiermacher is the human being thought within a model of the self's self-reflection.[43] To acknowledge God is to be affected by God's acknowledgment of the human being. Or, phrased otherwise, the human being's acknowledgment of God is an acknowledgment that has its origin in the one who is acknowledged (God). In the terminology of Schleiermacher this viewpoint can be expressed in the following way: to be aware of the feeling of absolute dependence is to be in relation with God. The structural similarity between Barth and Schleiermacher, which I suggest here, is based on a reading of Schleiermacher in which it is emphasized that it is God who,

40. Cf. Schleiermacher, *The Christian Faith,* p. 18.
41. Cf. Schleiermacher, *The Christian Faith,* p. 17.
42. Cf. Schleiermacher, *The Christian Faith,* p. 13.
43. My analysis of Schleiermacher differs from a more typical reading, where the main emphasis is on the self-consciousness rather than the God-consciousness.

from the outside, enables and initiates the human being's feeling of absolute dependence. Both Barth and Schleiermacher thereby accentuate the asymmetry between God and the human being, which can also be expressed as a maintaining of the Creator/creation distinction. In the theology of both Barth and Schleiermacher, revelation is understood as a divine action, an action that has an impact on the human being's self-awareness. Neither Barth nor Schleiermacher reduces this impact to a cognitive act, but includes the whole human being (knowing, feeling, act). Further, both Barth and Schleiermacher operate with a dialectical understanding of the human being's self-consciousness, which enables them to take account of both the passive and active side of the human being's self-consciousness. It is therefore not without good reason that Barth himself — in the beginning of his section dealing with acknowledgment — refers to Schleiermacher's use of the feeling of absolute dependence as a way to demonstrate and qualify the affective being of the human being:

> We cannot, of course, agree with 19th century thinkers when they say that "there is" or that "man has" a religious consciousness. But we might say that men can have a religious consciousness, or, in our own vocabulary, that the Word of God can become the ground and object of man's consciousness. Thus when Schleiermacher spoke of the Christian consciousness or of self-consciousness he had in view a "being affected" (to K. H. Sack, 9.4.1825, *Letters*, Vol. 4, p. 335) which is obviously very similar to our "being determined." (*CD* I/1, pp. 198-99)

Participation

Revelation has in itself a demand for participation. It contains a claim on each individual person who hears the revelation. It is not enough for each individual human being to understand its own life from the perspective of the revelation, as if the revelation could be understood as a pure intellectual exercise. Revelation must become internalized, which from Barth's perspective means that a transformation must take place, a transformation that can best be described as a demand for action. Consequently, revelation is only heard as such, when this demand is included.[44]

44. In his dialectic between the objective and the subjective aspect of revelation Barth is able to incorporate what Berkouwer defines as Scripture's call to faith. Berkouwer, how-

In its [the Word of God] reality we also have our own possibility, not to contemplate it, but only to *use* it. Contemplating it, we no longer hear, and we thus lose the reality and with it our own possibility that we want to contemplate. (*CD* I/1, p. 237; my emphasis)

An implication of the demand of participation is that theory and praxis cannot be viewed as two individual, independent approaches to reality. In fact, the gospel has only been heard as gospel when it includes a demand for action.

However, this should not be misinterpreted in a way that makes the gospel dependent on the response of the individual human being. The gospel refers to an interaction between God and the world, which — if it is to remain the gospel — has to be understood as a pure fact. The result of this particular event (the atonement) can therefore not be dependent on the human being's reaction; such dependence would destroy the message of the gospel from within.[45] The element of human self-involvement is always subordinated to or incorporated into the objective reality, which is established by God prior to the individual human being's acceptance of it. The reality is determined by God's action, not by the human being's acceptance or dismissal of this action (whether it be in the form of a simple denial or "just" pure indifference). Barth therefore often makes a distinction between *de jure* and *de facto*, when he writes about the connection between

---

ever, does not really acknowledge this, as Barth's emphasis on the call does not imply a similar emphasis on the one who is called. Berkouwer wants, not without sympathy for Brunner and Prenter's critique of Barth, to emphasize the necessity of the human being's decision of faith. Berkouwer's critique of Barth's "monism of grace" is already given away in the title of his book: *The Triumph of Grace in the Theology of Karl Barth*. Berkouwer states, in opposition to Barth, that it is possible at one and the same time to emphasize that God's salvation is sovereign, and that the human being's faith is necessary for salvation. Thus, the "mystery of the relationship between faith and salvation lies precisely in this, that *this* faith which does *not compete* is *necessary* and *saves*, and that therefore we are called to the acceptance of this faith." Gerrit C. Berkouwer, *The Triumph of Grace in the Theology of Karl Barth* (Grand Rapids: Eerdmans, 1956), p. 273. On this theme see also Alasdair I. C. Heron, "The Theme of Salvation in Karl Barth's Doctrine of Reconciliation," *Ex Auditu* 5 (1989): 107-22. In this article Heron states how Barth's view on the theme of faith and salvation is characterized by "a triple critical boundary: against pietistic individualism; against mystically-tinged ecclesiasticism; against mere dogmatic objectivism" (p. 113).

45. Here Barth disagrees with Brunner, who does not make the distinction between objective reality and the participation in this objective reality.

the reality established by God, the call for participation, and the actual participation or lack thereof.[46] A theology of revelation contains in itself a call to participate in the reality (the breakthrough of the kingdom of God) established by Christ. The drama enacted in the Christ-event has to become our drama, our story, our frame for understanding life (both in general and particular). In the words of Barth:

> We have also to ask how we succeed not only in thinking this distinction [the distinction between absolute and relative], i.e. achieving it as an idea and concept, but — and this is what makes it a serious thought — in so *making it our own* that it is not merely a *theoria,* a drama played out in front of us, but that we ourselves achieve it with *our lives,* in *our existence,* and the drama of it is *our drama?* For what sort of a knowledge of the priority of the absolute would that be which did not mean our acknowledgment of it, which did not include the authority of the absolute and our obedience to it, which was not in fact based on this obviously not self-evident acknowledgment, authority and obedience? (*CD* I/2, p. 498; partly my emphasis)[47]

To investigate the theme of transformation further, we need to take the dialectic between the believer's justification and sanctification into account. This dialectic is expressed in the idea of *participatio Christi* (in contrast to *imitatio Christi*). Justification and sanctification can only be fully understood when they are seen as two non-identical movements in the one act of God. They are united in their dependence on God's act in Christ (the atonement). Thus, neither of them can be granted a superior role at the expense of the other.

> Justification is not sanctification and does not merge into it. Sanctification is not justification and does not merge into it. Thus, although the two belong indissolubly together, the one cannot be explained by the other. It is one thing that God turns in free grace to

46. See for example Karl Barth, *Church Dogmatics* IV/2 (Edinburgh: T. & T. Clark, 1958), pp. 511 and 527; hereafter cited as *CD* IV/2.

47. The above-quoted passage from the *CD* demonstrates a continuity between the earlier more existentialistic writings of Barth and the *CD*. In continuation of the above quote Barth describes the divine law as the "*attack on our existence,* the act in which we have to recognize the priority of God" (*CD* I/2; my emphasis).

sinful man, and quite another that in the same free grace He con-
verts man to Himself. (*CD* IV/2, p. 503)

Sanctification no less than justification is an act that is established solely
by the will of God (and thereby a God-given fact). Justification and sanctification both reflect the same will of God: to enable the human being to
live in a partnership with him. It has always been God's intention that the
human being should be God's own partner. This partnership is expressed
in the covenant. Consequently, from the perspective of God, the human
being can be described as God's covenant partner.[48] For this reason the *a
priori* of this relationship can be said to be the will of God.

> Thus in its origin and basis, at the superior place where it is set in
> motion, the conversion of man is *a decision of God* for him which
> not only makes possible a corresponding decision of man for God,
> the free act of his obedience, but makes this act and obedience real,
> directly causing it to take place. (*CD* IV/2, p. 579; my emphasis)

The reciprocity that exists within any other kind of relationship is thus
claimed to be non-applicable to the relationship between God and the human being. Again, this does not exclude any kind of reciprocity in the relation, but does give it a derived instead of a foundational status. This status
comes to expression in the interpretation of the actual experience of the
relationship between God and human beings, as this has been described
under the heading "acknowledgment." Or, expressed in more religious categories: praise and thanksgiving. In one and the same movement God
turns himself toward the human being, and the human being toward
God.[49] The source of the human being's conversion is God. Justification
and sanctification express two different, but dialectically interwoven aspects of one and the same movement: God's coming to the human being
and the human being's coming to God. God is thereby the subject not only
of justification but also of sanctification.

Barth is here opposing an understanding of the relation between justification and sanctification in which justification is seen as the act of God
and sanctification as the human being's reply to this act.[50] The interpreta-

---

48. See also Chapter 8.
49. See *CD* IV/2, p. 505.
50. See for example *CD* IV/2, pp. 516-17.

tion of sanctification as a human reply to justification can be found in several variations, with a more or less subtle description of sanctification as a more or less synergetic act. These various thought models are united in the fact that the individual human person plays a constitutive role in sanctification. Further, this line of thought is most often combined with a soteriology in which the human being's acts or lack of acts are decisive for the final judgment of the individual human person. Barth's teaching concerning the relationship between justification and sanctification is worked out in opposition to such an emphasis on the individual human being's constitutive role in sanctification. Sanctification (as well as justification) has already taken place in Christ. The human being is sanctified in Christ; it is an event that has already taken place independently of each individual human being.

> The sanctification of man which has taken place in this One is their sanctification. But originally and properly it is the sanctification of Him and not of them. Their sanctification is originally and properly His and not theirs. (*CD* IV/2, p. 514)

Both the justification and the sanctification of the human being have happened substitutively in Jesus Christ. Sanctification is one aspect of the renewal of the human being that has taken place in Jesus Christ. In and through the justification and the sanctification of the human being, the human being obtains a new direction. From the perspective of the human being sanctification is a never-ending process. This open-endedness is due to its eschatological character.[51] This means that any question of merit in connection with the demand of good works is ruled out, due to the fact that it is only God who can unite the direction toward the goal (the acts of the human being) and the final fulfillment of the goal (the act of God). The question of good works has in this way clearly been separated from the question of the salvation of the individual human being.

---

51. A clear affinity between the protological eschatology in the *The Epistle to the Romans* and the *CD* can hereby be established. For a description of the protological eschatology in the work of the early Barth see Michael Beintker, *Die Dialektik in der "dialektischen Theologie" Karl Barths. Studien zur Entwicklung der Barthschen Theologie und zur Vorgeschichte der "Kirchlichen Dogmatik"* (München: Chr. Kaiser Verlag, 1987), pp. 66-71. The open-endedness in the *CD* is described as the human being's situation in between the recollection of the promises received and the hope for the future. See for example *CD* I/1, p. 197.

The good work is only good in Christ, which means that the good work is not good due to the actual agent (whether with regard to the good intentions, lack of self-interest, or non-objectification of the recipient of the good work). But what then can actually be claimed to be good about the good work, seen from the perspective of the actual doer? *Nothing* — which is exactly the point; nothing in the sense that any claim of doing good work (whether potential or actual) undermines the very claim itself from this perspective. Good works are characterized by their radical claimlessness and lack of self-righteousness, which, for example, can be expressed by the help of self-irony, self-criticism, and humor. On the anthropological level good works are characterized by a lack of smugness in respect to the good works (on behalf of the benefactor, the beneficiary, or God).

But this separation between soteriology and good works does not rule out the demand as such. The whole life of the human being is determined from the given *telos*. The human being has become a new center, whereby it is freed from its own self-centeredness.[52] It has not asked for this center, nor can it deny it — a center which, when it is first acknowledged as the center, radically changes the human being's self-understanding. This change cannot, from the perspective of Barth, be adequately described as a kind of circular, hermeneutical movement between two positions: the human being viewed as a sinner and the human being viewed as a justified and sanctified person. Such a circular understanding of the human being does not take the radicality of justification and sanctification into account. It would instead allow space for a merely static understanding of justification and sanctification, where it is reduced to a kind of hermeneutic key, through which the ambivalence of the dichotomy between ideal and real is explained. This does not as such exclude the inner dynamic between the understanding of the human being as a sinner and the human being as a justified and sanctified person. But the result of this dynamic is basically non-dynamic. The result of such a "non-dynamic dynamic" is an appraisal of the *status quo*.

Another objection is that such an understanding does not sufficiently

---

52. "But we must now be more precise. We really look away from ourselves, and therefore know ourselves genuinely and freely, only as we really look to Jesus Christ. We do not do so merely as we look formally away from ourselves and beyond ourselves, in a purely formal negation of that figure 'the self,' to an empty beyond" (*CD* IV/2, p. 284).

take into account the divine power to which justification and sanctification bear witness. To receive a new *telos* is not only to receive a call to participate in the work of Christ, but is also to be enabled to participate in it. This is not due to any intrinsic quality of the human being, but to the will and qualitative act of God. The structural similarities between revelation and justification and sanctification are here obvious. It is not only God who creates the possibility; it is also God who enables potentiality to become actuality.

The human being is in a new situation, as it is set in a new relation. This relation determines all other relations. Barth, quite surprisingly for a Protestant theologian, demonstrates what this radical change means for the human being by using the saints as an example of what it means to be justified and sanctified. One of the points here is to argue the case that the good work is an inalienable part of a Christian life. Further, the aim is to demonstrate that the saints became saints by the direction they were given. The divine power is in the power of the Word of God. The saints became saints not by their own efforts, but solely by the help of God.[53] The role of the saint is therefore not different from any other Christian, namely to be a witness to God's saving act in Christ.[54] I will now explore a bit further how Barth, as illustrated in his references to the saints, is able at one and the same time to describe the human being as a sinner and as a justified and sanctified person.

The human being is a sinner, whether it knows it or not. This is revealed to the human being through the gospel and not through the law. The law can neither have the function of enabling the human being to see its real situation before God, nor of setting the human being free to be in a new situation before God. The latter would presuppose that the human being was able to make a final decision to be for God. The former would presuppose that an abstract use of the law could at one and the same time break the self-centeredness of the human being and give the human being a new direction, whereby a gap between the old and the new person would have been established. However, according to Barth, the law can have nothing to do with either *vivificatio* or *mortificatio* of the human being.[55] The

---

53. See *CD* IV/2, pp. 522-23.

54. See *CD* IV/2, pp. 518-19.

55. Barth rejects the view that the law can in itself lead to a radical awareness of sin, as the law can always be overcome by the help of the law. This can for example be in the

dialectic between the *mortificatio* and the *vivificatio* is, instead, given in and through the revelation of the gospel. The gospel leaves the human being as a disturbed sinner (in contrast to an "undisturbed sinner," where the awareness of being a sinner is separated from the demand of participation).[56] The "disturbed sinner" has not only obtained an awareness of his or her own sinful status, but he or she has also acquired a new direction that requires action. The demand for action and the proclamation of the forgiveness of sins can therefore not be separated. Even a typical distinction, which combines justification with the latter and sanctification with the former, is thereby viewed as a false alternative due to the fact that such a distinction separates knowledge from praxis.

The "disturbed sinner" is a sinner who has been set free to act. The call from beyond the human being separates the act from the deed, which is to be seen in relation to the dismissal of any soteriological consequences of the acts. The disturbed sinner has thereby become a new form of existence, as he is now seen as God's covenant partner. Seen from the perspective of whom? *First,* viewed from the perspective of God. *Second,* viewed from the perspective of the human being — the latter with the elucidation that it is from the perspective of the human being, as the human being imagines itself being seen from the perspective of God.

> Sanctification is a *real change* even in this restricted sense — the creation of a new form of existence in which man becomes the true covenant-partner of God. As an undisturbed sinner he is always a covenant-breaker, unreconciled with God and unusable by Him.

---

form of either skepticism or apathy. The difference between the Reformed and the Lutheran use of the law hereby becomes clear: "It would simply be an abstract law — a law without any *locus* in a life fulfilling and embodying it, but merely advancing the arid claim that it is the law of God, and that as such it has the right to demand that man should be for God, and thus fulfil the condition under which God will also be for him. This abstract law has never yet led a man to conversion, even by killing him, let alone by making him alive" (*CD* IV/2, pp. 579-80).

56. According to Barth, the human being will always be able to absorb his or her own sin-awareness. From the perspective of the human being, there is no way out of its self-centeredness — which really is the core of sin. "In a purely formal sense no one, not even a Spanish mystic, has ever really looked away from himself and beyond himself, let alone transcended himself in a purely formal negation. If we try to do this, looking into an empty beyond, we are really looking quite cheerfully at ourselves again, however solemnly we may pretend that it is otherwise" (*CD* IV/2, p. 284).

The better he succeeds in achieving inner harmony, the less he can
be reconciled with God and used by Him. (*CD* IV/2, p. 525)[57]

Both justification and sanctification are an expression of God's judgment
and grace.[58] This eschatological judgment of God also has consequences
for the human person's life here and now, as human beings are not only
enabled but also allowed to see themselves from the perspective of God.

The schism between the disturbed and the undisturbed sinner, as
quoted above, leads us to the next question: How does Barth's understanding
of the relation between justification and sanctification fit with a Protestant
emphasis on *simul justus et peccator?* Let us from the very start note that
there are passages in *CD* §66 that can be read as arguments for an understanding of sanctification as process. Some will even claim that they can be
read as arguments for a progressive process of sanctification. Justification
and sanctification would in that case entail three different aspects: a once-
and-for-all aspect, an again-and-again aspect, and finally a more-and-more
aspect. I will try to show here that only the former two are intelligible in the
context of the overall line of thought in *CD* §61 and 66.[59] The element of
process embedded in Barth's description of sanctification and justification is
not of a quantitative character. Instead, it underlines the dynamic character

57. The English version translates here "sich selbst zu versöhnen" with "achieving inner harmony," which gives quite different associations. The German text says: "Heiligung
ist schon in dieser zurückhaltenden Beschreibung reale Veränderung, wirklich die
Schaffung einer neuen Existenzform, in der der Mensch Gottes rechter Bundesgenosse
wird. Gerade als ungestörter Sünder wäre und bliebe er ja der Bundbrüchige, der mit Gott
nicht Versöhnte, den Gott nicht brauchen kann: und das umso weniger, je besser es ihm
gelänge, sich mit sich selbst zu versöhnen." See Karl Barth, *Die Kirchliche Dogmatik* IV/2
(Zollikon-Zürich: Evangelischer Verlag A.G., 1955), p. 594; hereafter cited as *KD* IV/2.

58. The idea of *participatio Christi*, which unites justification and sanctification,
rules out any understanding of justification and sanctification that involves a shift in lev-
els regarding the preconditions and the subjects for the act of justification and sanctification. God cannot be the only subject in the one without being the subject in the other
also. The substitutionary act of Christ is essential for understanding not only the justification but also the sanctification.

59. George Hunsinger is an excellent proponent of what I here define as a progressive
understanding of justification and sanctification in the theology of Barth. However, I do
disagree with his interpretation of Barth's theology on this point, as I find he is overesti-
mating one particular strain of thought, at the expenses of the main line of thought in *CD*
§61 and 66.

of the argument. Justification and sanctification are described as an ongoing movement that happens throughout a person's whole life. It is, as said, a new direction given to the individual human being. It is a direction, not a predicate or quality of the individual human being.

Viewed from this perspective the human being will never get closer or more distant to its own justification or sanctification, as it has already taken place in Christ. However, this needs to be remembered, and to be retold again and again, so that it continues to have an impact on the individual human being. The dynamic is then placed between the once-and-for-all and the again-and-again aspects.

Another argument for this interpretation of justification and sanctification as a non-progressive process is that conversion (which includes justification as well as sanctification) concerns the whole human being. The whole human being cannot be split up into parts; the individual human being cannot be justified or sanctified in varying degrees. Such an understanding would — intentionally or not — leave space for a synergetic effect. It is therefore my claim that the more-and-more aspect would destroy the former two aspects from within. It is the whole human person who is a sinner. It is the whole human being who is called to conversion. It is the whole human being who is justified and sanctified. This is a dynamic understanding of justification and sanctification, where an inclusion of quantitative terms is ruled out.

> The man who today is confronted by that call to halt and advance, who today is set in that movement, in the *totality* of his existence and being, by the powerful truth that God is for him and he for God, is also today, and again in the *totality* of his existence and being, the sinful man of yesterday. (*CD* IV/2, p. 571; my emphasis)[60]

> No, the one who is under the determination and in the process of becoming a totally new man is in his totality the old man of yesterday. (*CD* IV/2, p. 571)

60. The German text emphasizes more strongly than the English translation the abruptness of the call and the fact that the human being is a slothful sinner: "Der heute mit jenem Halt! und Vorwärts! konfrontiert, heute durch die mächtige Wahrheit, daß Gott für ihn, er für Gott ist, in der Ganzheit seiner Existenz und seines Wesens in jene Bewegung versetzt ist, ist auch heute noch der in der Ganzheit seiner Existenz und seines Wesens sündenträge Mensch von gestern" (*KD* IV/2, p. 646).

The *totus-totus* aspect of justification and sanctification is thus strongly accentuated. The human person lives under a twofold determination: the old human being of yesterday and the new human being of tomorrow. Again the protological eschatological character is clear. The human person is a sinner. The human being is justified and sanctified. The human being is a justified and sanctified sinner. Hereby a "limit is set to their being sinners by the direction which they are given. Within this limit their being is still that of sinners. They still live in the flesh" (*CD* IV/2, p. 525). From the perspective of the human being both justification and sanctification are only penultimate since the ultimate change (the redemption) is fully eschatological.[61] There is no space open for a *partim-partim* understanding of justification and sanctification, where justification and sanctification can be understood in terms of an organic growth.

An argument against this rejection of the *partim-partim* aspect, based on its potential growth-motifs, could be that Barth uses terminology like "seed" and "sowing" to describe the divine power. But this is only to say that the power becomes further qualified as the power of the Word of God spoken in Jesus Christ. This means, *first,* that the human being has no influence on either the sowing or the outcome. *Second,* it means that it is the royal man Jesus who is sanctified, and that all human beings become a part of this in Christ. Jesus Christ is the one new human being, who cannot be imitated but only followed. Thus sanctification, just as much as justification, is dependent on its Christological content. Sanctification cannot be read off the lips or acts of any Christian — not even of any of the saints; the struggle between the new and the old human being is a never-ending struggle.[62] It is a struggle that has only been won in Christ, as Christ reveals not only the *verus deus* but also the *verus homo.*[63] The latter is qualified by radical God-obedience. To stress my critique of a progressive, processual understanding of sanctification in §66, let me quote the following passages:

> How can we say, in relation to our own persons or those of others, that we or these others have come out of darkness into light, that we have passed from death to life, that the old man has died and the

---

61. See *CD* IV/2, p. 530.
62. See for example *CD* IV/2, pp. 570-71.
63. See *CD* IV/2, p. 582.

new is risen, that we are in a state of *mortificatio* and *vivificatio*, or merely that we are converted or in the process of being converted? (*CD* IV/2, p. 583)

But everything is simple, true and clear when these statements are referred directly to Jesus Christ, and only indirectly, as fulfilled and effectively realised in Him for us, to ourselves. (*CD* IV/2, p. 583)

What remains, then, for us? Jesus Christ remains, and in and with Him everything, in and with Him the whole reality and truth that God is for us and we for God, and therefore the whole power of our conversion. (*CD* IV/2, p. 583)

The *partim-partim* understanding of sanctification is not a viable route, as it leaves a space open for a progressive-process understanding of sanctification, in which the individual human being can be more or less sanctified. This is due to the circumstance that a *partim-partim* understanding of sanctification separates the old human being from the new, which then again allows for what Barth describes as a psychological myth without any real substance.[64] The human being, in its entire life and as a whole, is in need of conversion. That it is the whole human being who is involved in conversion not only implies that it is impossible to quantify sanctification, but also that it is an ongoing movement spanning the entire life of each human being.

The conversion of each individual human being is imparted in the conversion of Christ. The *totus-totus* aspect is a description of two incompatible determinations of the human being that include all human beings. Again we can note that the difference between Christians and non-Christians is placed at the noetic and not at the ontological level. This distinction is often expressed with the help of the terminology *de jure* and *de facto*. All human beings are reconciled with God *(de jure)*, but not all human beings are aware of it *(de facto)*.[65]

---

64. See *CD* IV/2, pp. 582-84.

65. "The creation of man's new form of existence as God's covenant-partner is not, therefore, something which is merely before us, even as concerns ourselves. We have not to achieve it by imitation. Even if we could do this — and we cannot — we should be too late; just as we should be far too late in any attempted creation of heaven and earth. All that we can do is to live under the heaven and on the earth which God has created good. Similarly,

To conclude: with his emphasis on *telos* Barth wishes to avoid any misunderstandings that would misread the content of the Reformation as an acceptance of *status quo* in the sense that it is primarily seen as a theological explanation of the ambiguity of life. Barth would not, as earlier mentioned, reject the view that life is ambiguous. Nor would he claim that theology abolishes this ambiguity. But he tries to avoid an interpretation of justification and sanctification that would hereby legitimize the *status quo.*

As with Brunner, faith and not sin is the fundamental and original structure of the human being's relation to God and the world.[66] In and through the proclamation of the gospel the human being becomes aware of its status as a sinner. In and through the proclamation of the gospel the human being becomes aware that it is a reconciled sinner, that it — through Christ — has been reinstated in the covenant. The human being is justified and sanctified in Christ. Justification and sanctification cannot be separated into two different acts, where the one (sanctification) is seen as the answer to the other (justification). Sanctification of the human being, like justification of the human being, is an act performed by God. Sanctification is not an individual act performed by the individual human being, but an act that is enacted by God in Christ for all human beings. The substitutionary act of the one man Jesus thereby not only relates to justification, but also to sanctification.[67]

Sanctification is therefore not a question of *imitatio Christi,* as the act of sanctification is prior to any attempt of *imitatio Christi.* Neither sanctification nor justification can be described as some kind of private arrangement between Christ and us, as such a description would not properly take into account the dialectic between the objective and the subjective aspects of revelation.

---

our only option is to see and accept as an accomplished fact man's new form of existence, our sanctification, and to direct ourselves accordingly. He Himself has accomplished it in a way which is *effective and authoritative for all,* for His whole people and all its individual members, and ultimately for the whole world" (*CD* IV/2, p. 516; my emphasis). See also *CD* IV/2, p. 518.

66. Sin is absence of faith, faith not absence of sin (see also Chapter 6). Brunner states for example: "The concept of faith is more fundamental than the concept of sin; for sin is apostasy from faith. . . . We need not presuppose sin to speak about faith; but we must presuppose faith to talk about sin." See Emil Brunner, *Truth as Encounter,* trans. Amandus W. Loos and David Cairns (Philadelphia: Westminster Press, 1964), p. 110.

67. See *CD* IV/2, p. 519.

In this way both justification and sanctification acquire a specific Christological content that is to be interpreted within Barth's emphasis on the Chalcedonian pattern. In Jesus Christ we see both the electing God and the elected human being, the judging God and the human being judged by God. In Christ *all* human beings are not only judged but also elected. In Christ *all* human beings are not only elected but also judged. This emphasis on universal election and universal judgment gives space for an understanding of justification and sanctification as a universal act that includes all human beings. Barth criticizes Calvin's understanding of sanctification on exactly this point, as Calvin — due to his individualistic understanding of the doctrine of predestination — could not operate with such an inclusivistic understanding of sanctification. According to Calvin the eternal election in Christ is only for "those who in God's eternal counsel are foreordained to salvation and therefore to reconciliation, justification and sanctification in Jesus Christ, while His existence has no positive significance or consequence for those who are excluded from this foreordination, for the reprobate" (*CD*, IV/2, p. 520). The result of such a line of thought is that the "*participatio* or *communicatio Christi,* and the justification and the sanctification of man grounded in it, is a divine action which has only particular significance. For the reprobate Jesus did not die" (*CD* IV/2, p. 520).[68]

Barth differs here strongly from Calvin because of the way in which he combines a particularistic and a universalistic strain of thought: particularistic, as the human being can only obtain knowledge of its new relation to God through the revelation in Christ; universalistic, as all human beings are included in God's saving act in Jesus Christ. The universal strain in Barth's theology is thus placed in his soteriology instead of in his epistemology. A consequence of this connection between a particular grounded epistemology and a universally based soteriology (based in the one God, who is God for all human beings) is that the individual human being who understands itself in the light of revelation is called to give witness to the hope for salvation of all human beings. This is a consequence of the inner connection between God's primordial will and the revelation of this will in the particular history of Jesus Christ (witnessed through the story of Jesus Christ).

68. For a further elaboration of Barth's rejection of the double outcome, see Chapter 10.

PART II

THE HUMANITY OF THE CREATURE

And in all the seriousness of truth, hear this: without *It* man cannot live. But he who lives with *It* alone is not a man.

Buber, *I and Thou*

So why don't you ever put your head in the oven? I don't know. There's always a new Nirvana album to look forward to, or something happening in *NYPD Blue* to make you want to watch the next episode.

Nick Hornby, *About a Boy*

CHAPTER 5

The Human Being as a Being in Encounter

Introduction

According to Barth, a theological anthropology differs from any other kind of anthropology as it first and foremost defines the human being as being the creature of God.[1] The human being is informed about this basic relation between God (the Creator) and itself (the creature) through the Word of God. It is the Word of God that enables the human being to see itself as being the object (and not the subject) of theology. Through the Word of God the human being becomes aware of its special role within the creation.[2] The framework for understanding the particular relation between

---

1. Barth refers explicitly to two types of non-theological anthropologies in his development of the criteria for doing theological anthropology. The two types are categorized as the "speculative theory of man" and the "exact science of man" respectively (see *CD* III/2, pp. 22-24). The former is according to Barth hostile to theological anthropology, as it presupposes that the human being is able to be "both the teacher and the pupil of truth. Whether teaching of this kind includes or excludes the idea of God, and in what form it may perhaps include it, is unessential" (*CD* III/2, p. 22). The latter does not in itself contradict a theological anthropology, as it does not intend to tell the truth about the human being. It is *a priori* restricted to dealing with the appearance of the human being rather than with the true being of the human being: "To the extent that science is exact, it will refrain from consolidating its formulæ and hypotheses as axioms and therefore treating them as revealed dogmas" (*CD* III/2, p. 23); "As such, the exact science of man cannot be the enemy of the Christian confession" (*CD* III/2, p. 24).

2. See *CD* III/2, p. 19.

God and the human being is the covenant, and the place at which this covenant is revealed most clearly is in the election of the human being in Jesus Christ. The real human being is revealed in Jesus as the son of Man. The reason why the real human being is revealed in the person Jesus of Nazareth is that he is the Son of God, that he is Christ. Barth's anthropology is based on the Christological double claim: that Jesus is Christ and that Christ is Jesus. The precondition for Barth's theological anthropology is thus that only in Jesus Christ is true humanity revealed.[3]

However, this does not imply that anthropology can be derived solely from Christology.[4] Christology is not anthropology; anthropology is not Christology. But the essence and the nature of the human being can only be perceived in the light of the real man, as the real man is revealed in Jesus Christ. The true covenantal relation between God and the human being is revealed in Jesus Christ. Jesus Christ is unique as he is the *only* human being who represents God before men, and men before God. Consequently, the movement within a specific theological anthropology

---

3. Barth denies that it is possible for the human being to reach a neutral standpoint from where it can give an adequate description of itself, since such a description leaves the relation between God and the human being out of the center of the human being's being: "Who is the man who to know himself first wishes to disregard the fact that he belongs to God, that he exists because he stands in relation to the work of God, that he lives for the glory, under the lordship and in the service of God?" (*CD* III/2, p. 75). It is this critique of the human being's ability to obtain self-insight in and through itself that is at the very core of Barth's critique of naturalism, idealism, existentialism, and theistic anthropology. In short, all of these four approaches are only able to describe the phenomenon of man, but not the real man. See also Christofer Frey, "Zur theologischen Anthropologie Karl Barths," in *Anthropologie als Thema der Theologie,* ed. Hermann Fischer (Göttingen: Vandenhoeck & Ruprecht, 1978), pp. 42-43, 47, 60. However, they are not without value for understanding the phenomenon of man in the light of the real man. In the words of Bromiley: "*Naturalism* puts man in his creaturely setting. *Idealism* pinpoints his distinctiveness. *Existentialism* portrays him in his openness to a transcendental other. *Theism* understands him theonomously as a rational being responsible before God in historical decision. None of these leads us directly to real man but on the presupposition that real man is known they all offer genuine information about him. No conflict exists, then, between these anthropologies and theological anthropology so long as they do not pretend to present real man but are content to offer symptomatic human phenomena." Geoffrey W. Bromiley, *Introduction to the Theology of Karl Barth* (Edinburgh: T. & T. Clark, 1996), p. 127; my emphasis.

4. See for example *CD* III/2, pp. 47, 71, 222.

has to go from the particular person Jesus Christ to the general human being, and not vice versa as it is most often asserted within a modern theological anthropology.[5]

The Human Being in the Cosmos

The human being is embedded in a God-given reality. The human being is, in Barth's terminology, living under heaven and on the earth.[6] The human person can only understand itself when it sees itself in this twofold embeddedness. That the human being lives under heaven and on the earth is at one and the same time a description that contains several applications not only for the content of a theological anthropology but also for *how* this anthropology can be executed. The human person cannot be viewed as a human being independently of its embeddedness in the cosmos. The human being is a creature among other creatures, although the human being has a distinctive role among all the other creatures. Thus, the human being cannot be perceived as what it is, a *human* being, when it is viewed as one fortuitous creature among all other creatures, or as one animal among all other animals.

The reality of the human being is different from the reality of the cosmos in which it is embedded, but the dignity of humanity is equal to the dignity of the cosmos, as both the human being and the cosmos as such acquire their dignity from the Creator of the cosmos.[7] The high view of humanity that we are later to find in Barth's opus should therefore not be misunderstood as a kind of attempt to detach the human being from the cosmos. The human being cannot cease to be a creature among other creatures. The relation between God and the human being can only be fully explored when it takes the human being's relation to the cosmos into account. It is therefore not enough to view the human being in terms of an interpersonal relation between God and the human being. The human being cannot be understood as a creature that is addressed alone by God, nor

5. This way of structuring a theological anthropology implies further that the eternal will of God is decisive not only for the understanding of the essence and nature of God but also for the essence and nature of the human being.

6. See for example *CD* III/2, pp. 4, 12, 16-19.

7. See *CD* III/2, p. 4.

can the human being be perceived as a creature standing isolated before God. So, the emphasis on the covenantal relationship between God and the human being does not exclude an awareness of the fact that the human being is embedded within the cosmos. But this embeddedness is subordinated to the covenantal relation — as it is through the interpersonal encounter, not only between God and the human being, but also between person and person that the human being becomes conscious of its embeddedness in the cosmos.[8]

Barth rejects granting any kind of cosmology a theological validity, if it is merely a way through which the human being is understood without reference to its God-given determination. In Barth's perspective cosmology is equivalent to a purely secular worldview, in which there is no room for a Creator. Without a Creator it would not make sense to interpret the world as creation. Consequently, it would not be intelligible to interpret creation in the light of the purpose of the Creator. The world would then be left to itself.

When Barth uses the term "cosmos" positively, it serves to indicate the particular role of the human being: namely that the human being as the only creature among all other creatures lives *under* heaven *on* the earth. The human being is neither an animal nor an angel.

> We see him [man] as belonging to heaven and earth, and equally bound and committed to both. We see him in the proximity of angels and animals. If we forget that he must remain loyal to the earth, we shall never truly understand him; and even less so if we forget that heaven is above him. (*CD* III/2, p. 4)

The claim that the human being lives under heaven means that the human being is determined by the will of God. In the election of the human being as covenant partner, God has given the human being a *telos* from outside of the human being itself, which differentiates the human being from any

---

8. "We are concerned with man as set in the cosmos and therefore not with man as alone before God or alone addressed by Him; not with a cosmos concentrated in man, and perhaps having no independent reality, but being only the phenomenal world, as radical Idealism maintains, of the mind of man. We have to do with the man who in the cosmos is confronted by another reality, and who is the more conscious and sure of its true and genuine reality the more he is conscious and sure of his own humanity and therefore his own reality by the encounter of man with man and of God and man" (*CD* III/2, p. 4).

other species in the cosmos. This *telos,* as we have already seen, is only accessible for the human being through the Word of God. Barth's understanding of the cosmos can be summarized in the following six points:[9]

(1) Cosmos includes human reality, as it is only possible to understand the cosmos as the creation of God, when it places the covenant between God and the human being in the center.

(2) The human being cannot be understood apart from its embeddedness in the cosmos, and the cosmos cannot be understood without the central role of the human being in the cosmos.

(3) The human being cannot be understood solely from its relation to the cosmos, but neither can the cosmos be fully described from the centrality of the human being.

(4) The human being is a part of the cosmos *prior* to the human reflection on the relation between the human being and the cosmos.

(5) If the human being reduces cosmos to nothing more than an instrument for the purpose of the human being, the human being will in the end inevitably instrumentalize both itself and cosmos. The human being would then understand itself as both the start and the end of the cosmos, whereby the human being would see itself as the center of the cosmos, rather than being in the center of the cosmos. In the former case the human being is without God; in the latter the human being is placed on earth under heaven.

(6) The reality external to the human being cannot be reduced to a construction of the human mind. However, the human being only has access to the cosmos through the relation between humanity and cosmos. Not everything is said about cosmos in and through this relation, but the human being is, nevertheless, restricted to speaking about cosmos in and through this relation. Barth's Kantian heritage is here obvious. This further implies that no independent understanding of either the human being without the cosmos or the cosmos without the human being is possible.

In short: the election of the human being is central to understanding the meaning and purpose of the cosmos. Any given cosmology that does not place the covenant at the very center of the cosmos is according to Barth

9. See *CD* III/2, pp. 3-19.

unable to interpret the cosmos as the work of creation of the Christian God. The purpose of a theological cosmology is not to sacralize the cosmos, let alone to blur the distinctions between God and the world, but at one and the same time to restrict and empower the human being. The former consists in a rejection of an instrumentalization of the world, the latter in the demand for the human being's active participation in the coming of the kingdom of God. Barth's cosmology, if one dares to say that he has one, is worked out within the realm of eschatology.

The Vertical Dimension:
The Real Man and the Phenomenon of Man (I)

The Christological duality is, on the level of the human being, reflected in the distinction between the real man and the phenomenon of man. This distinction is eschatological at its very core. In short, this approach to anthropology implies that the human being is viewed as the object of divine grace. The human being cannot place itself outside of the grace of God. Thus, the human being is incapable of speaking either the first or the last word about itself. The human being's self-contradiction is not the first word spoken about the human being. Logically, what is contradicted (the human self) must be prior to the contradiction. But it (the human being's self-contradiction) cannot even be the last word about the human being, as the future of the human being belongs to God.

> If man is the object of divine grace, his self-contradiction may be radical and total, but it is not the last word that has been spoken about him. For with God and from God he has a future which has not been decided by his self-contradiction or the divine judgment which as the sinner guilty of this self-contradiction he must inevitably incur, but which by the faithfulness and mercy of God is definitely decided in a very different way from what he deserves. If he is the object of God's favour, his self-contradiction may be radical and total, but it cannot even be the first word about him. The fact that he became a sinner cannot mean that he has spoken an originally valid word about himself, even in respect of his own origin and beginning. For the fact that he covered his creaturely being with infamy cannot mean that he has annulled or destroyed it. The fact of

> his fall cannot mean that what he is eternally before God and from God, His Creator and Lord, has been changed. (*CD* III/2, p. 31)[10]

If God wants to be merciful and graceful toward the human being, the human being cannot — willingly or not — fall out of his mercy and grace. This is another way to stress that the human being does not — due to the grace of God — receive a fair trial.

Any theological description of the human being that has its foundation in the human being's sinful character must therefore be characterized as inadequate and misleading. Sin is a corruption of what is prior to sin. Hence, a theological anthropology has to operate within the dialectic between the real human being (as God in his will originally intended the human being to be), the actual phenomenon of the human being (the human being in its fallen state), and the fact that the human being is not just a fallen human being, but a forgiven fallen human being. On the one hand, it is this dialectic which enables Barth to emphasize the realistic character of the human person. The human being is capable of causing death and destruction for no other reason than death and destruction itself. But this acceptance of the human being's potential wickedness, on the other hand, does not lead Barth to an interpretation of the human being in which this capability for evil is viewed as the most fundamental expression of the being of the human being. The acceptance of the fact that the human being is a fallen human being does not lead to hopelessness or despair. The actual experience of the human being's ability to create suffering and pain is not the basis for understanding what real humanity is. Experience of the human being's wickedness is overruled, so to speak.

To be really human is to be without sin, and therefore there is only one real human being who has lived: namely Jesus Christ. The sinless character of Jesus includes both a vertical and a horizontal aspect. Sinlessness has not only to do with the relation to the Father, but also with the relation to fellow human beings. What is to be noted explicitly here is that this one real man is the light in and through which the phenomenon of man should be interpreted. In and through this light, the phenomenon of man can be in-

---

10. This quote demonstrates how closely protology and eschatology are interconnected in the theology of Barth. The reason for this is Barth's heavy emphasis on the eternal will of God.

terpreted as being the object of the grace of God. This gives the human being a wholly other basis on which and from which to live. The human being has hereby received a new future given from the outside; the human being is hereby enabled to live in hope and faith rather than in mistrust and despair.

To try to understand the human being apart from its relation to God is from a Barthian perspective to be evaluated as an abstract speculation. The human being can never cease to be in relation to God — and thereby to be determined by God — as God never ceases to be in relation to the human being (due to the will of God). The essence of the human being is thus determined by the will of God. Of course the human being can be viewed apart from the God-man relation, but it is then a description that is only able to take into account the phenomenon of man and not the real man. The purpose of the real man is to be found in the decision of God to create man as God's own partner prior to the actual creation of man. The real man is therefore the creature within creation that most evidently mirrors the will of God, and the most pure *imago dei* in the creation is therefore to be found in the real man (and not the phenomenon of man).

The next question that inescapably comes to mind is: How — after the fall of man — is it possible for the human being to acknowledge the real man? To answer this question thoroughly, a further investigation of Barth's understanding of sin is necessary, but before I analyze the relation between sin and nothingness in the theology of Barth, I will indicate the answer. The human being as such cannot be interpreted as the *imago dei,* due to the reason that the human being after the fall can only be described as some kind of shadow-man: namely, a shadow of what the human being originally was intended to be. The human being who is revealed is the human being who does not live in "the wholeness of his created being."

> The point is that the revelation of God does not show us man as we wish to see him, in the wholeness of his created being, but in its perversion and corruption. (*CD* III/2, p. 26)

However, this does not mean that the human being after the fall is Godless. God has the power to reject the human being's rejection of God. Due to the grace of God, the human being is never, with or without his or her will, without the grace of God. Nor does it mean that a new creation (the sinful human being) has removed the original creation (the human being as God intended the human being to be).[11] If this were the case there would be no possible connection between the human being before and after the fall. Such a radical understanding of the disconnection between the real man and the phenomenon of man would have some serious theological consequences. *First,* that the human being after the fall would be understood as a primarily evil being. *Second,* that the Marcionitic abyss between the God of creation (the evil God) and the God of the Redemption (the good God) is transformed into a hiatus between the human being before (the good man) and after the fall (the evil man). Hence, Barth acknowledges that there has to be some kind of connection between the phenomenon of man and the real man, but he stresses that this connection can only be seen from the perspective of the real man. Noetically and ontologically there is no way from the phenomenon of man to the real man. The epistemological structure for knowing the real man is thereby similar to the structure for knowing God. Both can only happen through God's own revelation of himself in the incarnation. In Christ the human being is enabled to see the human being as the human being originally was intended to be: a human being living in and out of its relation to God. Thus, Christ is the real man.[12]

Yet, one should notice that to argue that there is no direct way either noetically or ontologically from the phenomenon of man to the real man is not the same as to say that the phenomenon of man is theologically uninteresting. But it is a question of giving phenomenology its rightful place in a constructive doctrinal theology. When the distinction between the real man and the phenomenon of man is revealed, it is thus possible for the human being to see analogies between the phenomenon of man and the real man. In fact, analogies between the real man and the phenomenon of man are not only possible but also necessary in order to understand both of

---

11. "At this point it may be seen *how God sees man in spite of and through his sin,* and therefore how we ourselves are incapable of seeing him. What is impossible with man, but possible with God emerges at this point, namely, the vision of nature and essence which can be distorted by sin but not destroyed or transmuted into something different, because even in its sinful distortion it is held in the hand of God, and in spite of its corruption is *not allowed to fall*" (*CD* III/2, p. 42; my emphasis). "The fact that man sins does not mean that God ceases to be God and therefore man man. In this context, too, we must say that man does not accomplish a new creation by sinning" (*CD* III/2, p. 227). See also *CD* III/2, p. 26.

12. See *CD* III/2, p. 50.

them in the right perspective. On the one hand, the phenomenon of man must be understood in light of the real man, and in this light it can (retrospectively) be seen as analogous to the real man. On the other hand, the understanding of the real man can only be completed when the phenomenon of man is also taken into consideration — a connection between the real man and the phenomenon of man must be established. (In the case of Barth: anthropology is worked out with the help of insights from the I-Thou philosophy.) The real man is not a description of the human being as it actually is, but a description of the human being seen in the light of God's determination of the human being. This determination is revealed in God's act toward the human being in the man Jesus Christ. Jesus is at one and the same time a man like any other human person (if it were not so — the result would be a docetic Christology), and a man different from all other human beings (Jesus Christ is the one person who has full trust in and fully obeys the will of God).

If one wants to grasp the way in which Barth relates Christology and anthropology, it is essential to note that the real man is used as an eschatological category in which the human being sees itself under the final judgment and grace of God, both of which are fulfilled in Christ. The real man can only be found in Jesus Christ, in and through whom the kingdom of God has already arrived. A theological anthropology must therefore, according to Barth, be grounded in Christology even though they are not identical.

The Horizontal Dimension:
The I-Thou Encounter as the Basic Form of Humanity

The dialectic between the real man and the phenomenon of man is developed on the horizontal level in Barth's description of the basic form of humanity, in which he uses the terminology of the I-Thou philosophy to emphasize the relational character of the human being.[13] One needs only read

---

13. See *CD* III/2, pp. 222-85. This section of the *CD* plays an important role in Daniel Price's analysis of Barth's anthropology. See Daniel J. Price, *Karl Barth's Anthropology in Light of Modern Thought* (Grand Rapids: Eerdmans, 2002), esp. pp. 130-61. For a discussion of Buber's influence on Barth's anthropology see also Dieter Becker, *Karl Barth und Martin Buber — Denker in dialogischer Nachbarschaft? Zur Bedeutung Martin Bubers für*

a few pages of Barth's description of the basic form of humanity in the *CD* before one realizes how deeply Barth is influenced by the I-Thou philosophy (especially Martin Buber's).[14] Let me just state two examples here to demonstrate this:

> at the very root of my being and from the very first I am in encounter with the being of the Thou, under his claim, and with my own being constituting a claim upon him. And the humanity of human being is this total determination as being in encounter with the being of the Thou, as being with the fellow-man, as fellow-humanity. (*CD* III/2, p. 247)

> "I am" is not an empty but a filled reality. As I am, the other is like me. I am as I am in a relation. . . . What I am and posit as myself, I am and posit in relation to his [the Thou] positing and being, in distinction from and connexion with this alien happening which is

---

die Anthropologie Karl Barths (Göttingen: Vandenhoeck & Ruprecht, 1986), and Martin Leiner, "Martin Buber und Karl Barth," *Zeitschrift für Dialektische Theologie* 17, no. 2 (2001): 188-91.

14. Martin Buber (1878-1965) was the leading figure of the I-Thou philosophy, which is also known as the philosophy of dialogue. He was inspired by Chasidism (Jewish mysticism), which plays an inestimable role in his accentuation of the spirit as an intersubjective reality. I am here interested in the "late" Buber, who from around 1920 and onward started to develop a philosophy of dialogue, which first and foremost is represented in his appraised book *Ich und Du*. I will refer to Martin Buber, *I and Thou*, trans. Ronald Gregor Smith (New York: Scribner Classics, 2000).

Another important, but less known, thinker within the philosophy of dialogue was Ferdinand Ebner (1882-1931). He was a self-taught philosopher and theologian, who worked all his life as a schoolteacher. Like Buber, Ebner also tried to overcome an idealistic and naturalistic approach to humanity, but he seems — unlike Buber — to base the anthropological aspects of the philosophy of dialogue in a Trinitarian God-concept. Or to put it otherwise, it seems to be the Trinitarian understanding of God that enables the human being to participate in any intersubjective relation. See Ferdinand Ebner, *Das Wort und die geistige Realitäten. Pneumatologische Fragmente* (Wien: Herder-Verlag, 1952). The book did not receive any major public interest, but it had nonetheless an impact on several dialectical theologians (especially Emil Brunner, Friedrich Gogarten, and Karl Heim), whereby it also had an impact on the development of the dialectical theology as such. See also Christof Gestrich, *Neuzeitliches Denken und die Spaltung der dialektischen Theologie. Zur Frage der natürlichen Theologie* (Tübingen: J. C. B. Mohr [Paul Siebeck], 1977), p. 33.

characterised by the fact that I can see and recognise and accept this alien being and positing as one which corresponds to my own. This alien being and positing does not belong, therefore, to the general mass of happenings in the external world. In face of it I cannot refer back to myself, asserting and developing myself from myself as from a neutral point quite apart from it. The being and positing of this Thou reaches and affects me, for it is not that of an It, but of the Thou without which I should not be I. . . . My own being and positing takes place in and with the fact that I am claimed by that of the other and occupied with it. (*CD* III/2, p. 246)

Barth does not, though, at any place in the *CD* thoroughly account for his inspiration from and interpretation of the I-Thou philosophy. Instead he states that one should not be too excited if similarities can be found between his description of the basic form of humanity and Buber's description of the human being as a being in encounter. Not that he is ashamed of this, but the similarities and approximations are presented as merely coincident, as if Barth's theology were dependent on being independent of philosophy. Barth does refer explicitly to Buber at a few places in the *CD*, but here it seems to serve more to distract than to inform the reader of the connections and differences between the I-Thou philosophy's and Barth's interpretations of the human being as a being in encounter. Barth mentions for example the "Jew Buber" along the same line as "the pagan Confucius, and the atheist L. Feuerbach" (*CD* III/2, p. 277). It does not demand the skill of a professor to see that here the adjectives do not serve as much as a qualification as a disqualification of the mentioned thinkers.

In fact, Barth had not only read but also thoroughly analyzed and discussed Buber's book *I and Thou* in a part of his lectures on anthropology in the winter semester 1943/44 in Basel.[15] These until recently unpublished lectures served as Barth's preparation for *CD* III/2. The heading for the overall section, in which the analysis of Buber took place, was: "The Hu-

---

15. The manuscript is now available in facsimile on CD-ROM: Karl Barth, "Des Menschen Menschlichkeit," in *Unveröffentlichte Texte zur Kirchlichen Dogmatik. Supplemente zur Karl Barth-Gesamtausgabe 1*, ed. Hans-Anton Drewes (Zurich: Theologischer Verlag, 2005), pp. 1084-1109. Hereafter cited as *Des Menschen Menschlichkeit*. I will refer to this manuscript in the following. I will, where Barth quotes Buber's book, use the earlier-mentioned English translation of Ronald Gregor Smith. Consequently, the page numbers quoted of Barth will be changed to the numbers in the English translation.

manity of the Human Being" (Barth, *Des Menschen Menschlichkeit*, p. 1027).
I will in the following demonstrate how closely Barth had read Buber by
referring to some of the major points in his analysis of Buber. This includes
(also) some rather sharp critique of Buber (which is also "missing" in the
CD).

Throughout his presentation and analysis of Buber, Barth is aware of
the differences between the two, which means that he does not try to "baptize" Buber (as Brunner does in his book *The Truth as Encounter*). The differences are allowed to remain. Nevertheless, I find that Barth's anthropology is influenced so highly by the I-Thou philosophy that it is misleading
to trust Barth's own understatement of Buber's impact on the section of
anthropology in the *CD*.

To begin with, Barth gives Buber's book *I and Thou* a very positive
evaluation, which includes an acknowledgment of the impact Buber's
book has had on German Protestant theology. It is a book that due to its
depth and richness deserves respect and attention (Barth, *Des Menschen
Menschlichkeit*, p. 1084). With his fundamental distinction between two
types of relation — an *I-Thou* relation compared to an *I-It* relation —
Buber wishes to overcome a typical subject-object dualism. The I-It distinction is trapped within the Cartesian myth about the self-determined
subject, where the human subject is constituted as an I (read: an autonomous and independent subject) prior to the encounter with the encountering subject. Buber wishes to replace the I-It relation with an I-Thou relation, whereby the human being is freed from the illusion of being a self-
determined subject. The relation between the human I and the encountering Thou is symmetrical. The encountering Thou (let it be nature, fellow
human beings, or God) must not be transformed into an object owned by
the human I. A true encounter is first established when the encountering
object is seen as a subject (a "some*body*" instead of a "some*thing*"). The
human I must be opened from the outside; the "Thou-less" self must be
replaced by a relational self. A real human I is first established in its encountering with another subject (the I-Thou relation). This relation must
take place in a real encounter, and not in the form of a self-reflection, as
self-reflection still allows space for an autonomous, independent human I.
In other words, the encounter between two subjects dispels the I's illusion
of being a "Thou-less" I.[16]

16. Barth argues along the same line of thought in the *CD*, when he states that hu-

The human I first becomes a real subject in its encounter with another I (the I-Thou relation). Even prior to any awareness of this relation the being of the human person is a being in relation. The relation thus directs the subject back to its own ground or fundament. On the interpersonal level the encounter entails no pre-established order between the encountering subjects. They both receive their identity through the meeting. To be in relation can therefore not be viewed as an appendix to or an accidental capacity within the being of humanity. To be is to be-in-relation. The awareness of the differentiation between the I-It and the I-Thou relation frees the human being from the illusion of idealism that nothing can be conceived as real outside of the human being's consciousness. The philosophy of dialogue contains instead an immanent claim of realism: a pre-cultural, pre-historical *Entworfenheit* is presupposed. Thus the encountering subject must be viewed as the primary actor in the encounter — it is the Thou that comes to me, and not the other way round. The meeting between the two encountering subjects presupposes an openness that in itself excludes the idea of an "absolute and self-sufficient I," which again can be described as an "empty I."[17]

The human being becomes inhuman if it lives in a pure I-It relationship. Buber distinguishes here between person *(Person)* and individuals *(Eigenwesen)*.[18] The former demands an encountering subject, the latter an encountering object. One should note that Buber's distinction between the I-It and the I-Thou relation counts for all aspects of the encountering reality: nature, men, and spiritual beings *(den geistigen Wesenheiten)* (see Barth, *Des Menschen Menschlichkeit,* p. 1086).

---

manity is based on the interpersonal encounter between the human I and Thou. He writes for example: "Since I am not an It, but an I and therefore a Thou, he [the Thou] is reached and affected by me no less than I am by him. . . . In being myself, I cannot help being what I am for him. In this sense, too, there is no line of retreat to a place where I exist neutrally for him, where I do not affect him, where I do not owe him anything, where I with my being and positing do not have to take any account of his. The only line of retreat is again that of a retreat to inhumanity — to the inhumanity of a being without the Thou in relation to which I can be alone, to the 'I am' of an empty subject which cannot find fulfilment or really be a human subject, but is always, or always becomes again, an illusion" (*CD* III/2, p. 247).

17. See Barth, *Des Menschen Menschlichkeit,* p. 1084.

18. See Barth, *Des Menschen Menschlichkeit,* p. 1089; Martin Buber, *Das dialogische Prinzip* (Gütersloh: Gütersloher Verlagshaus, 2002), p. 67; Buber, *I and Thou,* p. 69.

The reason why nature can be seen as a possible partaker in an I-Thou relation is that God is in the being of the being, without being identical with it. God is being-itself, which means that God is the precondition for all being. Thus according to Buber the metaphor of God must not be restricted to a personalized one, as God then, willy-nilly, would be interpreted as one subject among other subjects. At one and the same time the difference and the identity between the creation and the Creator must be maintained. Buber differs here strongly from Barth, which becomes clear in his non-personalized description of the relation between man and God, as the "one boundless flow of the real life" (Barth, *Des Menschen Menschlichkeit*, p. 1093). This description is part of a longer passage, which Barth quotes from Buber. The aim of the quote is to show how Buber describes the difference between the relation to God and all other relations. In the words of Buber:

> This [the achievement of the power that works in the relation between God and man] does not mean that this one relation is set beside the others; for it is the universal relation, into which all streams pour, yet without exhausting their waters. Who wishes to make division and define boundaries between sea and streams? There we find only the one flow from *I* to *Thou*, unending, the one boundless flow of the real life. Life cannot be divided between a real relation with God and an unreal relation of *I* and *It* with the world — you cannot both truly pray to God and profit by the world. He who knows the world as something by which he is to profit knows God also in the same way. (102). (Barth, *Des Menschen Menschlichkeit*, pp. 1092-93)

Buber is a dialectical thinker who emphasizes the dialectical relation between God and the world. In fact, one could describe this relation with the help of a Chalcedonian vocabulary: "without separation, without confusion." Buber stresses very much the non-personal being of God. The purpose of this is pious enough: namely at one and the same time to secure the otherness and the sameness of God. One does not find God by leaving the world, nor does one find him by looking at the world.[19]

19. "To look away from the world, or to stare at it, does not help a man to reach God; but he who sees the world in Him stands in His presence. 'Here world, there God' is the language of *It*; 'God in the world' is another language of *It*; but to eliminate or leave be-

Barth and Buber share the conviction that humanity needs a transcendental form of reasoning, which goes beyond the boundaries of an "internal" form of reasoning. They are both aware that modern theology has to operate between the pitfalls of subjectivism and objectivism, naturalism and idealism. It is not enough to ground the constitution of the human I by an intersubjective I-Thou relation (in opposition to an I-It relation). A meta-level must be introduced between an eternal Thou (God) and a spatially and chronologically limited I. But they disagree in the way the encounter between the divine Thou and the human I takes place. It is probably this disagreement that makes it impossible for Barth to either see or to acknowledge the coherence between the dialectical structure in the philosophy of dialogue, as the I-Thou philosophy is also called, and his own theology of revelation. But before I elaborate Barth's critique of Buber, I will state two further points, where I find a close connection in their approach to defining the essence of humanity as relation-between-encountering-subjects.

On the anthropological level Buber operates with a distinction between reality and irreality. The irreality belongs to the human person who remains within the I-It relation, who does not take the step from the I-It relation to the I-Thou relation, who remains to look at the encountering reality as if it were mute, who remains to objectify the encountering reality, who remains within a self-absorbing reflection (in opposition to an open spontaneity), who keeps asking what good is in it for me. To be a human person is to live in reality, which again means to live in relation to other encountering subjects. If not, one is not to be defined as a person *(Person)*, but as an individual *(Eigenwesen);* one does not take part in the real being *(seiende),* but one becomes instead a spectator to one's own being *(soseiende).* Where the "person says, 'I am,' the individual says, 'I am such-and-such.' . . . Individuality in differentiating itself from others is rendered remote from true being."[20] Thus Buber distinguishes between a real I (real

---

hind nothing at all, to include the whole world in the Thou, to give the world its due and its truth, to include nothing beside God but everything in him — this is full and complete relation. . . . Of course God is the 'wholly Other'; but He is also the wholly Same, the wholly Present. Of course He is the *Mysterium Tremendum* that appears and overthrows; but He is also the mystery of the self-evident, nearer to me than my *I*" (p. 80). Barth, *Des Menschen Menschlichkeit,* pp. 1091-92. This is only a part of quite a long passage that Barth quotes from Buber.

20. See Buber, *I and Thou,* p. 68.

self) and a non-real I (an apparent self).[21] A structural similarity to Barth's distinction between the phenomenon of the human being and the real human being is obvious here.

However, Buber does not claim that a human person can be living in an I-Thou relation persistently. In fact, this is not possible. A shift *must* take place from an I-Thou relation to an I-It relation, as the I-Thou relation is so intense that one would be swallowed or burned out, if one should stay within this without interruption. One cannot live in pure presence.[22] The I-It relation is an inexplicable part of life. What concerns Buber is that the I-It relation must not be perceived as the most fundamental aspect of the being of the human person, as such an understanding would fail to take the spiritual reality into account. If the human being only lives in an I-It relation to the encountering world, the I of the human person would become empty.[23] The human being would live in the illusion that it was not only the center, but also the master of the universe. The encountering reality would then inevitably be instrumentalized, as its only aim would be to cover the actual requirements of the human being.

The fact that the human person cannot live consistently in the I-Thou relationship should not mislead the human being to think that the I-It relation is the basic form of humanity. A transformation *ought* to take place from an I-It to an I-Thou relation. But a major difference exists here between the necessity of the dialectical move between the I-Thou and the I-It relation, and the I-It and the I-Thou relation. The I-Thou relation will with certainty convert into an I-It relation, whereas the I-It relation might only transform into an I-Thou relation.

---

21. Barth, *Des Menschen Menschlichkeit*, p. 1085; Buber, *I and Thou*, p. 68.

22. Buber is here, according to my reading, more a realistic than an idealistic thinker. At this point of the interpretation I do disagree with Barth, who criticizes Buber for being a thinker stuck within idealism — more about this later.

23. Barth and Buber are here arguing along the same line. In the *CD* Barth states for example: "A pure, absolute and self-sufficient I is an illusion, for as an I, even as I think and express this I, I am not alone or self-sufficient, but am distinguished from and connected with a Thou in which I find a being like my own, so that there is no place for an interpretation of the 'I am' which means isolation and necessarily consists in a description of the sovereign self-positing of an empty subject by eruptions of its pure, absolute and self-sufficient abyss. The I is not pure, absolute or self-sufficient" (*CD* III/2, pp. 245-46).

The I-Thou-World inevitably transforms itself perpetually into the I-It-World.[24] It is not possible to live in the bare present. Life would be quite consumed if precautions were not taken to subdue the present speedily and thoroughly. But it is possible to live in the bare past, indeed only in it may a life be organised. We only need to fill each moment with experiencing and using, and it ceases to burn.

And in all the seriousness of truth, hear this: without *It* man cannot live. But he who lives with *It* alone is not a man. (44). (Barth, *Des Menschen Menschlichkeit*, pp. 1088-89)

But now the opposite, the other relation: The I-It world can transform itself into the I-Thou world.[25] The particular *Thou*, after the relational event has run its course, is *bound* to become an *It*. The particular *It*, by entering the relational event, *may* become a *Thou*. (43). (Barth, *Des Menschen Menschlichkeit*, p. 1089)

These two quotes help us to grasp the inner dialectic between the I-Thou and the I-It relation in the work of Buber. The emphasis on the presence, on the actual encounter, on the non-materialistic understanding of not only the human person, but of the cosmos as such, is not to be equated with a romantic or an idealistic concept of the human person that leaves out the ambiguity of life. No one can escape the tension, and duality, between the I-It and the I-Thou relation. In the words of Buber:

No man is pure person and no man pure individuality. None is wholly real, and none wholly unreal. Every man lives in the twofold *I*. "But there are men so defined by person that they may be called persons, and men so defined by individuality that they may be called individuals. True history is decided in the field between these two poles." (69). (Barth, *Des Menschen Menschlichkeit*, p. 1089)

When the encounter between the I and the Thou takes place, this takes place through a medium: the encountering I. The encountering I is here the medium of the divine Thou, which means that it is the divine Thou that enables the individual human person to enter into an I-Thou rela-

24. My translation.
25. My translation.

tion.[26] Thus the divine Thou is the precondition for the possible encounter between the human I and the encountering Thou (let it be in the form of nature, man, or spiritual beings). Without the gift of the Spirit it would not be possible for the human being to live in pure presence, which is what takes place in the actual encounter between the I and the Thou. With this reception of Buber in mind, one cannot help wondering why Barth in the *CD* avoids any reference to his own previous interpretation and analysis of Buber.

Barth's critique of Buber — that he is a thinker who is caught up in German idealism — is at best to be described as a caricature. Barth argues that Buber, if he really wanted to break the sovereignty of the subject, should have operated with a Thou-I relation, rather than an I-Thou relation.[27] According to Barth, the I remains master of the encountering reality; the I by itself can establish the shift from the I-It relation to the I-Thou relation, which in theological language is to say that the human person remains as the subject of its own redemption (see Barth, *Des Menschen Menschlichkeit*, p. 1099). The paradox is that although Barth seems to be very loyal to Buber in his presentation of him in his lecture "The Humanity of the Human Being," he obviously misses several of the discussed issues in his theological critique of Buber's work.[28] The dialectic between the *active* and the *passive* dimension of human action in the actual encounter (Barth, *Des Menschen Menschlichkeit*, p. 1091) is for example left out in Barth's rather rigorous critique of Buber: that the human I is able, by itself, to shift from an I-It to an I-Thou relation. Thus the change of relation is interpreted as an immanent possibility in the individual human person, which the individual human being can decide to potentialize or not. The human being becomes hereby its own potential savior. To talk about a fall of man would thereby become nonsense. One should rather define it as a dropout. Buber does not take into account that the honor of God has been discredited by the fall of man. Consequently, God is not the compassionate savior, who is risking his own life for the sake of the salvation of human beings, but rather the principle and foundation of the cosmos. Thus, the incarnation was not necessary for the salvation of the human being. Jesus was not the

---

26. See Barth, *Des Menschen Menschlichkeit*, p. 1090.
27. See Barth, *Des Menschen Menschlichkeit*, p. 1099.
28. See Barth, *Des Menschen Menschlichkeit*, pp. 1099-1109.

savior, but a good example of how human beings ought to live. When one says Jesus, one should also say Socrates and Goethe — all of them were good moral teachers.[29]

Perhaps one can explain the rigidity of Barth's critique by looking at the differences in the two thinkers' overall framework. The center in Barth's theology is the revelation of God in Jesus Christ. Barth is one of the Western theologians, if not *the* Western theologian, who has most strictly emphasized that God must be understood as a person. God is a radically free subject who acts according to his absolutely free will. This picture of God as an autonomous subject dominates Barth's doctrine of the Trinity, where God is described as one subject with three modes of being *(seinsweisen)*. The only place where the pure presence of the divine Thou is revealed is in the life, death, and resurrection of Jesus Christ, who, unlike any other human being, lived his life fully for others. The revelation of the real encounter must therefore take place in Christ.[30]

Any phenomenological analysis of the basic form of humanity must therefore be interpreted in the light of the Jesus-event. Without this it is not possible to see the real difference between the I-Thou and the I-It encounter. The need for the Christological foundation of the I-Thou relation regards the noetical aspect. The ontological aspect, the reason why the human being is a relational being, is to be found in the will of God. God created the human being as his own covenant partner, for which reason the human being is not secondarily but first and foremost a relational being. Humanity is in its very basis characterized by its interrelational character — but again, this can only be known through God's own revelation of himself in Jesus Christ.

Barth is either unable or unwilling to see the positive aspect of the method of Buber, who presupposes a non-personalized approach to God. This has, as already said, the pious purpose at one and the same time of preserving the otherness and the sameness of God. Barth dismisses such an approach, as he equals it with natural theology, where a hidden God re-

---

29. Barth, *Des Menschen Menschlichkeit,* pp. 1090 and 1109.

30. Barth makes this point very clear in the *CD,* where he for example states: "Jesus is man for His fellows, and therefore the image of God, in a way which others cannot even approach, just as they cannot be for God in the sense that He is. He alone is the Son of God, and therefore His humanity alone can be described as the being of an I which is wholly from and to the fellow human Thou, and therefore a genuine I" (*CD* III/2, p. 222).

mains outside of the revelation — for which reason he talks in the *CD* at several places about the absurdity of this understanding of a "God against God." It is not my topic to enter into a discussion with Barth on his rejection of a non-personalized interpretation of God here. Yet I think the reference to the two different approaches (non-personalized versus strictly personalized) to the being of God helps us see why Barth at the level of phenomenological analysis can be so highly inspired by Buber, but remain silent about it in his magnum opus, the *CD*.

I will proceed to a presentation and analysis of Barth's own use of the I-Thou terminology in his description of the basic form of humanity in the *CD*. The human I is constituted as an I in relation to a Thou. The "I am" includes a "Thou art." Humanity is in its very basis characterized by its interrelational character.[31]

> If we see man in and for himself, and therefore without his fellows, we do not see him at all. If we see him in opposition or even neutrality towards his fellows, we do not see him at all. If we think that

---

31. However, Barth misuses the I-Thou relation in *CD* III/2, pp. 285-324, where he opts for a specific gender understanding of the I-Thou relation. Of course, it should be noted that the overall emphasis here is to describe humanity as humanity in fellowship. But to make this fellowship concrete Barth describes the relation between male and female as a God-given relation, in which the woman is subordinated to the man (see for example *CD* III/2, p. 309). This idea of subordination is described not only with the "usual" references to the creation (for example Gen. 1:27 and 2:18-25), but also with the help of the asymmetry in the relation between the "I" and the "Thou." The asymmetry is here placed specifically at the distinction between the genders. This gender interpretation of the I-Thou relation is the background for Barth's sexual ethic in the *Church Dogmatics* III/4. See Karl Barth, *Church Dogmatics* III/4 (Edinburgh: T. & T. Clark, 1961), pp. 116-240. In short: the I-Thou relation is used as a way not only to describe but also to legitimize theologically an asymmetrical relation between men and women. This has been one of the reasons why most feminist theologians have been very critical of Barth's theology, which they have regarded as a kind of outdated male-biased Protestant version of scholasticism. It has also been labeled as speculative, non-contextual, ahistorical, neo-orthodox, and/or patriarchal. But more recently, especially on the theological scene in America, a more positive feminist approach to Barth's theology has emerged. Two positive feminist approaches are: Cynthia L. Rigby, "The Real Word Really Became Real Flesh: Karl Barth's Contribution to a Feminist Incarnational Christology" (Princeton, unpublished Ph.D. thesis, 1998), and Katherine Sonderegger, "Barth and Feminism," in *The Cambridge Companion to Karl Barth*, ed. John Webster (Cambridge: Cambridge University Press, 2000), pp. 258-73.

his humanity is only subsequently and secondarily determined, as
an incidental enrichment, by the fact that he is not alone, we do not
see him at all. If we do not realise and take into account from the
very outset, from the first glance and word, the fact that he has a
neighbour, we do not see him at all. (*CD* III/2, pp. 226-27)

The minimal definition of our humanity, of humanity generally,
must be that it is the being of man in encounter, and in this sense
the determination of man as a being with the other man. (*CD* III/2,
p. 247)

Thus, the human being cannot adequately be described with the help of an
emphasis on the human being's self-awareness.[32] This would reduce the
encountering fellow human being to an invention within the history or
myth of the I. At this stage of the argument it should be noted, however,
that Barth explicitly states that the relation between the human I and the
human Thou does not inform the human being about its own origin
(namely that it is created by God). The encounter between the human I
and the human Thou is "only" able to fill out the actual content of the creation (that humanity consists in fellow humanity). It is in the universality
of God, who has created and elected all human beings to be his own covenant partners, that fellow humanity is founded.

The emphasis on fellow humanity does not overrule the individuality of each individual human person.[33] That humanity consists in fellow
humanity is not the same as to suspend the individuality of each encountering subject. Each "being has its own validity, dignity and self-
certainty" (*CD* III/2, p. 248). In fact, Barth's use of the encounter between the I and the Thou stresses the individuality of each particular
human being, as both the I and the Thou — in the encounter — maintain themselves as individual subjects. Further, Barth uses the I-Thou en-

---

32. See *CD* III/2, pp. 229-31. Barth exemplifies his critique with the help of an extensive excursus on Nietzsche, whom he reads as the prototype for a perception of humanity
without the fellow human being. See *CD* III/2, pp. 231-42.

33. "I do not become Thou, nor Thou I, in this co-existence. On the contrary, as I
and Thou are together, their being acquires the character, the human style, of always being I for the self and Thou for the other. As we are in this encounter we are thus distinguished. On both sides . . . the being has its own validity, dignity and self-certainty" (*CD*
III/2, p. 248).

counter as a way to demonstrate that the being of the human being is dynamic. The encounter does not describe a relationship "between two static complexes of being, but between two which are dynamic, which move out from themselves, which exist, and which meet or encounter each other in their existence. The 'I am' and the 'Thou art' encounter each other as two histories" (*CD* III/2, p. 248). The human being is not describable with the help of the term *esse,* but rather with the help of the term *existere.*[34]

Barth operates with four categories in his description of the content of the actual encounter between the human I and the human Thou. In and through this encounter the humanity of each individual subject is confirmed.[35]

Mutual Seeing

The I is to look for a fellow human being in the encountering Thou. The I is not to look past or beyond the encountering person, as the I then looks at the Thou as an object among other objects. Eye contact between the two encountering persons is necessary for the establishment of a real encounter. But the I should not just look at the Thou as a fellow human being. The I should also let the Thou look at the I as a fellow human being. One has to open oneself, to let oneself be looked at, if this encounter is really to take place. Barth opts in this way for a "two-sided openness" between the two encountering subjects.

> To see the other thus means directly to let oneself be seen by him. If I do not do this, I do not see him. Conversely, as I do it, as I let him look me in the eye, I see him. The two together constitute the full human significance of the eye and its seeing. All seeing is inhuman in which the one who sees hides himself, refusing to be seen by the fellow-man whom he sees. The point is not unimportant that it is always two men, and therefore a real I and Thou, who look them-

---

34. See *CD* III/2, p. 248.

35. See here also Price's description of the fourfold basic form of humanity: Price, *Karl Barth's Anthropology,* pp. 146-58.

selves in the eye and can thus see one another and be seen by one another. (*CD* III/2, p. 250)

One cannot be seen without being vulnerable. One has to let the other see oneself, as one really is, and not just as one would like to be seen. Thus dignity is related to vulnerability in the opposite way to what is commonly thought. Barth's emphasis on the two-sided openness in the encounter between the "I" and the "Thou" as a basic characteristic for humanity might be quite surprising for many "opponents" or "followers" of Barth — especially in the Danish debate, where it has been very common to read Barth from an anti-Løgstrup perspective, and vice versa. Which of these "standard readings" of Barth would be able to incorporate the following quote?

> Where it [a two-sided openness] lacks, and to the extent that it lacks, humanity does not occur. To the extent that we withhold and conceal ourselves, and therefore do not move or move any more out of ourselves to know others and to let ourselves be known by them, our existence is inhuman, even though in all other respects we exist at the highest level of humanity. The isolation in which we try to persist, the lack of participation which we show in relation to others and thus *thrust* upon others in relation to ourselves, is inhumanity. The expression: "That is no concern of mine," or: "That is no concern of yours," is almost always wrong, because it almost always means that the being of this or that man is nothing to me and my being nothing to him; that I will neither see him nor let myself be seen by him; that my eyes are too good for him and I am too good for his eyes; that my openness reaches its limit in him. *But conversely, where openness obtains, humanity begins to occur.* To the extent that we move out of ourselves, not refusing to know others or being afraid to be known by them, our existence is human, even though in all other respects we may exist at the very lowest level of humanity. (*CD* III/2, p. 251; my emphasis)

Mutual Speech and Hearing

Mutual speech and hearing differs from seeing as encounter, as the latter is only receptive, whereas the former is also active and spontaneous. Mutual speech and hearing gives the actual encounter content. One (the I) is no longer exposed to the other's (the Thou's) speechless interpretation. One now has the chance to put oneself forward, to present one's own self-interpretation to the other. The aim of this self-presentation is not to gain popularity or to vindicate oneself in front of the other, but to establish a meeting between one's own self-conception and the other's conception of one and vice versa. This openness is necessary for a real encounter between two subjects. The act of mutual speech and hearing involves four part-actions: "reciprocal expression and its reciprocal reception, reciprocal address and its reciprocal reception" (*CD* III/2, p. 253). A reciprocal communication has to take place between the two encountering subjects. This communication can be split up in the following eight part-aspects:

a.[1] The I's self-expression to the Thou
a.[2] The Thou's self-expression to the I
b.[1] The I's reception of the Thou's self-expression
b.[2] The Thou's reception of the I's self-expression
c.[1] The I's self-addressing the Thou
c.[2] The Thou's self-addressing the I
d.[1] The I's reception of the Thou's self-addressing
d.[2] The Thou's reception of the I's self-addressing

I will limit myself here to sketching some of the elements contained in Barth's analysis of the content of the speech-act between the I and the Thou, the Thou and the I. *First,* the obligation of the I to make him- or herself clear and understandable to the Thou. One must speak to the other for the sake of the other. The other must have the chance to become acquainted with one's self-perception. The Thou is hereby taken seriously as an encountering subject, with whom I want to enter into a dialogue — and not to use for my own purpose (a more sophisticated version of seeing the Thou as an object, rather than an encountering subject). Self-communication has nothing to do with any kind of attempt to turn on the charm and thereby present oneself as well as possible.

Second, I am to hear the self-expression of the other with a real expectation of learning something more and new about the encountering other than I already have learned (or at least think that I have learned) through my own wordless perception of the other. This entails not only that the I as a recipient of the encountering Thou's self-communication is asked to let the Thou's word break through my suspicion (which is already there prior to the self-communication). It implies also that I keep being reminded of my "filter of interpretation," since it is an illusion to think that I can totally eliminate this disturbing filter. Instead, I have to be aware of its role and function — and thereby become enabled to diminish its role within the reception of the other's self-declaration. In other words: the encountering Thou "does not leave me to the picture which I have formed of him" (*CD* III/2, p. 255).

Third, the act of speech — through which communication between the encountering subjects takes place — is more than an act of self-expression. This could, in fact, take place in a degenerated form, namely, as two monologues instead of one dialogue. The self-addressing of the I to the Thou includes a claim on the Thou. The Thou is released from isolation through this address. "The word of address is necessary as a kind of penetration from the sphere of the one into the sphere of another being. As I address another, whether in the form of exposition, question, petition or demand, but always with the request to be heard, I ask that he should not remain in isolation but be there for me" (*CD* III/2, p. 256). The Thou becomes an encountering Thou — and thereby also an I through this address. To address the other is to take the other seriously as an individual and equal subject. This quest of the other entails a double-sided openness. On the one hand, I reveal myself in an address to the Thou. The Thou cannot look at me in the same way as before. On the other hand, I expect the Thou to open him- or herself in the answering of my address. This understanding of the address from the I to the Thou as a breakthrough of isolation is also one way to express the universal aspect within the particular encounter. In the particular encounter both the I and the Thou become part of an encounter, namely, the encounter with life. In the particular encounter one is reminded of life as such: to live with and for others.

Finally, the address of the encountering Thou has to be heard as an address that really does change the situation of the I. To hear the other "is not just a matter of the other but of myself" (*CD* III/2, p. 259). If one does not listen with the attitude of openness and the desire to receive, if one does not listen with the expectation of and willingness to be changed, one does not listen in a human but in an inhuman way! Barth here opposes a self-imposed humility, in which one thinks everything is done by listening to the other in humility. In fact, this can be just another type of arrogance. To listen in humility just for the sake of listening is inhuman! Thus, the other person is not being seen as an equal, encountering subject. Barth stresses this point when he states that one should listen under the compulsion that one is affected by hearing what the encountering human person says.[36]

The most intriguing element in this analysis of the verbal encounter between the I and the Thou is the dialectic between the subject (the one who speaks) and the object (the one who listens). Barth here turns the normally perceived relation upside down. He states that the speaker should speak for the sake of seeking and helping the other (one does not speak for the sake of placing oneself in the center of the communication, to obtain acceptance, etc.), and the hearer needs to listen for the sake of the hearer him- or herself (one does not listen for the sake of helping the other, to give the other time, etc.). The motive behind the verbal encounter between the I and the Thou decides whether one looks at the other as a subject or an object, whether one acts humanly or inhumanly.

Mutual Assistance in the Act of Being

The encounter between the I and the Thou is completed in acts, where the I puts him- or herself into the service of the Thou, and vice versa. As in the previous aspects of the relation this is based on a reciprocal structure. The helper needs one who is to be helped as much as the one to be helped needs the helper.[37] The distinction between humanity and inhumanity is not identical with the distinction between altruism and egoism. "Egoistic activity — for there is a healthy egoism — can be thoroughly human if, without denying itself as such, it is placed at the service of the summons issued by the Thou to the I" (*CD* III/2, p. 261). And altruistic activity can be inhuman if it does not respect the other as an equal subject. Altruistic activity is supremely inhuman "if it does not derive from the summons of the one to the other, but the one acts under the illusion that he does not need the other just as much as the other now seems to need him" (*CD* III/2, p. 261).

36. See *CD* III/2, p. 259.
37. See Price, *Karl Barth's Anthropology,* pp. 151-52.

Further, if one does not hear the call of others one plunges into inhumanity. The real loser is thus the one who withholds his or her help to the other, as he or she may be described as an empty subject. An empty subject is a subject who either rejects receiving help when help is needed, or who refuses to give help when help is called for. An empty subject is a subject who wants to live in an illusion of being self-sufficient — and thereby distances him- or herself from the essence of life: to live in the encounter. This is not, however, to be misunderstood as if one can or should live the life of the other. Only Christ can — due to his divinity — represent other men fully. Human beings must not play each other's God. The result of this would inevitably — despite the helper's best intentions — end up in an assault on the one who cries out for help. To wish to live another's life is just another way of expressing a disrespect for the other human person — whether it takes place in the form of misperceived goodness or disrespectful paternalism. Perhaps the mutual assistance in the act of being can best be described with Barth's description of the need for rendering mutual assistance:

> My humanity depends upon the fact that I am always aware, and my action is determined by the awareness that *I need the assistance of* others as a fish needs water. It depends upon my not being content with what I can do for myself, but calling for the Thou to give me the benefit of his action as well. (*CD* III/2, p. 263; my emphasis)

> My humanity depends upon the fact that I am always aware, and my action is determined by the awareness that *I need to give my assistance to* the Thou as a fish needs water. It depends upon my answering the call of the other, and acting on his behalf, even in and with what I do for myself. (*CD* III/2, p. 264; my emphasis)

Mutual Gladness

All of the above three stages in the description of humanity would be empty (that is: inhuman) if they do not happen with gladness on the part of both the encountering subjects.[38] The question Barth puts forward is whether the human being is in a position in which it can decide to act

38. See *CD* III/2, p. 265.

gladly or reluctantly toward the other. If the human being were in such a position the encounter with the fellow human would be subordinated to the human being as an autonomous subject. The relational character of the being of the human being would then — despite its character of necessity — be accidental. If the human being can choose how to relate in the relation, and if one way to interact (gladly) is as valid as the other (reluctantly), the relation is not seen as belonging to the very essence of the being of the human being.

> In his [man's] essence, his innermost being, his heart, he is only what he is gladly. If we do not speak primarily of what he is gladly, we do not speak of his essence, of himself. If it is an open question whether he is human and engaged in the encounter of I and Thou gladly or reluctantly, this means no more and no less than that it does not belong to his essence as man to be human. . . . Humanity is alien to him. It is a kind of hat which he can put on and take off. It is not intrinsic to him. (*CD* III/2, p. 267)

The mutual relation of the I and the Thou would then be alien to the innermost being of the human being, which would leave man in the "waste of isolation" (see *CD* III/2, p. 273). It belongs, on the contrary, to the very essence of the human being to live in relation. Hence, the human being must live gladly in this relation.[39]

But (and this is important to note) the emphasis on the mutual encounter does not imply a suspension of the particular human being's individuality. In fact, the encounter can only take place when the individuality of each encountering subject is maintained. Two potential and opposite errors are obvious here: self-sacrifice and self-redoubling.[40]

Self-sacrifice takes place when one totally neglects one's own life and task and only wishes to live for the sake of the other. A noble course, one might think, but the other has hereby acquired the doubtful honor of being the center of and the aim for my own life. The distance between me and the other is thereby abolished, which not only makes the one who sac-

---

39. It should here be noted that the opposite of gladly is not, as one might think, reluctantly, but neutrally. Consequently, the differentiation between gladness and reluctance is subordinated to the distinction between gladness and neutrality. See *CD* III/2, pp. 266-69.

40. See *CD* III/2, pp. 269-71.

rifices him- or herself vulnerable; it is also an interference in the other person's sphere of intimacy. So the self-sacrifice is not only problematic due to the case that one (I) loses oneself totally for the sake of the other (Thou). It is also problematic that this seemingly unselfish act is really a transgression of another person's boundaries. By binding oneself to another in this self-sacrificing way, one deeply injures the other person — not only because one breaks into his sphere of intimacy, but also because one does not encounter the other as an individual and particular human being. The other is thereby deprived of the possibility of being enriched in the mutual encounter. The self-sacrifice also sacrifices the other. The other expects me to be a singular subject, a genuine counterpart. Instead he or she becomes a self-willed slave, whereby the other has been turned into a tyrant.

Self-redoubling takes place when one wants to find him- or herself in the other person. The encounter is then reduced to a striving for self-redoubling, as the encounter only serves to "extend and enrich and deepen and confirm and secure" the being of the I (CD III/2, p. 270). Again, the relation is broken, as no encounter takes place between two individual subjects. The wish to find oneself in the other person is a wish that inevitably ends up in a wish to possess the other person. This is similar to the structure of a relationship in a "cheap love-story" in which the encounter is described as a "campaign of conquest" (CD III/2, p. 270).

One consequence of this self-seeking I is that the I will always be left on his or her own. The I has hereby deprived him- or herself of the possibility of being enriched by the encounter with the Thou. The wish to own the other is then not only a wrongful claim on the other, it is also a road into self-isolation, as no real mutual interaction between the two encountering subjects takes place. The final result of such a striving for self-confirmation will therefore very likely be a "mutual attack or a mutual withdrawal" (CD III/2, p. 271).

However, Barth's heavy use of the encounter between the I and the Thou does not intend to disguise the acknowledgment of the "fact of life": that each individual subject is "really quite alone" (see CD III/2, p. 270). It does not pretend that the feeling of alienation can be replaced by an idealistic Christian perception of fellowship. I cannot own the encountering Thou (and thereby redouble myself), nor can I be owned by the encountering Thou (and thereby lose myself). Freedom and mutuality are necessary preconditions for a perception of the basic form of humanity as a meeting between the I and the Thou.

In a togetherness which is accepted gladly and in freedom man is neither a slave nor a tyrant and the fellow-man is neither a slave nor tyrant, but both are companions, associates, comrades, fellows and helpmates. As such they are indispensable to one another. As such they intend and expect and seek one another. As such they cannot be without one another. As such they look one another in the eye, and speak and listen to one another, and render mutual assistance. All this is impossible if they meet as tyrant and slave. Between tyrant and slave there is no genuine encounter, and even genuine encounter ceases to be genuine to the extent that it is understood and actualised on the one side or the other as the encounter of tyrant and slave. Only in the atmosphere of freedom can it be genuine. Companions are free. So are associates. So are comrades. So are fellows. So are helpmates. Only what takes place between such as these is humanity. (*CD* III/2, p. 271)[41]

This quote demonstrates very clearly how Barth subordinates mutual bondage and limitation to mutual freedom and reciprocity.

An understanding of the being of the human person that does not have the relation between fellow human beings at its very core is, according to Barth, not a description of humanity but of inhumanity. When the encounter takes place in gladness, the human being fulfills its own determination — and this is what Barth describes as freedom. Freedom is not to be equated with a plurality of choices, where the individual human being can choose freely between various options.[42] Freedom would then be confused with freedom of choices. Such a perception of freedom presupposes not only that the human person — from a neutral platform — can choose between the various options, but also that the individual human being determines its own *telos*. In that case, there would be no schism between the general ability to choose and the actual choice. But, freedom is not the

41. On the interpersonal level Barth agrees with Hegel's critique of a unilateral relation, where a one-sided power structure exists between the two encountering subjects. Barth differs, however, from Hegel in the way he emphasizes that the subject is first established as a subject in, and not prior to, the encounter between the two encountering subjects. See also my comparison of Barth with Hegel and Schleiermacher in Chapter 4.

42. From the perspective of Barth this would rather be to describe a tyranny of options. Freedom is then viewed abstractly, and not concretely.

ability to decide which possibility is to be transformed into reality (freedom would then be confused with power). Freedom is not to define one's own *telos* (freedom would then be confused with autonomy). Rather, the freedom of the human being consists in the ability to live in and out of its determination. This determination consists on the vertical level in the human being's call to be the covenant partner of God, and on the horizontal level in the mutual bonds — and thereby also mutual limitations — between fellow human beings.[43] The human being is therefore to live out its humanity in gladness, as this corresponds to the only adequate response to the covenant: praise.

This emphasis on gladness relates to a stress on the human being's spontaneity. In spontaneous acts the necessity through which the act takes place can no longer be described purely in terms of an external law. It has also become an inner law. If the human being breaks out of the interpersonal fellowship, or if the human being lives reluctantly instead of gladly in this fellowship, the human being contradicts its own nature. Such a contradiction cannot be described as freedom. Instead, it is sin.[44]

> But this means that if we are to embrace human nature as such, as created and given by God, then we must grasp as its motivating element the decisive point that man is essentially determined to be with his fellow-man gladly, in the indicated freedom of the heart. By nature he has no possibility or point of departure for any other choice. If we have to maintain that he has this choice in fact, it does not derive from his nature. For we cannot make God his Creator responsible for this fatal possibility. And it is even worse if we praise the Creator for obviously giving man the possibility of a different choice. For this is to praise Him for allowing and enabling man to choose in his heart inhumanity as well as humanity, and therefore to be in his heart inhuman as well as human, or both perhaps alternately. (*CD* III/2, p. 273)

43. For a description of the connection between freedom on the vertical and the horizontal level, see Wolf Krötke, "Gott und Mensch als Partner. Zur Bedeutung einer zentralen Kategorie in Karl Barths Kirchlicher Dogmatik," *Zeitschrift für Theologie und Kirche*, Beiheft 6 (1986): 166-68, who unites them both under the heading: "Das Geschöpfh als Partner Gottes."

44. See *CD* III/2, p. 273.

It is sin to withdraw from mutual fellowship with other human beings because this withdrawal contradicts the nature of the human being created by God. When the human being withdraws from this fellowship, the human being turns life into death.

It is really interesting to note here that Barth argues with reference to the creation and the nature of the human being. Does Barth contradict himself here? Has he suddenly become more positive toward a theology of creation — or perhaps even of a theological use of a natural law? Is the law given in the heart of a human being? Not really, because the nature of the human being here refers to how God has intended the human being to live. When the human being refuses to live in accordance with the intention of God, this is not to be seen as a genuine expression of the human person's freedom. It is instead an expression of the human being's capacity for self-destruction and self-denial.[45]

I find that this is the horizontal correlate to what Barth elsewhere describes as the impossible possibility: the human being's wish to live without God. Here it is enough to note that, viewed from the horizontal level, sin is to live in a wasteful and self-willed isolation. When the human being is acting against its nature, the human being is acting in an inhuman and unnatural way.[46] Consequently, Barth would not be able to support a theology that evaluates the fall of man positively by arguing that it is in the fall that the constitution of the human being has taken place. Freedom would then be interpreted as a freedom to fall. This does not imply, however, that Barth means it is possible to go behind the fall. The human being is the fallen human being. But it means that the fallen human being can only be

---

45. On the vertical level this has taken place in the human being's rejection of being God's covenant partner. As the apostasy from God is no real option — the apostasy from the fellow human being is no real option either. Both are an expression of the depravation that takes place when the human being turns life into death. One main difference between the two is that the former can be overruled by the one who first is thought ruled out (from an eschatological perspective the final words belong to God — not only there and then but also here and now). The latter means the waste of life here and now. The rejection of fellowship might here not be overruled.

46. The knowledge of the human being's nature cannot, obviously, be derived from a pure empirical or phenomenological analysis of the being of the human person. Barth's analysis of the basic form of humanity presupposes that it is the revelation of the real man in Jesus Christ that enables the human being to see the correlation between the real man and the phenomenon of man.

understood as what it is — a fallen human being — when the human person is viewed in the perspective of what it has fallen from. The human being, despite its fallenness, has not fallen out of the grace of God. A new creature has not been created in and through the fall. I will clarify this point under the next heading: sin and nothingness. What is important to note here is that human beings' ability to reject their relation to either God and/or fellow men is not the same as human freedom.[47]

47. Barth opposes here a trend within theology, where the human being's ability to reject God is viewed as an expression of the freedom that God in his love has granted the human being. See *CD* III/2, p. 227. This line of thought is often in recent theology combined with a modernistic approach to and use of the teaching of the double outcome. The perception of freedom that lies behind this approval of the human being's ability to reject God is the idea that the human being is an autonomous being who is able to withdraw itself from the love of God. Such an interpretation emphasizes, willy-nilly, the human being's own decision. Christianity can then be communicated through fear as well as love. The question: "Where do you want to spend your eternity?" becomes hereby a relevant question. But this line of thought would eliminate the difference between God and the human being, as the love and grace of God would then be reduced to operating under the same rules of reciprocity as the interpersonal encounter does. I will later argue, in my analysis of Barth's reinterpretation of the double outcome (see Chapter 10), that Barth is an exponent of the idea of universalism.

CHAPTER 6

Sin and Nothingness

The Real Man and the Phenomenon of Man (II)

I have already demonstrated some of the elements implied in Barth's distinction between the phenomenon of man and the real man. The whole presupposition behind this differentiation is that the human being is no less able to describe him- or herself in the light of God's purpose with the human being than the human being is able to describe God. The radical distinction between God and the human being includes therefore a radical distinction between the human being as it is viewed from the perspective of God, and the human being as it is viewed from the perspective of the human being itself.

Harmatology and anthropology are closely connected in *CD* III/2 and *CD* III/3.[1] The human being is on the one hand described as a sinner, totally corrupted and pervaded in its nature.[2] On the other hand, the human being is described as the reconciled human being, who despite its sinful being is called to live out of the covenant according to its "creaturely being and essence":

> Only in the light of God's Word is his [man's] radical and total self-contradiction clear to him, and only in this light may he look be-

---

1. Karl Barth, *Church Dogmatics* III/3 (Edinburgh: T. & T. Clark, 1960); hereafter cited as *CD* III/3.
2. See *CD* III/2, p. 28.

121

yond this self-contradiction to the creaturely being and essence preserved in spite of it. (*CD* III/2, p. 31)

This paradox must be seen in connection with the distinction between the real man and the phenomenon of man. This distinction is subtler than it at first appeared. The phenomenon of man is not only a description of the human being without the Word of God, but also a description of the human being as a sinner in the light of the Word of God. The real man is not only a description of Christ as the one real man, but it is also a description of the reconciled human being. What is real for Barth is not what empirically can be seen and said about the human being (this is just a shadow of the real), but is instead how the human being is seen in relation to God from the perspective of God's election. God is the point through which reality can be described. I will clarify the above distinction between phenomenon of man and real man with the help of the following four points:

(1) **The phenomenon of man I:** The human being viewed without the Word of God is only a shadow of what the human being ought to be.
(2) **The phenomenon of man II:** Only through the Word of God can the human being obtain an awareness of its real situation: the radical corruption and depravation of the human being's nature.
(3) **The real man I:** In Jesus Christ the true human being is revealed. Jesus *is* the real human being.
(4) **The real man II:** The reconciled human being, who in and through Jesus Christ is reinstated as God's own covenant partner.

The result of this double understanding of the phenomenon of man and the real man is that we seem to be left with a paradox. The Word of God not only informs the human being about its *status corruptionis,* but also informs the human being about the God-given fact that the human being is constituted by God. On the one hand, the human being can know nothing of its God-given nature, because of the fall. On the other hand, the human being is to be aware of its creaturely essence and being prior to the fall. One of Barth's ways of describing this paradox is this:

We must insist on two points. On the one hand, the realisation of the *total* and *radical corruption* of human nature must not be weakened. The shame which covers it is unbroken, and therefore there can be no question of gaining an insight into man as unaffected by sin. On the other hand, *the question of human nature as constituted by God is reasonable and necessary.* We have no right to be frightened by the difficulty which seems to make the answering of this question almost hopeless. (*CD* III/2, p. 29; my emphasis)

Consequently, the task for a theological anthropology must be to take into account both the radical corruption of humanity and the God-willed nature of the human being. The distinction between the phenomenon of man (I and II) and the real man (I and II) functions as a way through which the same human being is described from different perspectives, whereby sin in its full radicality is taken into account, without letting this (the description of the human being as a sinner) be the final theological characterization of the human being. The real man is the human being who is not first and foremost looked upon as a sinner, but who is first and foremost looked upon as a redeemed sinner. But two questions remain:

(1) How can the human being obtain access to both the phenomenon of man I and II and the real man I and II?

(2) How can it be possible to claim that the essence and being of the human being at one and the same time refer to the creaturely essence and being of the human being prior to the fall, and that the essence and being of the human being are totally corrupted and perverted?

From the perspective of the human being the solution can only be regarded as a paradox. Any knowledge grounded in the human being cannot lead to the distinction between the real man and the phenomenon of man, nor can it possibly demonstrate the connection between them:

If there is a necessary connexion between the realisation of our sin and that of our creaturely being, it is not within our power to establish this connexion or to derive the second of these insights from the first. We are capable neither of the one nor of the other, and therefore we cannot connect the two. (*CD* III/2, p. 31)

That they are connected is in itself an act of the grace of God. This connection is another way of explaining Barth's dialectic between God's Yes and No, No and Yes to the human being. The grace of God can in this way be described as a secret, since the Word of God at one and the same time tells us what we ourselves cannot know (that all human beings are sinners, and that despite their sinfulness they are still God's creatures) and that by ourselves we cannot know this.

Again, the human being should not be viewed primarily as a sinner. If this were the case, the sinner would turn into a new and second creation without any similarity to the human being created by God before the fall. If this sinful human being were a new and evil creation, the human being would not only be at war with itself and God, but would possibly be without God entirely. One consequence of the latter would be the possibility of a final damnation of the human being. The discrepancy between the phenomenon of man and the real man would in this case be an invincible discrepancy — both for the human being and for God. But the discrepancy is overcome in God. The human being as sinner is still the creature of God.

> We will not neglect to "bedenken," of course, that even as sinner the human being remains and will remain the creature of God. If his nature is wholly controlled by the fact that he has fallen away from God and can only be at odds with himself, yet this nature is not effaced, and *he cannot succeed in destroying it and making himself unreal. The distortion or corruption of his being is not the same thing as its annihilation.* Death itself does not spell annihilation. We cannot say, therefore, that he has ceased to exist as the one whom God created. (*CD* III/2, p. 27, rev. trans.; my emphasis)

How does this connect with the relation between the human being viewed as a sinner and the human being viewed as a redeemed sinner? The point is that the human being should see itself as it is looked at from the perspective of God, meaning that the human being should see itself in the light of God's grace and judgment. And looked at from this perspective the human being is at one and the same time both a sinner and a redeemed sinner. But the latter is the more final and it is therefore a sin (and a subtle one, that is) when the human being is so preoccupied with its sinful state that it becomes the very foundation for a theological anthropology.

EXCURSUS: THE DEBATE BETWEEN BARTH AND BRUNNER

Barth finds that the connection between God the Creator and God the Redeemer is missing in Brunner's work *Man in Revolt*.[3] Barth finds that Brunner — despite various statements in which he stresses that the Word of God is the essential background and foundation through which an ontology and a theological anthropology can be constructed — is only capable of reaching a description of the phenomenon of man (instead of the intended description of the real man). The problem, according to Barth, is that Brunner tries to synthesize two non-synthesizable points of view. Brunner at one and the same time claims that the human being is determined by the Word of God, and that the human being has a neutral capacity to decide whether it wants to be determined by the Word of God or not.

The free will of the human being thus plays an essential role in the human understanding of itself — not only in relation to fellow human beings but also in relation to God. The human being has the freedom to withdraw itself from the covenant. The human being's status as covenant partner is therefore also determined by the human being's own decision, whether the human being wants it to be so or not.[4] With his emphasis on a neutral capacity in the human being Brunner wishes to establish a connection between a general understanding of the human being and the human being seen in the light of the Word of God. This connection is established with the help of the free will. But such an accentuation of the free will results in a harmatology, where sin — from the perspective of the human being — is seen as a non-necessary part of the creation. Sin is in this way a possibility given within the creation itself. Hence sin cannot be described as an impossible possibility (a rejection of the essence of the human being: to be God's covenant partner), as Barth describes it. Thus, sin cannot be claimed to be negated through God's rejection of the human being's rejection of God. Instead, sin seems to acquire a constitutive role in the being of the human being, as it then belongs to the essence of the human being to

3. Emil Brunner, *Man in Revolt: A Christian Anthropology* (Philadelphia: Westminster Press, 1947). The following investigation is based on Barth's analysis of Brunner's book in *CD* III/2, pp. 128-32, originally published in 1948. The discussion with Brunner takes place here in a much more restrained tone than the discussion in 1934. However, this debate is still very much in the background of Barth's polemic against Brunner in 1948.

4. See *CD* III/2, p. 131. Barth opposes Brunner's perception of the relation between the free human will and the covenant. The human being can break the covenant, but the human being cannot dissolve it. The human being cannot set itself outside of the covenant. The breaking of the covenant is still an act that happens within the covenant. The human being can reject God, but the human being cannot reject God's rejection of the human being's rejection of God. See also *CD* III/2, pp. 33-34.

be able to choose to obey or disobey the Word of God.[5] The possibility of sin is therefore to be regarded as one of the possibilities given within the creatureliness of the human being. The result, then, is that the Word of God as constituted in the historical revelation of Jesus Christ can only be said to constitute man on a noetic but not on an ontic basis.[6] Ontically, the Word of God determines the being of the human being in the sense that the universal *Logos* is revealed in Jesus Christ.[7] The being of the human being is thereby constituted in the strictly formal sense that the human being as created by God is able to hear and live by means of the Word of God. But the human person does not necessarily do so. The Word of God does not include in itself a determination of the human person. Viewed from a Christological angle this implies that God has not decided over all human beings in the event of Christ. Consequently, Brunner has to operate with two distinctly different forms of the Word of God: the Word of God as Creator, and the Word of God as Redeemer.[8] This difference is not only formal, but also material. The result, from Brunner's perspective, is that it is possible to establish a theological anthropology that can be combined with a philosophy of existentialism. From Barth's perspective the result of Brunner's effort is an unsuccessful "crossbreed." Barth's judgment is that Brunner has inconsistently tried to combine two contradictory lines of thoughts: (1) that the human being is determined by the Word of God, and (2) that the human being is constituted by its own free will. The result is that Brunner has been forced to separate the Word of God the Creator and the Word of God the Redeemer formally as well as materially. Thus the salvation of the human person is not only determined by God, but the human being's own self-determination has acquired a soteriological force.[9] Barth's solution, uniting the Word of the Creator and the Word of the Redeemer, can be described as a "reversed Brunner." It is not the free will of the human being but the free will of God that constitutes the essence of the human being. The human being is not allowed to fall out of God's love toward humanity.[10] The life, death, and resurrection of Christ do not reveal the meaning of life in the abstract (as a possible possibility), but reveal the concrete love of God toward the human being. In the life, death, and resurrection of Jesus Christ God has reconciled the human being with God. The Christ-event

5. See *CD* III/2, p. 131. See also Christofer Frey, "Zur theologischen Anthropologie Karl Barths," in *Anthropologie als Thema der Theologie,* ed. Hermann Fischer (Göttingen: Vandenhoeck & Ruprecht, 1978), 46; Hendrik Van Oyen, "Bemerkungen zu Karl Barths Anthropologie," *Evangelische Ethik* 7 (1963): 297-99.

6. See *CD* III/2, pp. 131-32.

7. See *CD* III/2, p. 132.

8. See *CD* III/2, p. 132.

9. See also Gerrit C. Berkouwer, *The Triumph of Grace in the Theology of Karl Barth* (Grand Rapids: Eerdmans, 1956), pp. 263-67.

10. See *CD* III/2, p. 42.

thereby acquires an ontologically determining role for all human beings, whether they are aware of it or not.

The sinful state of the human being cannot be granted the status of being the primary theological description of the human being. The fall would thereby be overemphasized at the cost of reconciliation, which has already happened in Christ. If harmatology does not take the dialectic between the awareness of sin and the forgiveness of sin into account, harmatology would inevitably end up in a self-centered tribute to the *status quo*. Further, if the awareness of sin and the forgiveness of sin were separated into two distinctly different modes of time, the awareness of sin would then in itself become an independent source of revelation. The awareness of sin would in that case function as a general revelation of the *status corruptionis* of the human being. If this really were the case the fall would become more determinative than redemption for an understanding of theological anthropology — which Barth strongly opposes in his critique of Brunner. With his emphasis on the inseparable relation between the fall and redemption, redemption and the fall, Barth wants to avoid an understanding of the human being that stops at the *status corruptionis*.

That the human being is a sinner and always will remain a sinner does not neglect the fact that the human being is a redeemed sinner. It is in one and the same movement that the human being becomes aware that it is a sinner, and that it is a redeemed sinner. What sin is cannot be realized through the human being's general experience of the more unpleasant sides of life, such as for example mistrust, betrayal, failure, evil, etc. This is connected with the well-known fact that Barth reorganizes the Lutheran order of the relation between law and gospel to a relation between gospel and law. No human being can reach the gospel through the law; no human person can through the experience of life's wickedness reach an understanding of what sin is. Sin is much more radical than individuals' experience of what they themselves may define as sin.[11] To let sin be the final description of the human being is in itself a sin, as it is one way to not take fully into account the redeeming act of God in Christ. "We are forbidden to take sin more seriously than grace, or even as seriously as grace" (*CD* III/2, p. 41).[12] Thus, a theological anthropology should not focus so much on the fall (which does not mean that the fall can or should be neglected in any way) as on the redemption, which reinstates the human being in its original relationship to God. Both the first and the last word about the human being are to be found in God's decision, prior to creation, to create the human person as God's own covenant

11. A practical example of the devaluation of the term "sin" that takes place as soon as it is redrawn from its religious context and meaning is the way it is often used today as a favorite expression of various "health-prophets" when they describe the desire to eat food that exceeds the magic fat-limit of 3 percent.

12. See also *CD* III/2, p. 37.

partner. In the theology of Barth protology and eschatology are very closely inter-connected, as they both are rooted in the eternal will of God to be God for the human being.

It is not the fall — the human person viewed as a sinner — that constitutes what the human person is. Instead it is the eternal election of the human being in Jesus Christ. In the reconciliation of the human being, the human being has been restored to the covenant. The human being has a future with God, which only God decides. And it is the working of this future in the present that determines the life of the human being (a future we know from the past: the election of the human being prior to creation, revealed in Jesus Christ). This implies that the human being is not so much determined by what it is now (a sinner), as by what it will be (a saved sinner in the judgment of God). This hope for the future (the hope for salvation) is a hope that already in the present changes the situation and self-understanding of the human being (as the human being — also here and now — sees itself in and from this perspective of hope).[13] What determines the being of the human being is then not so much what the human person has been or is, but what the human person can be. The future is decisive for the present, more than the present is decisive for the future. Thus, the present is not the most adequate modality of time for describing the being of the human being.

The Problem of Nothingness

Nothingness as a Theological Problem

The world may not be as it looks at a first glance from the perspective of the human being. As the human being can only be understood as real in the light of the covenant between God and the human being, the cosmos can be perceived as the creation only in the light of the covenant between God and the human being. The whole creation is elected by God — not just the human being. The creation can be regarded as both the phenomenon of creation (the cosmos) and as the real creation (the creation as elected and created by God). The latter expresses the real *Sein* of the creation, the former the *Schein* of the creation (the being of the cosmos). It is from this perspective of the creation as elected and willed by God that Barth confronts the

---

13. In a painstakingly clear and succinct way, Gerhard Sauter describes the eschatological foundation of theological anthropology. See Gerhard Sauter, "Mensch sein — Mensch bleiben. Anthropologie als theologische Aufgabe," in *Anthropologie als Thema der Theologie,* ed. Hermann Fischer (Göttingen: Vandenhoeck & Ruprecht, 1978), p. 93.

question of nothingness.[14] Barth uses a well-known term here, but gives it a twist (as he often does) that gives it a new content.[15]

The description of nothingness is more than a description of what is not (nothing). The theological description of nothingness receives its specific content from the relation between God and creation. Nothingness is and cannot be seen as an attribute either to God or to the human being. Nor can nothingness in a strict and direct way be rooted in either the acts of God or in the acts of the human person.[16] It is important to note that Barth rejects the possibility of solving the problem of nothingness on a theoretical level.[17] Nothingness must not be granted a divinely willed purpose. Barth thus rejects the many and various ways found in the tradition in which the problem of nothingness (which Barth very much equals with the problem of evil and thereby also the problem of theodicy) has been solved. For Barth it is important that this problem is handled in a way that neither neglects the problem of evil, nor derives evil from God. Instead, the problem must be handled in a way that takes into account both the radicality of nothingness (a realistic perspective) and the radical grace and love of God (a perspective of grace). The "power of nothingness should be rated as low as possible in relation to God and as high as possible in relation to ourselves" (*CD* III/3, p. 295).

The problem of nothingness is essential to understanding the connection between the human being as a sinner and the human being as a redeemed sinner. Humanity is only perceived as humanity when the duality between the human being living on earth and under heaven is taken into

---

14. The material content of nothingness cannot be reduced to one singular topic. Barth notes that the concept of nothingness entails such different issues as real evil, real death, real devil, real hell, and real sin. It is the latter that mainly occupies Barth in his description of nothingness in *CD* III/3 §50, pp. 289-368. Consequently, it will be this aspect of nothingness that I will focus on in the following analysis.

15. According to Barth, nothingness is an annihilation of the relational being of the human subject. In contrast to this view, the modern philosophy of existence (Barth refers here explicitly to Heidegger and Sartre) claims that nothingness is a basic existential condition, which the human being has to become aware of to understand its own self. The human subject is thrown *(entworfen)* into nothing, which implies that an individualistic understanding of the human subject must be prior to a relational or a collectivistic perception of the human subject. See *CD* III/3, pp. 334-49.

16. See *CD* III/3, p. 292.

17. See *CD* III/3, p. 293.

account. Barth's paragraph on nothingness in *CD* III/3 (§50) will here be read as a case study on how the Christian faith determines the Christian's approach to reality.

The first attempt to dig more deeply into Barth's line of argument regarding the question of nothingness is to see which positions he wants to avoid — and thereby also to see how he lines up the field for what he defines as a Christian approach to the question of nothingness. Roughly speaking, Barth wants to avoid two pitfalls: to place the responsibility for nothingness solely on God or solely on the human being. In the case of the former the human being's picture of God would become dubious (as God also becomes the Creator of nothingness). In case of the latter God would become impotent (as the human being in this way would have the power to obstruct the will of God for good). This classical dilemma (normally called theodicy) is evaded in Barth's treatment of the question of nothingness. Instead Barth relates the issue of nothingness to God's eternal election. This must be seen in relation to Barth's soteriological universalism. Thus, a specific Christian approach to the question of nothingness must be established:

(1) Nothingness must not be evaluated as a third instance that is without any reference to God at all. Nothingness would then turn into a kind of anti-God and the result would be a dualistic perception of God and an anti-God.[18] Nothingness can only be described theologically when it is subordinated to the power of God. But it must be subordinated in such a way that it does not destroy the understanding of God as the loving and compassionate God. Nothingness does not belong to the being of God.[19]

(2) An independent understanding of nothingness, in which it is not subordinated to God, would eliminate the joy of Easter. In the event of Easter nothingness is already judged by God in Jesus Christ and thereby turned into nothing.[20]

(3) This judgment of nothingness (which destroys the power of total destruction in nothingness) is a judgment in which each individual hu-

---

18. See *CD* III/3, p. 293.

19. Barth defines the being of God as a being in grace, and the being of nothingness as the very negation of this being. See for example *CD* III/3, p. 353.

20. See *CD* III/3, p. 293.

man being participates in faith. God's overcoming of nothingness through Jesus Christ can from the perspective of the human being only be seen within the category of hope.[21] The human being should have confidence in God. The human being should be humble toward God. Both have to be said to avoid an unreasonable pessimism or a "cheap" optimism. Both are ways through which nothingness gains power over the human being. In the case of the former the human being rejects God's victory over nothingness in and through Jesus Christ. In the case of the latter the human being underestimates the power of nothingness.

(4) It will never be possible to solve the problem of nothingness at a theoretical level. This would either destroy the monism of God, or reduce the radical character of nothingness. Nothingness would then be given a purpose — and thereby be granted a meaning. But in Barth's perspective nothingness is — and has to be viewed as — meaninglessness. In other words, nothingness cannot be subordinated in some kind of inner dialectic within God or in some kind of outer dialectic between profane history and salvation history.

Thus on the one hand Barth wants to take into account the radical character of nothingness (as it is viewed from the perspective of the human being) and on the other hand to keep in mind that nothingness is always subordinate to God (as it is viewed from the perspective of God). One way to express this duality is to say that nothingness witnesses to the break between the Creator and the creation.[22] God is never directly (in and by himself) threatened by the power of nothingness, as this would imply a dualistic understanding of God and nothingness. But God is indirectly threatened, as the creation is threatened by the nothingness.

Real nothingness is without any God-given *telos*.[23] Real nothingness is

---

21. The victory is then a victory that can never turn into a principle owned by man. Hence it can never be separated from the fear of and faith in God: "Again, it is no less clearly wrong if this victorious might of faith is treated as if it were a principle at our own disposal, or if it is forgotten that the victory over nothingness can be ours only through hope in Jesus Christ, or if we think and speak of this adversary, who was certainly not defeated by us, in any other way than in the fear of God and the seriousness of faith" (*CD* III/3, p. 293).

22. See for example *CD* III/3, pp. 293-94.

23. Cf. Wolf Krötke, "The Humanity of the Human Person in Karl Barth's Anthro-

a purely destructive force whose aim is to destroy what already is.[24] Nothingness cannot be creative, but only destructive. Thus the being of real nothingness is different from both God and creation. But to say that nothingness is without any *telos* and without any meaning is a statement that asks for further clarification. This is provided by Barth's distinction between the positive and the negative aspect of creation.

The Positive and the Negative Aspects of Creation

Nothingness has nothing to do with the negative aspect of creation, which is still a part of creation and therefore also still an expression of the positive will of God. Both the light and the shadow side of creation belong to the wholeness of creation as it was intended and created by God. Thus the shadow side of creation and nothingness are not identical.[25] The shadow side of creation belongs to the fullness and the essence of creation. Death, for example, is a basic condition of life, which is given within creation itself. Barth distinguishes here between *sterben* ("the natural termination of life"), and *Tod* ("the ultimate irruption and triumph of that alien power which annihilates creaturely existence and thus discredits and disclaims the Creator").[26] The problem here is that nothingness has often been misinterpreted as a synonym for the ending of life (the transformation of being into non-being). But life itself is characterized by being lived out in a tension between the two poles of birth and death, creation and destruction. It belongs to the very essence of creation that it is stretched out in the tension between life and death, between what it is and what it will become.[27] This movement does not — not even when the movement finally

pology," in *The Cambridge Companion to Karl Barth*, ed. John Webster (Cambridge: Cambridge University Press, 2000), p. 165; Wolf Krötke, *Sünde und Nichtiges bei Karl Barth*, 2nd ed. (Neukirchen-Vluyn: Neukirchener Verlag, 1983), p. 48.

24. See Krötke, *Sünde und Nichtiges bei Karl Barth*, p. 46.

25. See *CD* III/3, p. 296.

26. See *CD* III/3, p. 310; Karl Barth, *Die Kirchliche Dogmatik* III/3 (Zollikon-Zürich: Evangelischer Verlag, 1950), p. 353; hereafter cited as *KD* III/3.

27. See also Krötke, *The Humanity of the Human Person in Karl Barth's Anthropology*, pp. 171-73. Krötke emphasizes here that death is not to be regarded as a result of original sin: "Barth did not understand this [mortality] to be an evil or negative fate which the Creator imposed upon us as a result of our sin" (p. 171). Finitude is a part of being a crea-

ends with death — end in nothingness. Nothingness is not a term describing what does not exist any more in the form that it formerly had. Instead, it is a term for the misperception — and thereby destruction — of what already is.

The ambiguity of life belongs to creation itself (the left side of creation) and cannot be seen as either a lack or a mistake in creation. It belongs to the fullness of creation and of each individual creature's life that it exists in contrasts and antitheses. The Yes (the positive side of creation) and the No (the negative side of creation) are dialectically connected, such that the one is unthinkable without the other. Viewed from this dialectic between the Yes and the No, creation is still a good creation.[28] In the incarnation God himself became a part of the Yes and the No that are given within the creation, as God hereby made himself "the Subject of both aspects of creaturely existence" (*CD* III/3, p. 296). God thereby embraces the whole creation in its antithetical character.

However, this dialectic between the right (the positive) and the left (the negative) side of creation does not transform the negative side of creation into a positive one. The individual human being's experience of the negative side of creation will still in each particular case be experienced as an accusation against God. Yet it is to be accepted as the frame in and through which life takes place. This presupposes that the creation as such — seen from an overall perspective — is good. The distinction between chaos and order, darkness and light, is good. The negative side will always remain as a reminder of the threat of chaos.[29] This chaos — due to the will of the Creator — will never be able to break out in its fully destructive potential again.

The reason why Barth puts such a high emphasis on the positive understanding of the dialectic between the positive and the negative side of creation is that he wants to avoid any confusion between the negative side of creation and nothingness. Such confusion would in itself be a victory for nothingness. Nothingness would then be understood as a part of creation itself — which it is not. Nothingness is the enemy not only of the

---

ture. Thus, "'eternal life' did not mean the negation of the mortality of the human, but rather the 'redemption' of his this-sided, finite and mortal being by the eternal, gracious God" (p. 172).

28. See *CD* III/3, pp. 296-97.
29. See *CD* III/3, p. 352.

creatures, but first and foremost the enemy of God. In other words: nothingness is not only the enemy of life; it is also the enemy of the power of life.[30] Therefore only God can win this battle against nothingness.[31] At this point it might be relevant to add that Barth has two different lines of approach when he treats the question of nothingness. At some places it seems to be the problem of evil that frames the whole question of nothingness. Nothingness is then understood within the framework of theodicy. At other places it seems more to be the question of nihilism that sets the agenda for discussion of nothingness. In what follows, the first aspect of nothingness (the problem of evil) should lead us to an investigation of how nothingness became reality. How did nothingness come into existence, and how does its existence coexist with the being of God? The second aspect (nihilism) should lead us to a questioning of the content of nothingness.[32] Finally, both aspects ask for a clarification of its effect on the human being: What power does it have over the human being? And in case this power can and should be broken — how?

The Existence of Nothingness

Barth does not give us an answer to the question of theodicy as such.[33] Why nothingness exists has to remain a riddle, but Barth radically changes the way in which this riddle is treated. He rejects a traditional metaphysical

30. See *CD* III/3, pp. 300-301.

31. One should notice here the inner dialectic within Barth's description of nothingness. We have previously seen the statement that God is not directly threatened by nothingness since nothingness is subordinate to God. Thus, it is the human being who is most directly threatened. But this indirect threat is a real threat since it is a threat against the creation of the Creator. Barth can therefore also state that nothingness is first and foremost an enemy of God.

32. See also Robert W. Jenson's analysis of the relation between evil and nihility in *Alpha and Omega: A Study in the Theology of Karl Barth* (New York: Thomas Nelson & Sons, 1963), pp. 33-46.

33. See Karl Barth, *Church Dogmatics* IV/3 (Edinburgh: T. & T. Clark, 1961 and 1962), p. 177: "It will always be obscure, unfathomable and baffling that something which is merely opposed to the will of God can have reality. We do not understand how this can be. But it is of a piece with the nature of evil that if we could explain how it may have reality it would not be evil." This volume will hereafter be cited as *CD* IV/3.

understanding of God without rejecting a theistic understanding of God. Nothingness is gaining reality in a different way than the rest of the creation. However, nothingness is still coming into existence through an act of God. Otherwise nothingness would not be subordinated to God — and would thus be beyond God's control. This, taken to its final consequence, would lead to a destruction of a monistic perception of God.

Election and Rejection

Nothingness is the negative consequence of election, as it expresses what is not elected. This argument is based on the logic that an election in itself always includes a rejection, that is to say, the rejection of what is not elected. But when the election from the beginning is universal, this must then imply that it finally includes a rejection of the rejected, whereby the universal election has reached its aim. I will elaborate on this point in Part III. Here I want to state that nothingness obtains reality through the election. Nothingness is nothing in itself, but consists only in a reference to (that is: a negation of) the election.[34] Nothingness comes into existence as the negative consequence of God's own election. This has to be strictly differentiated from the creation of God, which is created due to the positive will of God. Nothingness is given existence through God's rejection.

> Nothingness is that which *God does not will.* It lives only by the fact that it is that which God does not will. But it does live by this fact. For not only what God wills, but what He does not will, is potent, and must have a real correspondence. What really corresponds to that which God does not will is nothingness. (*CD* III/3, p. 352; my emphasis)

The distinction between what is elected and created by God due to the positive will of God and what is given a reality *sui generis* due to the power of the election (including the rejection entailed in election) is described with the help of a distinction between *opus proprium* and *opus alienum*.[35]

The *opus proprium* includes God's ongoing reign over and preservation of creation, which, together with election and creation, can be sum-

34. See *CD* III/3, p. 351.
35. See *CD* III/3, pp. 352-59.

marized as the grace of God toward creation. The *opus alienum* exists then as a rejection of the grace of God. *Das Nichtige* is hereby defined in specific Christian terms as the being that rejects, neglects, and suppresses the ultimate grace of God. It belongs to the honor and right of God to be gracious toward the creation. It belongs to the right and salvation of creation that it can receive and live in and out of the grace of God. What is real is the grace of God toward creation.[36] Both the right of God (to be gracious) and the right of the human being (to receive grace) is discharged by nothingness. Hence, nothingness consists in a depravation of what really is. Nothingness is a destructiveness that devastates the human being's ability to perceive the cosmos as creation.

The destruction implied in nothingness does not have a *telos* that goes beyond the destructiveness itself. The destruction can therefore only be described as evil. Nothingness cannot be absorbed in any kind of dialectic, in which the destructiveness is interpreted as the necessary negative stage of intermediation, which leads to a final and positive stage in and through which the former positive and negative stage is absorbed. Nothingness has nothing to do with either the essence of God or the essence of creation. Due to the fact that nothingness is a privation, given as the negative side of the election, and that nothingness is directed primarily against God, it is only God who can reduce nothingness to nothing.

But how can God eliminate nothingness? By fighting it on the premises of nothingness? If this were the case, God would then have to destroy nothingness in the sense of showing no grace toward it. The result would then be that nothingness, and not God, would be the real winner. Nothingness would thereby be confirmed — although in a strictly dialectical way — by God himself. The No of God toward nothingness therefore has to be a No that at one and the same time eliminates nothingness without creating a new — and even more radical — nothingness. The rejection of God has to be a rejection that also — dialectically, in one and the same movement — rejects its own rejection. The *opus proprium* will at the end be the only opus left, as the *opus alienum* will be embraced in the *opus proprium.*

36. Härle correctly emphasizes that nothingness is a negation of God's grace. Härle states further that grace is the embodiment of the positive will of God. Ergo, nothingness is an expression of what God does not want to happen, what goes against the grace of God. See Wilfried Härle, *Sein und Gnade. Die Ontologie in Karl Barths Kirchlicher Dogmatik* (Berlin: Walter de Gruyter, 1975).

The *opus alienum* exists only at the border of the rejection given within the election *(opus proprium I)*. When this rejection is rejected the border is eliminated, so that there is nothing left that is not embraced in the grace of God. The nothingness *(das Nichtige)* has in this way become nothing *(Nichts)*. The *opus proprium (opus proprium II)* has then — seen from the perspective of God — become the only opus left.[37]

But how has God been able to transform nothingness into nothing? According to Barth this is exactly what has happened in the Christ-event. God incarnated himself to become a part of the creation. In the incarnation God himself experienced finitude. God hereby also took the *opus alienum* on himself. The decision to do this is to be found solely in God's love and faithfulness toward creation. The act of God toward creation is therefore both in the acts of election, creation, and atonement an act of pure grace and love which nothingness cannot destroy. The being of God is the only being that nothingness cannot corrupt. The being of God is the only being in which grace will always remain not only its center but also its very foundation.

The Defeat of Nothingness

The grace of God is an all-embracing grace, which is also able to encounter nothingness. By God's entering into nothingness, nothingness has lost its power. To save the creation from nothingness, God became a part of creation. In the life and death of Jesus Christ we can see what it means to live in and out of the grace of God. The annihilation of nothingness is fulfilled in the death of Jesus Christ. This annihilation has two main features, which are both revealed in Jesus Christ: the eternal decision of God to take the punishment of human beings upon himself in the singular man Jesus, and Jesus' obedience toward God. This double movement expresses the only way through which nothingness can be defeated: by the willingness to give up life for the sake of life. Nothingness is defeated in the interrelation between the death on the cross and the resurrection. The latter is a proclamation of faith: that God finally and once and for all has conquered nothingness. To believe in God is thereby also to believe in the final destruction of nothingness:

37. See *CD* III/3, p. 360.

But it is no less true that this divine *opus alienum,* the whole activity of God on the left hand, was fulfilled and accomplished once and for all, and therefore deprived of its object, when it took place in all its dreadful fulness in the death of Jesus Christ. Nothingness had power over the creature. It could contradict and oppose it and break down its defences. It could make it its slave and instrument and therefore its victim. *But it was impotent against the God who humbled Himself, and Himself became a creature, and thus exposed Himself to its power and resisted it.* Nothingness could not master this victim. It could neither endure nor bear the presence of God in the flesh. It met with a prey which it could not match and by which it could only be destroyed as it tried to swallow it. *The fulness of the grace which God showed to His creature by Himself becoming a threatened, even ruined and lost creature, was its undoing.* (*CD* III/3, p. 362; my emphasis)

The life, death, and resurrection of Jesus show the all-embracing character of grace — and thereby also — the destruction of nothingness in the following seven ways (though this list may not be exhaustive).[38]

(1) Trust in God, which is expressed in the way Jesus lives and dies.
(2) Willingness to die as one accused of blasphemy.
(3) The prayer of forgiveness from the cross ("Father, forgive them, for they do not know what they are doing" [Luke 23:34]) demonstrates in full clarity the all-embracing character of grace.
(4) The collapse of reciprocity due to the structure of this prayer.
(5) The "ultimate" combination of self-abandonment and self-sacrifice. The prayer demonstrates that this sacrifice cannot be used as a tool of power. Power, for example, that could be expressed in the sentence: "All this I did for you!" where the main message is that the object is in debt to the subject.
(6) The overcoming of the fear of death. Life is worth dying for. The price that has to be paid to stay alive can in some circumstances be too high

---

38. It should be noted that the first six arguments are worked out from the perspective of the man Jesus. Barth operates here — so to speak — with a Christology from below. However, as we will see in Part III, Barth does not operate with a schism between a Christology from above and a Christology from below. They are united in the belief that Jesus is Christ, and that Christ is Jesus.

(whereby life in itself would turn into death). The willingness to die for others is an act of grace that in itself passes the boundaries of death.

(7) The resurrection: God's confirmation of the destruction of nothingness.[39]

Thus, the reason that nothingness is unable to conquer God is that God in Jesus Christ is able to resist its power, its ability to return evil with evil. Self-sacrifice and self-abandonment are the ultimate actions against nothingness:

> Everything ultimately depends on this one point, and we remember that it is not a theory or notion but the concrete event at the core of all Christian reality and truth — the self-giving of the son of God, His humiliation, incarnation and obedience unto death, even the death of the cross. It is here that the true conflict with nothingness takes place. And it is here that it is unmistakeably clear that it is God's own affair. All the statements and delimitations which we have made rest on this point and can be made only on this noetic and ontic basis. (*CD* III/3, p. 360)

Nothingness has hereby been defeated. Thus the *kenosis* of God (an active act) implies the emptiness of nothingness (a passive act). But this presentation of the structural pattern in the relation between God's *opus proprium* and God's *opus alienum* and the content in the life and death of Jesus Christ in relation to God's *opus proprium* and God's *opus alienum* is not exhaustive. To complete this description it must further be taken into consideration that one of the main differences between the *opus proprium* and the *opus alienum* consists in the fact that the *opus alienum* is not actively elected by God. It is not created due the eternal election of God, which again implies that it does not have a share in the eternity of God. Ergo, the *opus alienum* is — in contrast to the *opus proprium* — limited in time.[40] If it had a share in the eternity of God it would have been possible for it to turn into an ongoing dialectic in God's Yes and God's No. But as it is created passively instead of actively it does not have such a share. It will have an end, a limit, where the *opus proprium* has no

39. See also Chapter 12.
40. See *CD* III/3, pp. 360-63.

limit.[41] The *opus alienum* can therefore be finally defeated and overcome. There is no eternal dialectic between election and rejection.

In Christ nothingness has already been defeated. The defeat is not a defeat that has yet to take place. In Christ nothingness has been devastated. This implies that each individual Christian is called to understand him- or herself (and all other human beings too!) in the light of the actual defeat of nothingness. This interpretation might at first seem very odd, since it is much easier to perceive the world in the light of nothingness than it is to interpret the world in the light of the grace of God. And the only point through which this is possible is the life, death, and resurrection of Jesus Christ. Death is no longer the final limit through which the human being has to understand/accept its life.[42] Christians live in the tension between the resurrection (remembrance) of Jesus Christ and the Second Coming of Jesus Christ (expectation). According to Barth the "anxiety, legalism and tragedy" (rev. trans.) that reflect the most obvious experience of and approach to the world is disqualified. This is because they do not take the event of Christ seriously into account. "It is no longer legitimate to think of it [nothingness] as if real deliverance and release from it were still an event of the future" (*CD* III/3, p. 364). So when Barth claims that nothingness is overcome already and that nothingness already has been turned into nothing, this is an assertion expressed from the perspective of the human being, with the belief that it is viewed from the perspective of God. The statement is in itself an expression of faith and hope in the ultimate grace and love of God toward the human being.

To sum up: the problem of nothingness is a problem that cannot be solved theoretically. Instead, it must be treated at a practical level (which not only includes praxis but also reflection on praxis). As God's partner the human

---

41. See *CD* III/3, p. 361.

42. Barth's critique of Heidegger and Sartre regarding their treatment of nothingness can be summarized as follows: they both see death as the final limit, which the human being for intrinsic reasons has to come to terms with. Barth is well aware that Heidegger and Sartre do this in two quite different ways, but he unites them nevertheless on this one point: that the overcoming of death happens solely according to the will of the human being (let it be in acceptance, repression, or affirmation). See further *CD* III/3, pp. 334-49. Instead, Barth claims that death is overcome in Christ. In the proclamation of the life, death, and resurrection of Jesus Christ, life has acquired a meaning that death cannot break.

being is asked to fight against nothingness. The human being is thereby given the place as the secondary subject in the coming of the kingdom of God. This is a way through which God's sovereignty in the coming of the kingdom of God is strictly maintained, without leaving the human being in a totally passive role, where *Erwartung* is equated with act-less waiting.

Nothingness has nothing to do with God in the sense that it is willed by God. But nothingness cannot be understood as nothingness without its relation to God. Nothingness is subordinate to the will of God, as it is the negative consequence of God's election (the rejection that is included in an election). This excludes the idea that nothingness can receive a *telos* apart from God. The only aim that nothingness has is to destroy God's grace toward his creation. The content of nothingness is therefore a content that can only be described in negative terms: in what it is not, as it only has the power to destroy and not the power to create. The only power that can destroy the destructiveness of nothingness is the power of the ultimate love and grace of God. In the life, death, and resurrection of Jesus Christ nothingness has been destroyed. Thus, the human being should not live as if this conquest of nothingness has not taken place. However, this is not to be misread as if the world has hereby turned into a utopia where there is no pain and no sorrow. Such a claim would confuse nothingness with the left side of creation. The *opus proprium* contains in itself a distinction between the left and the right side of creation.

To defeat nothingness is not to defeat the ambiguity of life or to defeat the tensions that are given within life (such as for example joy and sorrow, happiness and grief, life and death, love and hate), but to defeat a self-centered perception of life. Life is not a game where the human being sets its own rules; life is not a neutral playground without a given *telos*. Life is worth dying for, and therefore life is worth living. It is God who enables the human being to see what nothingness really is: a life without a goal, a life where grace is not the foundation. To believe in Christ is to believe that nothingness has been destroyed in Christ. Mistrust, anxiety, and despair have been overruled in the Christian faith, hope, and love.

PART III

CHRISTOLOGY AND ATONEMENT

[Reason] cannot bring herself to believe that God is good if he acts in this way, but setting aside faith, she wishes to feel and see and understand how he is good and not cruel. She would, of course, understand if it were said of God that he hardens no one, damns no one, but has mercy on all, saves all, so that with hell abolished and the fear of death removed, there would be no future punishment to be dreaded. That is why she blusters and argues so in the attempt to exonerate God and defend his justice and goodness. But faith and the Spirit judge differently, for they believe that God is good even if he should send all men to perdition.

Martin Luther,
The Bondage of the Will

Christ is the God of victims primarily because he shares their lot until the end. It takes little thought to realize that nothing else is possible. If the logic of this God shares nothing in common with that of the God of persecution and its mystifying mimesis, the only possible means of intervention in the world is that illustrated by the Gospels.

René Girard, *Job*

CHAPTER 7

The Chalcedonian Pattern

Introduction

Barth's Christology is worked out within the framework of the *Versöhnung* (the German word *Versöhnung* includes the meaning of both "atonement" and "reconciliation").[1] The "Doctrine of the Reconciliation"

---

1. I have, wherever possible, chosen to translate the German word *Versöhnung* with the English word "atonement." I am well aware that at most places in the *CD* it is translated with the word "reconciliation." The reason why I nonetheless chose the term "atonement" is that it indicates an emphasis on the new situation that has emerged for the human being in and through the life, death, and resurrection of Jesus Christ. The human person has become a new *telos*, which I have described in Part I as a transformation of the self. The use of the term "atonement" indicates also that I am opposing a traditional interpretation of Jesus' substitutionary death in which the community between God and the human being is reestablished through a necessary sacrifice of God's innocent Son. Such an interpretation of Jesus' death implies an inner conflict in God between his mercy and his righteousness. As a result of this line of thought, the death of Jesus has often been described with the help of legalistic (penal substitution) or commercial (ransom) terms. However, this does not imply that I reject the whole concept of a substitutionary death in my reading of Barth — but rather that I reinterpret it in the light of René Girard's analysis of the relation between violence and the sacred. Human beings' ongoing judgment of each other functions in Barth's teaching of the atonement as an anthropological *a priori*. A rejection of this human striving for judgment includes in its most extreme consequence the willingness to take on the judgment of others, without judging the ones who judge. This leads inevitably to death. This death is substitutionary, but its aim is no longer to overcome an internal obstacle within God himself. I will elaborate on this in Chapter 11.

is the heading for *CD* IV, in which part of the *CD* the Christology is most profoundly elaborated on. In *CD* IV it becomes obvious that Barth's approach to Christology is determined by a strong emphasis on an all-inclusive soteriology. This inclusiveness determines not only the picture of God, but also the way the relation between God and human beings and the interhuman relations are worked out. To say that soteriological inclusiveness determines the content of our picture of God is — of course — not quite appropriate, since it is God himself who is the first and primary subject of this all-embracing love. It is this all-embracing love that is expressed in inclusive soteriology. So, both noetically and logically, it is God who gives radical grace content (and not the other way around). It is through the revealed love of God in Jesus Christ that God can be known as God. Two major presuppositions should be noted here. *One*, that the essence of God cannot be understood apart from the acts of God. This is due to Barth's actualistic perception of being, where acts determine being and not vice versa. *Two*, that Barth in his Trinitarian framework maintains a traditional distinction between the immanent and the economic Trinity, without subjecting himself to the traditionally stated consequences of this distinction. By using the Chalcedonian pattern as the structuring principle for not only Christology, but also for the perception of the relation between the immanent and the economic Trinity, Barth succeeds in avoiding an inner conflict of motives in God, without letting the immanent Trinity become absorbed by the economic Trinity.[2] This is exactly what takes place in many modern non-metaphysical perceptions of God, where the claim that God *became* human has been turned into the claim that God *is* human. The divinity of God has then been replaced by the humanity of God, whereby the content of God has been reduced to the human quest for love and solidarity. Such a perception of God is based on an interpretation of the incarnation in which the distinction between the immanent and the economic Trinity has been dissolved. In fact such a reading does not even give space for an old heretical version of the Trinity: modalism. In opposition to this Barth not only maintains but also qualifies the transcendence of God in the way he connects a Christological approach with a Trinitarian framework, in which the dif-

---

2. The Chalcedonian pattern is, according to George Hunsinger, the clue to understanding Barth's Christology. See George Hunsinger, *Disruptive Grace: Studies in the Theology of Karl Barth* (Grand Rapids: Eerdmans, 2000), pp. 131-47.

ferentiation between the immanent and the economic Trinity is vital. Thus a distinction between the history of God and God's history with the human being is maintained.

To grasp the impact of Barth's use of the Chalcedonian pattern, one must see it in relation to his use of covenant and election. That Christ is truly human and truly God means that Christ must be seen as both the God who elects the human being, and as the human being who is elected by God. To know God, as he is in and for himself, is to know him as the One who prior to the creation of the human being elects the human being to become his covenant partner. To know the human being, as the human being is intended to be by God, is to know the human being as elected by God.

That Christ is fully human and fully God means that Barth's Christology is classic in the sense that he first and primarily operates with a Christology from above. But this description is not quite adequate. Barth also operates with a Christology from below, but his use of the term differs heavily from the common understanding of it. Usually it implies a refusal of Jesus' divinity, in the sense that the man Jesus of Nazareth cannot be claimed to be pre-existent and partaker in the eternal being of God. But in fact the pre-existence of Jesus Christ is included in Barth's Christology from below. Within Barth's theological universe the aim of a Christology from below is to elaborate the second element of the election (Jesus Christ as the elected human being).

The interaction between a Christology from above and a Christology from below is for Barth another way of describing the relation between the pre-existence of Christ and the earthly Jesus of Nazareth. The precondition for this dialectical relation is that the order between the Christology from above and the Christology from below is fixed:

(1) The Christology from above is the logical precondition for the Christology from below.
(2) The Christology from below serves to fill out the content of the Christology from above.
(3) The dialectic between the Christology from above and the Christology from below belongs within the relation of the Trinity. We have not seen Christ if we only see Jesus of Nazareth (Christology would then have been replaced by Jesuology). But we have only seen Christ when we see him in and through Jesus of Nazareth.

In what follows I will aim to place Barth's Christology within the tradition with the help of the distinctions between the teaching of the en- and anhypostasis, and the λόγος ἄσαρκος and λόγος ἔνσαρκος.

Enhypostasis and Anhypostasis

At first glance Barth's Christology might seem to be very orthodox in both form and content. It is structured by means of the old Chalcedonian distinction between the two natures of Jesus Christ. Barth hereby places himself in the line of tradition from Nicea (325) and Chalcedon (451). What is important here, however, is to see not only how Barth revitalizes this pattern, but also why he does so. My argument is that Barth in fact reformulates the tradition in such a radical way that it can no longer be claimed as a Christology that is a "simple" extrapolation of the tradition.[3]

Barth uses the Chalcedonian pattern to reformulate some of the original insights from Nicea and Chalcedon. His Christology can be read as an attempt to balance the Alexandrian and the Antiochian types of Christology. Neither the deity nor the humanity of Christ should be overemphasized.[4] Barth maintains the Christological balance with the help of a twofold approach to the election in which he partly looks at Jesus Christ from above (the electing God) and partly from below (the elected human being). Jesus Christ is thereby regarded as "complete in deity" (the electing God) and "complete in humanity" (the elected human being). The description of Jesus Christ as being both the electing God and the elected human being is also an attempt to incorporate both the Johannine and the synoptic traditions. At one and the same time and without confusion, Jesus Christ is both the Son of God and the Son of Man. Jesus Christ is not a kind of hybrid between God and man. In the words of George Hunsinger:

> No harmonization of these different statements [that Jesus of Naza-
> reth on the one hand is depicted as the Son of God; and that the Son

3. Regin Prenter argues this point very well. See Regin Prenter, "Karl Barths Umbildung der traditionellen Zweinaturlehre in lutherischer Beleuchtung," in *Theologie und Gottesdienst*, ed. Erik Kyndal, Gerhard Pedersen, and Anna Marie Aagaard (Aarhus: Aros Forlag, 1977), p. 40.

4. See Hunsinger, *Disruptive Grace*, pp. 131-40.

of God, on the other hand, is depicted as Jesus of Nazareth] is either possible or appropriate.[5]

The dogma of the two natures hereby acquires what Hunsinger defines as a regulative function.[6] Chalcedon thus turns into a hermeneutical key by which the various Christological statements within the New Testament can be interrelated. The different Christological traditions in the New Testament are then not seen as competitive, mutually exclusive types of Christologies. Instead they are viewed as different ways of referring to one and same claim of faith: that Jesus is Christ.

In line with the ecumenical councils of Nicea and Chalcedon, Barth assumes that the act of atonement presupposes that Jesus, the Son, has the same being *(homoousios)* as God the Father. At this point he finds himself very much in line with the neo-Chalcedonian tradition, and its teaching of Christ's en- and anhypostasis.[7]

The teaching of the enhypostasis incorporates the hypostasis of the human nature of Christ into the hypostasis of the logos. The human nature of Christ cannot be viewed as an independent hypostasis; it can never be viewed autonomously, separated from the incarnated logos. The nature of man in Christ is absorbed into the nature of God in Christ. It is the logos, which exists in eternity (that is: prior to creation of time and space), that is incarnated in the one man, Jesus Christ (and thereby limited in time and space). The human nature of Jesus Christ does not have its own independent hypostasis (i.e., person), but is the manifestation of the hypostasis of the logos.

A typical claim against the teaching of the enhypostasis is that it may have a docetic tendency. The argument behind this accusation is that the teaching of the enhypostasis allows no room for the individuality of Jesus Christ: that Jesus Christ should not "have an independent existence as a man like us" (*CD* IV/2, p. 49). To answer this claim Barth quotes Hollaz: "*Perfectio rei ex essentia, non ex subsistentia aestimanda est*"[8] and adds:

---

5. Hunsinger, *Disruptive Grace*, p. 135.

6. See Hunsinger, *Disruptive Grace*, p. 133.

7. Barth refers explicitly to the teaching of the en- and the anhypostasis in *CD* I/2, pp. 163-65, and *CD* IV/2, pp. 49-60, 90-91. The teaching of the en- and the anhypostasis tries to solve the dogmatic problem: How is it possible to claim that there is only one person but two natures at one and the same time?

8. The perfection of a thing should be estimated from the essence (ουσια), not from

It is true enough that the *humanum* exists always in the form of actual men. This existence is not denied to the man Jesus, but ascribed to Him with the positive concept of *enhypostasis*. But it is hard to see how the full truth of the humanity of Jesus Christ is qualified or even destroyed by the fact that as distinct from us He is also a real man only as the Son of God, so that there can be no question of a peculiar and autonomous existence of His humanity. (*CD* IV/2, p. 49)[9]

This should be seen together with the teaching of the anhypostasis, where Christ's human nature is described as impersonal. It cannot exist apart from the incarnated *Logos* and thus it can never be fully perceived as separate from the incarnated *Logos* in the person Jesus Christ. This does not imply that Christ should be "reduced" to a manifestation of an eternal idea (the result of which would be pure docetism). Christ is like any other person, a particular, unrepeatable, and incomparable individual. But this feature of individuality is a common feature for all human beings. What is really distinct about Jesus Christ is that the *Logos* in him has adopted the human essence. Thus, it is only this man who can be perceived as being complete man and complete God.

Essentially, the teaching of the en- and anhypostasis rests (at least as Barth depicts and uses the terms in the *CD*) on the same foundation: namely that the pre-historical *Logos,* which belongs to the essence of God's Trinitarian being, is incarnated in a particular human being. The reason why the human nature of Christ can be said to have no hypostasis (person) on its own is that it shares or, better, is absorbed into the hypostasis of the divinity of Christ. So the *aufnehmende logos* and the *aufgenommene menschliche Natur* have the same hypostasis (i.e., they are one person). Thus, the human nature of Christ cannot be granted any independent or

---

the independent existence (ὑπόστασις) of it. This translation of *subsistentia* is rooted in Barth's earlier explanation on page 49 where he states that ὑπόστασις, *persona,* meant the independent existence (the *propria subsistentia*) of Christ's humanity.

9. The second part of the English translation here is inaccurate. The German passage says: "Es ist aber nicht einzusehen, daß eben die vollkommene Wahrheit der Menschlichkeit Jesu Christi dadurch tangiert oder gar aufgehoben wird, daß Er im Unterschied zu uns Anderen allen nur als Gottes Sohn auch ein wirklicher Mensch ist, daß also von einer eigenen, selbständigen Existenz seiner Menschlichkeit keine Rede sein kann" (*KD* IV/2, p. 53).

autonomous status; it is impossible to separate the two natures of Christ, as they are united in the one person.[10] There are, consistently with this position, several references to the *unio hypostatica* or *unio personalis* of Christ in *CD* IV/2.[11]

The dialectic between the en- and anhypostasis also enables Barth to reinterpret the traditional teaching of the *status duplex*. Due to the interrelation between the two natures of Christ (united in the one hypostasis), it is possible to describe the humanity of Jesus Christ as exalted instead of humiliated. The reason why it is possible to turn the traditional use of the *status duplex* upside down and still remain within a neo-Chalcedonian framework is that the human nature of Christ is absorbed into the being of God. The human nature of Christ cannot be separated from the *Logos* incarnated, and the incarnated *Logos* cannot be fully understood if it is not seen in relation to God's Trinitarian being. The being of God (which includes a differentiation between an inner- and an economic-Trinitarian being) is determined by the will of God. Barth's characteristic way of combining the *status duplex* with the doctrine of the two natures of Christ is based on his emphasis on the eternal and original will of God: to be a God for the human being. In the incarnation God has not only humiliated himself but has also exalted the human being into fellowship with him. Thus, the locus of the human being's exaltation is not (as assumed in a traditional teaching of the *status duplex*) the resurrection, but the incarnation.

Very much in line with Barth, Eberhard Jüngel has used the distinction between the an- and enhypostasis to describe the relation between the word of Jesus and Jesus as the Word of God. This is closely connected with the question as to how the historical Jesus interrelates with the proclaimed Christ. In the actual life of Jesus Christ the anhypostasis is historically revealed in Jesus' preaching of the kingdom of God. Jesus of Nazareth understands himself in terms of the kingdom of God he is preaching. His "lack" of an autonomous hypostasis, independent of the being of God, hereby becomes clear within history. In the resurrection these words of Jesus are revealed as being God's own word. In the resurrection the work and words of Jesus are confirmed as being the work and words of Christ, whereby the

10. See *CD* IV/2, p. 49.
11. See *CD* IV/2, pp. 51, 66, 105.

enhypostasis is revealed.[12] The enhypostasis of Jesus Christ is thus hidden prior to Easter, whereas the anhypostasis of Jesus Christ is revealed in history prior to Easter. Thus, the an- and the enhypostasis can be fully understood only when they are seen in relation to each other. The an- and the enhypostasis refer to one and the same being (the Trinitarian being of God), and they are both — seen in their inner relation — an attempt to verify how, at one and the same time, one can believe in a monotheistic God and claim that this God has incarnated himself in a specific human being. Jüngel describes this interrelation between the an- and the enhypostasis with the help of the Heideggerian distinction between ontological and ontic.[13]

The an- and enhypostasis share the same ontological identity, but they nevertheless differ in their manifestation at the ontic level in the life of Jesus of Nazareth. The anhypostasis is revealed in and within history. Jesus of Nazareth lives in relations that all are determined by one particular relation: the relation to God. The relation between God the Father and Jesus the Son is revealed in the time before Easter in his preaching of the power and the kingdom of God. As such it is perceivable within the frame of history. The enhypostasis, which is the precondition for the anhypostasis (the possibility that creates the possibility of the anhypostasis), is first revealed in the being of Jesus Christ as resurrected. But this a-historical event can only be fully perceived in the light of what has happened in the actual history of Jesus of Nazareth prior to his death and resurrection. Thus, a typical Bultmannian separation between the *kerygma* (the proclamation of Jesus as Christ) and the authentic words of Jesus (the historical Jesus of Nazareth) is not really helpful, since it is unable to account for the being of God prior to history and the being of God within history, the aseity of God

---

12. See Eberhard Jüngel, "Jesu Wort und Jesus als Wort Gottes. Ein hermeneutischer Beitrag zum christologischen Problem," in *Unterwegs zur Sache* (München: Chr. Kaiser Verlag, 1972), pp. 126-44.

13. See Jüngel, "Jesu Wort und Jesus als Wort Gottes," p. 137: "We have to distinguish between and correlate en- and anhypostasis as two different relations at the same time which differ in an ontic way while they are ontologically identical. This is due to the pre-easterly Jesus historically existing and thus revealing the anhypostasis of his being (which he can do ontologically because of the power of the enhypostasis of his being in the form of logos). On the other hand the enhypostasis which enables and characterizes his whole being is being revealed in the form of the resurrected as the existence of Jesus Christ" (trans. Michael Waltemathe).

and the incarnation of God — in short: the interrelation between the history of God and the history of the world. So the particular human being (Jesus of Nazareth) cannot be fully understood from the perspective of history, as it does not take into account the references to the incarnated *Logos* (more specifically: the reference between *logos incarnandus* and *logos incarnatus*). The incarnated *Logos* transcends the limits of history — whereby to a certain extent it can also be claimed to relativize — or perhaps even historicize — history.

Barth's use of the Chalcedonian pattern, including the teaching of the anhypostasis and the enhypostasis, can be summed up in the following words, in which he describes the relation between the divinity and humanity of Jesus Christ:

> But the fact that He is not only *a* true man, but *the* true man, is not exhausted by His likeness with all other men. He is not only completely like us, but completely unlike us — and it is only when we add this complementary truth that we realise the full meaning of the *vere homo* as it applies to Him. But the unlikeness consists in what must necessarily become, and has become, of "human nature" when He assumed it in likeness with us, of flesh when it became His. It relates to the particularity of the history which took place when He became man, and still takes place as He, the Son of God, is man.
>
> His unlikeness with us does not consist, of course, only in the fact that He is something that we are not — the Son of God, very God. Rather, because He is the Son of God, it consists in the unlikeness of His humanity and ours. Because and as He is the Son of God, He is *exactly the same* as we are, but *quite differently*. If we do not have regard to the *totality*, we do not see what has to be seen. (*CD* IV/2, pp. 27-28; my emphasis)

The final question, which ought to be answered in relation to Barth's use of Chalcedon and the teaching of the an- and enhypostasis, is: Why does he find it so important to maintain a high view of Christ's person?[14] The

---

14. George Hunsinger distinguishes between a high and a middle type of Christology. He claims that there has to be a correlation between the understanding of the work and the person of Christ. A high conception of Christ's saving work implies therefore a high view of Christ's person and vice versa. In *Disruptive Grace* Hunsinger states in oppo-

answer to this question is "classical." The unity between God and the human being in Christ is necessary for at least the following three reasons. *First*, it is God who meets human beings as a human being in Jesus Christ. *Second*, the human being meets God as God in Jesus Christ. Jesus *is* God and not just a human reference to God (for example, a priest or a prophet). This implies not only that the incarnation entails no alteration of God (Jesus Christ is not a man "into whom God has changed Himself"; *CD* IV/2, p. 49), but also that "the *unity* in which *as man* He is the Son of God, and *as the Son of God* man" is kept (*CD* IV/2, p. 49; my emphasis). Barth's Christology is worked out in a continuation of a traditional soteriological emphasis on this particular God-man who was fully God and fully man. If he was not fully God, the reconciliation could not have a universal effect, as only God can reconcile all human beings with himself in one singular act. If he was not fully human, the punishment of the human being — which takes place in the reconciliation — could not have been substitutionary for the human being. *Third*, such a high view of the work and person of Christ leaves neither room nor need for a deepening, reiteration, or extension of this one act of reconciliation. In Chapters 9 to 11 I will elaborate on how the punishment of God and the substitutionary death of Jesus Christ can be interpreted in a much less neo-orthodox way than the heavy use of traditional terms suggests.

Λόγος ἄσαρκος and λόγος ἔνσαρκος

This leads us to an investigation of the relation between λόγος ἄσαρκος and λόγος ἔνσαρκος.[15] This distinction served in the Reformed tradition to maintain the omnipresence of the *Logos*, even after the *Logos* had been spatially circumscribed in the human nature of Jesus Christ. The *Logos* is still ubiquitous outside of Christ (as it was in the beginning prior to cre-

---

sition to what he defines as modern Christology: "Insofar as modern Christology has typically abandoned a high view of Christ's person, it has also abandoned the correspondingly high conception of Christ's saving work that Chalcedonian Christology is meant to sustain" (pp. 131-32). See also Hunsinger, *Disruptive Grace*, pp. 263-67.

15. In my analysis of the relation between the λόγος ἄσαρκος and the λόγος ἔνσαρκος, I am in debt to Bruce L. McCormack's article, "Grace and Being: The Role of God's Gracious Election in Karl Barth's Theological Ontology," in *The Cambridge Companion to Karl Barth*, ed. John Webster (Cambridge: Cambridge University Press, 2000), pp. 92-110.

ation).[16] The Lutheran tradition not only labeled this as an *extra calvinisticum,* but also fiercely rejected it, seeing in Calvin's teaching a "'Nestorian' separation of the divine and the human natures" (*CD* IV/1, p. 181). But it is worth noting here that the distinction between λόγος ἄσαρκος and λόγος ἔνσαρκος in both the Lutheran and the Reformed traditions served to qualify the unity and differentiation between the *Logos* (as a part of the Trinity) before and after the incarnation.[17] Further, the distinction between the λόγος ἄσαρκος and the λόγος ἔνσαρκος serves to affirm that God is the same (read: unchanged) before, during, and after the incarnation.

Barth keeps this distinction between λόγος ἄσαρκος and λόγος ἔνσαρκος for two reasons: epistemological and ontological. Epistemologically, it relates to God's excess in revelation. God is the subject of revelation. Not only is it God who decided to reveal himself in the man Jesus of Nazareth, it is also God who enables the human being to perceive the revelation as a revelation. Ontologically, it relates to the excess in the being of God. This means, on the one hand, that the λόγος ἄσαρκος is the content of a "necessary and important concept in Trinitarian doctrine when we have to understand the revelation and dealings of God in the light of their *free* basis in the inner being and essence of God" (*CD* IV/1, p. 52; my emphasis).[18] The emphasis on the λόγος ἄσαρκος serves thereby also to secure the absolute freedom and sovereignty of God. On the other hand it means that it is impossible for the human being to gain any access to the "*Logos* itself."

---

16. Calvin's accentuation of the omnipresence of the *Logos* expresses a dogmatic tradition that goes back to Athanasius and Gregory of Nyssa. The important passage from Calvin's *Institutio,* which the Lutherans mark as *extra calvinisticum,* is to be found in book II, chapter XIII, section 4: "For even if the Word in his immeasurable essence united with the nature of man into one person, we do not imagine that he was confined therein. Here is something marvelous: the Son of God descended from heaven in such a way that, without leaving heaven, he willed to be borne in the virgin's womb, to go about the earth, and to hang upon the cross; yet he continuously filled the world even as he had done from the beginning!" John Calvin, *Institutes of the Christian Religion,* trans. Ford Lewis Battles, ed. John T. McNeill (Philadelphia: Westminster, 1960), p. 481. See also *CD* IV/1, pp. 180-81.

17. See also McCormack, *Grace and Being,* p. 95.

18. See also Karl Barth, *Church Dogmatics* III/1 (Edinburgh: T. & T. Clark, 1958), p. 54, where Barth states that the λόγος ἄσαρκος, despite being an abstraction, "has turned out to be indispensable for dogmatic enquiry and presentation."

However, this hiddenness of the *"Logos* itself" should not be misinterpreted as an argument for a traditional metaphysical use of the hidden God, where the hidden God serves as the final explanation for all uncalled acts and incidents in the world. The hiddenness of the *Logos* itself is not a synonym for a hidden meaning. The traditional distinction between *deus absconditus* and *deus revelatus* is replaced in Barth's theology by the differentiation between the λόγος ἄσαρκος and the λόγος ἔνσαρκος. In this way Barth succeeds in emphasizing the ultimate hiddenness of God, without letting this hiddenness end in a theological dead end, where the human being should fear a God *(deus absconditus)* behind God *(deus revelatus)*.[19] God can have no other motive toward the creation than the one he has actually revealed in the incarnation. In this sense there is no hidden God behind Jesus Christ.

> Under the title of λόγος ἄσαρκος we pay homage to a *deus absconditus* and therefore to some image of God which we have made for ourselves. And if we were to deal with a figure of this kind, we should be dangerously susceptible to the temptation, indeed we could hardly escape it, of asking whether the revelation and activity of this "Logos in itself" can altogether and always be confined to this phenomenon, the incarnation in Jesus Christ. (*CD* IV/1, p. 52; my emphasis)

The atonement, which has happened once and for all in Christ, is determinative for the human being's understanding of God. It is here that the human being cannot only intellectually but also existentially grasp the drama in which the *deus pro nobis* is revealed.

> But since we are now concerned with the revelation and dealings of God, and particularly with the atonement, with the person and work of the Mediator, it is *pointless,* as it is *impermissible,* to return to the inner being and essence of God and especially to the second person of the Trinity as such, in such a way that we ascribe to this person another form than that which God Himself has given in willing to reveal Himself and to act outwards. (*CD* IV/1, p. 52; my emphasis)

19. Such a perception of God is closely linked to a soteriology in which the general precondition is that not only do all human beings deserve eternal punishment, but most people will also receive eternal reprobation. See Chapter 10.

The distinction between λόγος ἄσαρκος and λόγος ἔνσαρκος has approximately the same structural function as the distinction between the immanent and the economic Trinity. The one (λόγος ἄσαρκος) is the logical presupposition for the other (λόγος ἔνσαρκος). This maintains a distinction between God and history, so that God is not destroyed as God when he enters into history. Barth connects this distinction with the idea of the immutability of God.[20] God can absorb the experience of the human being (including the death of the human being) without changing his "own personality."[21]

> He could be obedient even to death, even to the death of the cross. He had this other possibility: the possibility of divine self-giving to the being and fate of man. He had the freedom for this condescension, for this concealment of His Godhead. He had it and He made use of it in the power and *not with any loss, not with any diminution or alteration of His Godhead.* That is His self-emptying. It does not consist in ceasing to be Himself as man, but in taking it upon Himself to be Himself in a way quite other than that which corresponds and belongs to His form as God, His being equal with God. (*CD* IV/1, p. 180; my emphasis)[22]

God continues, in the incarnation, to be the same God, as God has always been. The life and death of Jesus Christ does not create any change within God himself.[23] God is still the same as he was before the incarnation. How can Barth make this strong claim? Only through an emphasis on the eternal and original will of God, which enables an unbroken continuity between λόγος ἄσαρκος and λόγος ἔνσαρκος. Time and again Barth states that prior to the creation God had decided to be a God in relation to the

---

20. Traces of the young Barth, who was very much inspired by Kierkegaard's dialectic between eternity and time, are easy to detect here.

21. See also McCormack, *Grace and Being,* p. 98.

22. See also *CD* IV/2, p. 85.

23. In Chapter 11 I will elaborate on how Barth interprets and uses the endlessness of the cross through an analysis of his references to the outcry from the cross. Does Barth take the full consequences of his own approach? I will argue against Barth's way of connecting the radical freedom of God (as an *a priori* condition) with the impossibility of change in God's inner being. In opposition to Barth it is my claim that if God did not change through the experience of the absence of God on the cross, God did not really absorb the experience of Jesus Christ on the cross.

human being. It thereby becomes possible at one and the same time to describe the incarnation as a new constitutive act for the relation between God and the human being (seen from the perspective of the human being) and to claim that this constitutive act does not bring about any change in God himself (seen from the perspective of God).

As will be seen in Chapter 13, I am critical toward Barth's way of combining the dialectic between eternity and time, and the immutability of God. I opt, with inspiration from other aspects of Barth's theology, for a less static, more dynamic interpretation of the being and essence of God. Such a reading gives room for a positive evaluation of the possibility that God might change. One must admit, however, that this presupposes a change in Barth's way of describing the Trinity. Rather than describing it as the one absolute subject's three modes of being, we should describe it as a unity of the mutual interrelations between the three subjects of the Trinity.

An Actualistic Understanding of the Being of God

The being of God is constituted by the acts of God. The essence of God is not "something" prior to the acts of God, nor are the acts of God an "outpouring" of the essence of God (which then would exist prior to the acts). Rather, God's essence is constituted by the acts. The being of God is a being in act. The free will of God (potentiality) and the acts of God (actuality) are united in the essence of God. God's will and God's action are, as noted in Part I, inseparable. Thus the essence of God in the immanent Trinity cannot be interpreted independently of the essence of God in the economic Trinity and vice versa. Neither can the λόγος ἄσαρκος, as seen above, be interpreted independently of the λόγος ἔνσαρκος. The relation between the immanent and the economic Trinity and the relation between the λόγος ἄσαρκος and the λόγος ἔνσαρκος are not only *noetic* but also *ontological* in character. If this were not the case, the essence of the *deus absconditus* would not necessarily be congruent with the essence of the *deus revelatus*.

So, from the perspective of human beings there can be no hidden God who differs from God the Creator and Redeemer in his essence. The essence of God the Creator and the Redeemer can be perceived only in the light of the actual revelation in Christ (which is possible due to the inner relation between the incarnation and the resurrection).[24] Again, we are back at the inner dialectic in Barth's theology, in which the movement always goes back and forth between the precondition for revelation (the essence of God in and for himself prior to history) and the actual revelation of this essence (the essence of God as revealed to human beings in Jesus Christ in history). The two are not identical. The latter is dependent on the excess of the former. It is God who has established this relation due to his own free will. If this were not the case the immanent and the economic Trinity would become identical in such a way that God would become dependent on the relation between God and the world. From the perspective of Barth this would not only do away with the nature of grace, but it would also turn the whole interaction between God and the world into a kind of principle (or would at least make it possible to interpret this divine action as a divine principle). God would thereby become subjected to an extrinsic necessity, which is incompatible with his free will. Such an interpretation would — to follow Barth's own understanding of his theology's inner logic — presuppose an essentialistic instead of an actualistic understanding of the being of God.[25] One consequence of this would be that God is turned into an abstract idea (such as the ultimate being) without any concrete starting point. God would then no longer be the God who proclaims: "Ye shall be my people"; and the adequate answer to this proclamation would

---

24. Barth is aware of the fact that his use of the λόγος ἄσαρκος leaves room for a concept of a hidden God behind the *deus pro nobis*. But Barth here places the mystery in the fact that God due to his own inner free will has decided to be God for human beings. This decision is revealed most clearly in the life, death, and resurrection of Jesus Christ. Where Luther urged his fellow Christians not to speculate about the hidden God, as they then no longer would be able to differentiate between God and the Devil, Barth encourages them instead to allow the speculation as the necessary place for the mystery of the saving act of God. Barth states for example: "The second 'person' [λόγος ἄσαρκος] of the Godhead in Himself and as such is not God the Reconciler. In Himself and as such He is not revealed to us. In Himself and as such He is not *deus pro nobis*, neither ontologically nor epistemologically. He is the content of a necessary and important concept in Trinitarian doctrine when we have to understand the revelation and dealings of God in the light of their free basis in the inner being and essence of God" (*CD* IV/1, p. 52). The text continues with the passage I have already quoted on p. 156, where Barth makes clear that human beings are not permitted to ascribe to the second person of the Trinity any form or content other than that which God himself has already revealed in Jesus Christ.

25. See McCormack, *Grace and Being*, p. 98.

then no longer be obedience, gratitude, and worship.[26] To be obedient is to be thankful.[27] And the liturgical expression of this thankfulness is given place in the community's worship of God.

Barth's Critique of Hegel

From Barth's point of view it is impossible for God to undergo any change, even in the incarnation, as this would make God dependent on the world (time and space). God is the same from eternity to eternity. Barth's critique of Hegel might not really be all that sophisticated on this point, but it is nevertheless worth consulting as a help to elucidating his own position. Barth criticizes Hegel's historical understanding of God, according to which God needs history to become himself in and through history. In Barth's understanding of Hegel, the incarnation can be construed as a necessary move within God's self-development. God becomes himself through the incarnation in the world. The incarnation therefore not only happens for the sake of humanity but also for the sake of God himself. God had to incarnate himself to become real God.

In opposition to Hegel, Barth interprets the incarnation as a pure result of God's radical love and grace toward the human being. The incarnation is not a necessary stage within God's own self-development. God would still have been God without his entering into the world. Instead, the incarnation is the most complete expression of God's eternal decision: to be God for human beings. This decision will always relate to history in the same way due to its eternal origin. God does not collapse into history, but history is rather the place where God's history of salvation is enacted.

God is not only the precondition for history but also the foundation underpinning the history, without which history would collapse into a line of singular events. The event of Christ — which can be summed up in the atonement — is not restricted to a strict time line. It is the very foundation

---

26. See for example *CD* IV/1, pp. 15-16, 20, 42-44, 69. The three modes of reactions are reactions that happen within the covenant. They express human beings' adequate reaction ("we with God") to the proclamation: "God with us."

27. "For the other partner in the covenant to whom God turns in this grace, the only proper thing, but the thing which is unconditionally and inescapably demanded, is that he should be thankful" (*CD* IV/1, p. 41).

for the history of human existence — regardless of whether they lived before, during, or after the historical actualization of this event.

> But is it [that all men, "even those who lived thousands of years before Jesus," should have their being in the history of Jesus, that the history of human existence should derive from that of the man Jesus] so inconceivable, does it need such a great imagination to realise, is it not the simplest thing in the world, that if the history of Jesus is the event of atonement, if the atonement is real and effective because God himself became man to be the subject of this event, if this is not concealed but revealed, if it is the factor which calls us irresistibly to faith and obedience, then how can it be otherwise than that in this factor, and therefore in the history of Jesus, we have to do with the reality which underlies and precedes all other reality as the first and eternal Word of God that in this history we have actually to do with the ground and sphere, the atmosphere of the being of every man, whether they lived thousands of years before or after Jesus? (*CD* IV/1, p. 53)

The thought structure behind this argument is twofold:

(1) God does not change. God has a history, but this does not make God historical.
(2) God is the foundation for all human beings. This foundation of humanity is established prior to time and creation. Thus, the actual revelation of God's essence in time is constitutive for all time.

God's self-revelation in Jesus Christ thereby has an all-determining impact both backward and forward in history. Time is Christologically determined, as it is understood from the perspective of Christ, who is, who was, and who will come again. The focus here is on the relation between the eschatological hope and the protological commitment and promise (both grounded in the original will of God). The present is not understood in the light of the past. The future is not anticipated in the light of the present. The eternal will of God is instead decisive for the understanding of the present, in the way the actual present is determined by the dialectic between the original and basic will of God and the expectation of the second coming of Christ. The latter is anticipated in Christ; the former is revealed in Christ.

It is not my aim here to go into a detailed critique of Barth's critique of Hegel (its affinity to Kierkegaard's Hegel-critique is almost too obvious). What I want is simply to elucidate how important a role the emphasis on God's sovereign free will plays in Barth's whole thought structure. The emphasis on the sovereignty, the majesty, and the free will of God occasionally leads Barth into some not entirely clear statements about God's radical freedom and God's wish to be God for human beings. I find that Barth, in places, overemphasizes the claim that God could have acted otherwise than he actually did. According to Barth God would be no less God without the creation. Within the relation of the immanent Trinity God would have remained a God of love (Barth's Augustinian heritage becomes obvious here). Barth states for example:

> It is not as though the object of this relationship, the other, constitutes a part of the reality of God outside of God. It is not as though it is in any other way comparable with God. It is not as though God is forced into this relationship. It is not as though He is in any way constrained or compelled by this other. As we have often enough seen and asserted, there can be no question of any such compulsion coming upon God from without. God is love. But He is also perfect freedom. Even if there were no such relationship, *even if there were no other outside of Him, He would still be love.* (*CD* II/2, p. 6; my emphasis)

> In the inter-Trinitarian life of God the eternal generation of the Son or Logos is, of course, the expression of God's love, of His will not to be alone. But it does not follow from this that God could not be God without speaking to us. . . . *God would be no less God if He had created no world and no man. The existence of the world and our own existence are in no sense vital to God,* not even as the object of His love. (*CD* I/1, p. 139; my emphasis)

In reading these passages, the reader must inevitably ask him- or herself whether God could still be God without the creation. Could God still act otherwise? Could God withdraw from his merciful acts toward human beings? Of course, Barth's intention is to illustrate the precondition for the graceful act of God. The logic here seems to be: the more uncertainty, the more grace. But the question remains: If God could have done otherwise, can God then still do otherwise? Can God in his radical freedom withdraw from the human being — and still be the same God? From reading the *CD*, the overall answer to this question must be No, even if there are certain passages that, read in isolation, could seem to indicate the opposite. The No has its reason in the revelation, where the actual decision of God is revealed to the human being. Barth can therefore also state:

> But positively, in the free decision of His love, God is God in the very fact, and in such a way that He does stand in this relation, in a *definite* relationship with the other. We cannot go back on this decision if we would know God and speak accurately of God. If we did, we should be betrayed into a *false abstraction* which sought to speak only of God, not recognising that, when we speak of God, then in consideration of His freedom, and of His free decision, we must speak also of this relationship. (*CD* II/2, p. 6)[28]

Does Barth really need to stress the majesty of God so heavily in order to ensure that grace is understood as pure grace, or could there be more at stake here? To answer this question, I will again refer to the distinction between an essentialistic and actualistic ontology.[29] The former is at play in the work of Calvin, as he "knows of a mode of being or existence on the part of the λόγος ἄσαρκος which is independent of his being/existence as Redeemer."[30] This distinction is built on a gap between the λόγος ἄσαρκος and the λόγος ἔνσαρκος, where the essence of the former is "understood to be complete in itself apart from and prior to all actions and relations of that [divine] Subject. And divine 'essence,' on this view, is something hidden to human perception and, finally, unknowable."[31] But the essence of God is, according to Barth, "not an independent 'something' that stands behind all God's acts and relations. God's being is a *being-in-act*. First, as a being-in-act in *eternity* and then, corresponding to that, as a being-in-act *in time*."[32]

This implies (1) that the essence of God can only be understood through the redemptive act of God, and (2) that there is no essence of God

---

28. See also *CD* IV/1, p. 52, where Barth describes the Christ-event as binding, inescapable, and irrevocable.

29. Cf. McCormack, *Grace and Being*, p. 98.

30. McCormack, *Grace and Being*, p. 98.

31. McCormack, *Grace and Being*, p. 98.

32. McCormack, *Grace and Being*, p. 99.

that is in opposition to God's being-in-act. In the essence of God, there is no valid distinction between act and will. It is this actualistic understanding of the being of God that enables Barth to describe Jesus Christ as the one who is not only elected, but also as the one who elects. The latter is only possible when there is no essentialistic gap between λόγος ἄσαρκος and λόγος ἔνσαρκος. In Jesus Christ we see the God who elects from eternity.

CHAPTER 8

The Covenant

Barth's way of using the dogma of the two natures is unique in the sense that he combines the teaching of the two natures *(verus deus, verus homo)* and the teaching of the two states *(status exinanitionis* and *status exaltationis)* with the teaching of the covenant. All three aspects should again be seen in relation to Barth's emphasis on God's eternal election of all human beings in the one man Jesus Christ. The true God is the electing God; the true human being is the elected human being. The close connection between Christology and soteriology is hereby given in itself.

The covenant has been established solely by the act of God. This includes both the old and the new covenant. God was not obliged to establish this covenant between himself and human beings. It is an act of pure grace and therefore a covenant of grace. The covenant demonstrates that God has decided to be God for human beings in a way that involves God himself. The covenant thereby expresses God's own self-willed commitment toward the human being.

In and through the covenant God has established a fellowship between himself and humanity. The human being is elected by God to become God's own covenant partner. Thus the human being has to answer adequately to this fellowship — in short, to express his or her own gratitude toward God.[1] "χάρις always demands the answer of εὐχαριστία" (*CD* IV/1, p. 41). It is natural here to see some structural similarities between Barth's interpretation of the covenant in the Old Testament and his own attempts

---

1. See *CD* IV/1, p. 41.

to clarify what it means here and now to be the covenant partner of God. One of Barth's points is that the human being cannot put itself in a neutral position toward God: "man cannot first be neutral towards God" (*CD* IV/1, p. 42) and then — in this space of neutrality — decide if it is feasible to believe 'in God. "He [man] cannot simply know about God, or believe 'in a God'" (*CD* IV/1, p. 42).

The Covenant and the Two-State Theory: Barth and Prenter in Discussion

According to Barth, the humiliation of God and the exaltation of the human being is a single act.[2] It is not possible to separate the humiliation of God and the exaltation of the human being in a chronological or a spatial way.

> The reconstitution and renewal of the covenant between God and man consists in this exchange — the *exinanitio,* the abasement, of God, and the *exaltatio,* the exaltation of man. It was God who went into the *far country,* and it is man who *returns home.* Both took place in the one Jesus Christ. It is not, therefore, a matter of two different and successive actions, but of *a single action* in which each of the two elements is related to the other and can be known and understood only in this relationship: the going out of God only as it aims at the coming in of man; the coming in of man only as the reach and outworking of the going out of God; and the whole in its original and proper form only as the being and history of the one Jesus Christ. (*CD* IV/2, p. 21; my emphasis)

So, God's movement toward the human being includes a movement from the human being toward God. Both aspects of this movement have taken place in Jesus Christ. The teaching of the two states is thus combined with the doctrine of the two natures. It is God who is humiliated and the human being who is exalted. To say that God is exalted or that the human being is humiliated would according to Barth be a tautology.[3] It is pointed

---

2. See also George Hunsinger, *Disruptive Grace: Studies in the Theology of Karl Barth* (Grand Rapids: Eerdmans, 2000), p. 141.

3. See *CD* IV/1, p. 134. Nothing is said here that can be said to exceed the common ex-

out at several places in the *CD* that the true God is the God who humiliates himself, and that the true human being is the human being who due to the grace of God in Jesus Christ has been exalted to true fellowship with God. Jesus Christ is the mediator through whom the double movement (humiliation and exaltation) takes place. To illustrate this, let me quote the following three examples from §64 in the *CD:*

> In virtue of this humiliation of God, as He became mean and poor, as His eternal Word was made flesh, and took human essence and existed as a man among men, this man, Jesus of Nazareth, was and is elevated and exalted man, true man. He was and is this unique man among all others, this Sovereign. *His human work runs parallel to the work of God. In His speech and action, in His person, there is actualised the kingdom of God drawn near.* (*CD* IV/2, p. 292; my emphasis)

> What we have called the way of the *Son of God* into a far country and the homecoming of the *Son of Man,* and what older dogmatics called the *exinanitio* and *exaltatio* of Jesus Christ, are *one and the same event at the cross.* The humility and obedience of the Son of God, and the corresponding majesty of the Son of Man, coincide as they are represented in the event of Gethsemane and Golgotha. The Word was really made real flesh. It was really God who really reconciled the world to himself — in the One who was *true God,* omnipotent in the depth of His mercy, and also (in His death and passion) *true man,* allowing free rein to this omnipotent mercy of God. . . . The secret of the cross is simply the secret of the incarnation in all its fulness. (*CD* IV/2, pp. 292-93; my emphasis)

> He had exercised and confirmed and maintained His kingdom and lordship in His death. He comforted and claimed His people from the place where there can be no question of the possession and exercise of human help and authority. He was the confidence for their

---

perience. A main argument that lies behind Barth's emphasis on God's humiliation is the critique of religion — especially as it is presented in the work of Feuerbach. His critique of religion had a long-lasting influence not only on Barth's understanding of Christianity in relation to religion (and vice versa), but also on Barth's understanding of how it is possible to talk with theological adequacy about God.

> own life from the place where all the confidence reposed in man can only fall because it loses its object. He was their hope where every human hope fails. *He was exalted as the One who was abased.* The light of His resurrection was the light of His cross. (*CD* IV/2, p. 295; my emphasis)

The humiliation of God and the exaltation of the human being both take place in the life, death, and resurrection of Jesus Christ. The exaltation is not strictly connected to the resurrection, nor is the humiliation strictly connected to the cross.[4] The humiliation and the exaltation take place as two dialectical movements within the one act of God in Jesus Christ.

The Danish Lutheran theologian Regin Prenter (1907-1990), who at one and the same time was very much inspired by and critical toward Barth's theology of revelation, claims that Barth's way of combining the act of atonement with the humiliation and the exaltation of Jesus Christ is problematic. In Prenter's reading of Barth, the act of atonement takes place in the resurrection (and not in the death) of Jesus Christ. Jesus, as the substitute for the disobedient human being, had to die. However, the main issue is not that Jesus had to suffer "what we ought to have suffered" (*CD* IV/1, p. 253). Rather, the point is that Jesus at the cross had "delivered up us sinners and sin itself to destruction" (*CD* IV/1, p. 253). And this destruction could really have been the end! Thus, the passion and death of Jesus Christ does not in itself include the conquest of our death. The final damnation of the human being could have taken place at the cross (the cross in itself does not save the human being from eternal destruction). In fact, even if the destiny of the cross had been the final outcome, God would still have been righteous! Human beings are not in a position to demand anything from God; nor does God need to save humanity from death as the final limitation. But God did in fact choose to limit the limitation of death through the incarnation of the eternal *Logos* in Jesus Christ. According to Prenter's interpretation of Barth this happens solely in the act of the resur-

---

4. See also *CD* IV/2, p. 299, where Barth states: "It is quite easy to understand, therefore, why earlier theology described His resurrection as in some sense the *datum* of His exaltation. If we have read the New Testament aright, the datum of both the humiliation and the exaltation of Jesus Christ is the whole of His human life including His death. But His resurrection is the event, and not merely the datum, of the revelation of the One who is exalted in His lowliness."

rection, where God raises Jesus Christ from death. Thus, no act of human love partakes in this overcoming of death. This means (again according to Prenter) that the incarnation and the resurrection are linked very closely together, as they are both to be seen as the outpouring of the eternal will of God. Barth hereby commits a Christological error due to his lack of emphasis on the humanity of Christ. Thus the atonement is not a drama of life or death. It is rather a well-played script.

This rather dubious description of Barth's teaching on the atonement enables Prenter to create a big gap between Barth and Athanasius, whom Prenter uses as an example for what he (in the tradition of Gustaf Aulén) defines as a classical teaching of the atonement.[5] Prenter states with reference to Athanasius that the death of the human being has already been overcome through the death of Jesus Christ, and not first in the resurrection of Jesus Christ. The being of the *Logos* is love, which again is the essence of life. This love has been expressed in the will of Jesus Christ to die on the cross for the sake of others. Death has hereby been overcome through death. The love of God hereby also includes the love of a human being.

Prenter uses his interpretation of Athanasius as a platform for developing his critique of Barth. This critique is twofold:

(1) The passion of Jesus Christ is directed solely toward God. The aim of the passion is the destruction of the old man (the old Adam). This destruction is a necessary precondition for the creation of the new man (the new Adam).[6]

(2) Human love has not become a part of the atonement. When the atonement is placed at the act of the resurrection, and this act is solely an act of God, then the love and suffering of Jesus Christ do not play a role within the atonement. The life and death of Jesus Christ are more like the enacting of an already-written script, where all is known prior to the actual performance. Jesus' death is hereby reduced to a necessary precondition for the resurrection.[7]

---

5. See Regin Prenter, "Karl Barths Umbildung der traditionellen Zweinaturlehre in lutherischer Beleuchtung," in *Theologie und Gottesdienst. Gesammelte Aufsätze,* ed. Erik Kyndal, Gerhard Pedersen, and Anna Marie Aagaard (Aarhus: Aros Forlag, 1977), pp. 77-91.

6. See Prenter, "Karl Barths Umbildung der traditionellen Zweinaturlehre," p. 85.

7. See Prenter, "Karl Barths Umbildung der traditionellen Zweinaturlehre," pp. 80-83.

However, Prenter's attempt to describe Barth's teaching of the atonement as a kind of dialectical logic — in which (a) there is no dialectical relation between the death and the resurrection of Jesus Christ (as if it is only the death of Jesus that should be interpreted in the light of the resurrection, and not vice versa); where (b) the act of the atonement excludes an aspect of human love, and (c) the resurrection at the end can be reduced to a demonstration of God's eternal Yes to himself[8] — simply does not hit the target. In fact, it is really hard to understand how Prenter can manage to misinterpret Barth so consistently. One reason could be Prenter's animosity toward Barth's emphasis on the universality of atonement. In Barth's *CD*, judgment and salvation are interwoven in such a way that one cannot be interpreted without the other. The life and death of Jesus are not, as claimed by Prenter, empty preconditions for the resurrection. The resurrection cannot be reduced to God's eternal Yes to himself. In fact, it is the dialectic between the life, death, and resurrection of Jesus Christ that enables me to make an interpretation of Barth's teaching of the atonement in which the revelation and judgment of the human being's wish to judge (an anthropological constant) plays a major role (see Chapter 9).

With the help of the combination of the *status duplex,* the two natures, and the covenant, Barth has established a Christological basis for a universal salvation in which all human beings not only potentially can be, but actually have been included in the saving act of God. Instead Prenter wants to make sure that a clear distinction between the invitation to salvation *(Heilsangebot)* and the acceptance of salvation *(Heilsaneignung)* is maintained. Prenter opposes the view that the act of incarnation should in itself be a saving act of God.[9] Prenter, despite his disapproval, sees

8. See Prenter, "Karl Barths Umbildung der traditionellen Zweinaturlehre," pp. 80-83.

9. Prenter summarizes Barth's point of view in the following way: "God is the Reconciler, man is the one being reconciled. God is the one humiliating Himself, offering grace, man is the reconciled man, the one who is being elevated, exalted, the one who finds grace. There can be no mistake here. At the same time the Divine and the Human cannot be divided. The degradation, the humiliation of the Son of God is his becoming man, his acceptance of human nature, and the elevation of the Son of Man is man's return to God, to real human life taking part in God's life. If this has become true in incarnation it has been for the single and irreversible condition: that the self-humiliation of God and the elevation of man is the same act. This act is *without any possibility that God's self-humiliation does not reach its goal of elevating man* and makes sure that man — after God's

rightly that the interrelation of the *status duplex* with the incarnation and the covenant enables Barth to interpret the incarnation as the ultimate manifestation of God's eternal mercy toward all human beings.[10] It is therefore possible to claim that there is no chronological or spatial separation between the humiliation and the exaltation.[11] What happened in the life, death, and resurrection of Jesus Christ was already anticipated in the incarnation. But, one should note that this is not the same as to say that it was all predetermined.

The judgment of Jesus takes place through human beings' judgment. Human beings' judgment contains, however, not only human beings' judgment of God (the rejection of Jesus' self-proclamation, which is demonstrated most ultimately on the cross), but also God's judgment of human beings (that God judges himself substitutively on the cross). The human being is judged due to the fact that God in Jesus Christ takes the judgment of the human being onto himself. The question is: How is this judgment executed and what is the content of this judgment? The sacrifice, if it should be called a sacrifice at all, is *not* necessary in the sense that God had to please himself through this sacrifice. The sacrifice is necessary "only" in the sense that it is the only way through which God can demonstrate and fulfill his radical love toward the human being (a love that includes not only self-devotion but also self-deliverance). The aim of this sacrifice is to exalt the human being into a partnership with God. From this perspective the word "sacrifice" cannot be restricted to describing the death of Jesus Christ on the cross. It includes the very act of the incarnation — in which God humbled himself to become a ser-

---

self-humiliation has happened — cannot be at home anywhere but by God, that divisiveness between them becomes unthinkable." See Prenter, "Karl Barths Umbildung der traditionellen Zweinaturlehre," p. 40; my emphasis (trans. Michael Waltemathe).

10. See Prenter, "Karl Barths Umbildung der traditionellen Zweinaturlehre," p. 38: "The elevation of the Son of Man is always the elevation to the destiny man was created for, to true human existence with God. The act of incarnation, in which the Son of God and the Son of Man become *one* person, is the realization of the covenant-history itself. What can be said about elevation of other humans into coexistence with God has thus been said. Therefore pneumatology, ecclesiology and eschatology can *only* be treated as part of the testimony for the reality of incarnation" (trans. Michael Waltemathe).

11. Cf. Eberhard Jüngel, "Der königliche Mensch. Eine christologische Reflexion auf die Würde des Menschen in der Theologie Karl Barths," in *Barth Studien* (Gütersloh: Gütersloher Verlagshaus, 1982), p. 242.

vant for human beings. In the introduction to §64 in the *CD* Barth states:

> Jesus Christ, the Son of God and Lord who humbled Himself to be a servant, is also the Son of Man exalted as this servant to be the Lord, the new and true and royal man who participates in the being and life and lordship and act of God and honours and attests Him, and as such the Head and Representative and Saviour of all other men, the origin and content and norm of the divine direction given us in the work of the Holy Spirit. (*CD* IV/2, p. 3)

To grasp that one owes one's life to God and not to oneself is one way through which the human being's self-centeredness and self-sufficiency are destroyed. According to Barth, self-centeredness and self-sufficiency are expressed most clearly in the human being's wish to judge other people. The human being's judgment of itself and others leads to death instead of life. My interpretation of the role of the judgment in Barth's teaching of the atonement — and thereby also the meaning of sacrifice, substitution, and solidarity — is indicated in the introduction to §59 in the *CD*, where it says:

> that the eternal Son of the eternal Father became obedient by offering and humbling Himself to be the brother of man, to take His place with the transgressor, to judge him by judging Himself and dying in his place. (*CD* IV/1, p. 157)

A connection is established here between the judgment and the substitution in the sense that the judgment of the human being consists in the fact that God takes the place of the human being, and thus — in contrast to the human being — lives a life that is not centered around the will to judge oneself and others. Again this implies that the act of atonement cannot be reduced to the cross; nor can the cross be left out of the very same act of atonement. What this further implies will be demonstrated under the headings: "The Judge Judged in Our Place" (Chapter 9), "The Double Outcome" (Chapter 10), and "The Punishment and Wrath of God" (Chapter 11). But prior to these investigations of the various aspects of judgment, I will analyze how Barth's use of the covenant relates to the so-called federal theology.

Federal Theology

"Federal theology" is a label for a "school" within the older Reformed Church, where the covenant plays a very decisive role.[12] John Coccejus (1603-1669), one of the most important theologians within this movement, gave federal theology its classical and systematic form in his *Summa doctrinae de foedere et testamento Dei* from 1648.

Barth refers positively to federal theology in the sense that it "tried to understand the work and Word of God attested in Holy Scripture *dynamically* and not statically, as an *event* and not as a system of objective and self-contained truths" (*CD* IV/1, p. 55; my emphasis). Federal theology was thus the first movement that in principle tried to historicize the activity and revelation of God (see *CD* IV/1, p. 55). It read the Bible as a series of events in and through which the Christian truth is revealed. The content of the Christian doctrine can thereby no longer be explained with the help of static concepts. It is instead the task of theology to unfold the history of God and human beings as this history is revealed in Holy Scripture.

Barth further recognizes that parts of federal theology incorporate a strong universalistic strain. Both Zwingli and Bullinger state that *the covenant is from the very first open to the whole race*.[13] However, this potentiality is not to be equated with actuality. "The people or Church of the covenant is not identical with the whole race " (*CD* IV/1, p. 57). But both Zwingli and Bullinger nonetheless saw the potentially all-including aim of the covenant: "it is the destiny of all men to become and to be members of this covenant" (*CD* IV/1, p. 57).

But this "universalism in the thought of the covenant was" unfortunately "quickly obscured if not obliterated" (*CD* IV/1, p. 57). In line with the work of Calvin (especially his emphasis on double predestination), federal theology developed various distinctions through which it wanted to separate those who were elected for salvation (those who were included

---

12. The following is based on Barth's excursus regarding federal theology in *CD* IV/1, pp. 54-66.

13. For Bullinger the new covenant given with Christ is the "fulfilment of the covenant with Abraham, and as such it is also the ratification of the *fœdus Dei æternum* with the whole human race, which did not cease to be a covenant of grace, or to apply to all men, because of the intervention of the law of the covenant with Israel" (*CD* IV/1, p. 57).

in the covenant) and those who were elected for reprobation (those who were outside the covenant actually as well as potentially). Thus a split is established between creation and election. Consequently, creation and election are not united in the covenant. The focus here is on the elected people, who have either failed or fulfilled the demands of the covenant.

But does this not entail a gap between God the Creator and God the Reconciler? One way to avoid this dead end is to distinguish between various types of covenants. This type of solution was already present in some of the works of the early reformers and their followers. Barth mentions for example Wolfgang Musculus's (1497-1563) and Stephan Szegedin's (1502-72) differentiation between *foedus generale* and *foedus speciale,* Zacharias Ursinus's (1534-83) distinction between *foedus naturae* and *foedus gratiae,* and Franciscus Gomarus's (1563-1641) division between *foedus naturale* and *foedus supernaturale.* All these differentiations make it possible for the covenant to refer to both a universal creation and a particular salvation (rooted in double predestination).

I will not go into details regarding the — at places quite subtle — differences between these distinctions, but only explain what is at stake with the help of the above-mentioned division between *foedus generale* and *foedus speciale.* Surprisingly enough, it is the *foedus generale* that is the temporal covenant and the *foedus speciale* that is the eternal. The temporal covenant refers to God's covenant "with the *universe,* the earth and man as a part of the creation" (*CD* IV/1, p. 58; my emphasis), whereas the eternal covenant refers to the ones who in all eternity have been elected by God: "the true seed of Abraham" (*CD* IV/1, p. 58). In the history of salvation the elected ones are "split up into three periods, *ante legem, sub legem, post legem*" (*CD* IV/1, p. 58).

The continuity between the various historical forms of the election has been established through the common reference back to God's eternal election. They are all expressions in time of one and the same eternal election. The general covenant serves only as the necessary precondition for the execution of the eternal one. The creation has to be created, so that parts of it — according to the eternal election (an election that goes from Abraham forward) — can be saved. The distinction here is neither between Jews and Gentiles, nor between law and gospel as they are ordered in historical sequence. This sequence is — as we have seen — overruled by the eternal decision of God. To understand the content of the covenant it is necessary to go behind its actual historical shape — and back to its eternal foundation (the will of God). This strong emphasis on God's eternal will goes back to Calvin, who, according to Barth, claimed that

> the covenant made with the fathers was already the *foedus evangelii*, of which Christ was not only the fulfilment but the eternal basis. The distinctions between the fathers and us do not any of them relate to the substance of the covenant, which was and is the same, but only to the *modus administrationis*. It is only its *accidentia, annexa accessoria*, which have been abrogated and made obsolete by the appearance of Christ. We live with them, and they lived with us, by the same promises, under the same command, by the same grace. (*CD* IV/1, p. 58)

Barth notes with satisfaction that chapters IX-XI in the *Institutes* (where Calvin treats the covenant of grace) have hardly been touched by "the shadow of his [Calvin's] doctrine of an eternal double predestination" (see *CD* IV/1, p. 58).

By referring to both federal theology and the Reformers, whom he partly sees as forerunners of federal theology, Barth has been able to establish a space for his own covenantal theology, in which he unites the free will of God with an eternal election of all human beings. This election has reached its goal in the life, death, and resurrection of Jesus Christ. By now it should be obvious why the covenant is viewed as the presupposition for the atonement in the *CD*. But, before going into an interpretation of the meaning of Jesus' life, death, and resurrection as it is described in the *CD*, this section will conclude with a description of the most essential points of the critique that Barth directs toward the final outcome of federal theology. The exposition of this critique serves as another way of clarifying Barth's own use of the covenant.

Federal theology presupposes that the covenant of grace has its reason in an intra-Trinitarian decision. In Barth's account of federal theology the eternal basis of the covenant is described as "a freely accepted but legally binding mutual obligation between God the Father and God the Son" (*CD* IV/1, p. 64). But if this intra-Trinitarian decision takes place in a mutual pact between the Father and the Son, a split is established between the essence and the will of God, as God first becomes a God of grace when he has made this binding agreement with himself. The need for such an intra-Trinitarian settlement would then have its reason in the presupposition of an original split between the mercy and the righteousness of God, which can only be overcome by an intra-Trinitarian contract.[14] Thus, not only is a gap established between the mercy and the righteousness of God, but it may also be asked whether the covenant can really be trusted as the eternal will of God. A hidden God, a God *in abstracto* who might not be merciful toward the human being, is thus intelligible.[15]

If God needed to make an intra-Trinitarian commitment to establish the covenant of grace, whereby mercy and righteousness were united, then what about the eternal will of God prior to this decision? Barth's aversion to a theological emphasis on the *deus absconditus* who can potentially be different from the *deus revelatus* is once again seen here. Instead Barth wants to make sure that the covenant established in Jesus Christ is nothing more and nothing less than the revelation of the eternal free will of God.

Barth also criticizes such a mutual contract between the Father and the Son from a Trinitarian perspective. It splits up the being of God into various autonomous subjects, instead of describing the Trinity as the one God's three modes of being. According to Barth the unity of God is hereby dismissed, which leads to what he defines as a possible dualism within God. Now, the problem is not "only" the possible conflict between different predicates of God, but also that God from this perception of the Trinity consists of not one but three individual subjects, each with their will. Again, the unconditional validity of the covenant of grace is threatened.[16] Furthermore, the problem with this two-subject theory is that the two partners between

14. See *CD* IV/I, p. 64.

15. "For God to be gracious to sinful man, was there any need of a special decree to establish the unity of the righteousness and mercy of God in relation to man, of a special intertrinitarian arrangement and contract which can be distinguished from the being of God? If there was need of such a decree, then the question arises at once of a form of the will of God in which this arrangement has not yet been made and is not yet valid. We have to reckon with the existence of a God who is righteous *in abstracto* and not free to be gracious from the very first, who has to bind to the fulfilment of His promise the fulfilment of certain conditions by man, and punish their non-fulfilment. It is only with the conclusion of this contract with Himself that He ceases to be a righteous God *in abstracto* and becomes the God who in His righteousness is also merciful and therefore able to exercise grace. In this case it is not impossible or illegitimate to believe that properly, in some inner depth of His being behind the covenant of grace, He might not be able to do this" (*CD* IV/1, pp. 64-65).

16. See *CD* IV/1, p. 65.

whom the covenant is established are God the Father and God the Son. Federal theology fails to describe the covenant as an outer relation between God and the human being. Instead it describes the covenant as a relation of God with himself. The result is that the human being seems absent from the covenant.[17] Barth is, in fact, very critical of federal theology's way of uniting the will of God in an inner-Trinitarian decision that had to take place prior to the establishment of a correlation between the mercy and the righteousness of God. With his emphasis on the radical freedom of God, he wants to secure the dialectic between the righteousness and the mercy of God, without presupposing a conflict between the two that first has to be overcome in an inner-Trinitarian act of decision. The covenant is a covenant of grace rooted in God's free election of grace.[18]

To conclude: in the covenant it is most clearly demonstrated that God never wanted to be a God for himself. The covenant is the external expression of God's wish and will to be a God for the human being. To think of either God or the human being in isolation from this relation is to think of them *in abstracto*. The election of the human being has been fulfilled in the election of Jesus Christ, who is therefore not only the middle and the end but also the beginning of the covenant. The various types of covenants must therefore all be interpreted from Christ as the center, and not from a historical chain with an investigation of the inner-historical development of the covenants. The connection between the old and the new covenant is hereby established due to the essence of the covenant and not due to the *accidentia, annexa,* or *accessoria* of the covenant.

17. A similar critique has been raised against Barth's own covenantal theology. Prenter has argued that Barth's way of combining election, covenant, and Christology not only lacks a sense of the humanity in Christ, but also a participation of the human being in the covenant. The result is allegedly that the salvation of the human being that takes place in the act of atonement is described as "nothing more" than God's eternal love to himself. See Prenter, "Karl Barths Umbildung der traditionellen Zweinaturlehre," pp. 96-99, 106. Falk Wagner shares, although from quite another perspective, this critique of Barth. He finds that Barth leaves no space for the human being as the real otherness from God. For a further description of Wagner's critique see Chapter 13.

18. See *CD* IV/1, p. 66.

CHAPTER 9

The Judge Judged in Our Place

The vocabulary and phrases that Barth uses to describe the act of atonement are at places very traditional. In fact, they are so traditional that one might ask if Barth really adds anything new to the tradition, or if he simply repeats it. Occasionally in the *CD* the patterns of the atonement appear to be structured very much like Anselm's teaching of an objective atonement. The human being is under the judgment of God (due to the sin of the human being). This judgment will inevitably lead to a destruction of the human being. The only way this destruction can be avoided is if God takes the righteous punishment of the human being upon himself. The righteousness of God would thus be fulfilled without a destruction of the human being. Here is just one example (among many) from the *CD*, where this kind of theological language game is at play:

> Everything happened to us exactly as it had to happen, but because God willed to execute His judgment on us in His Son it all happened in His person, as His accusation and condemnation and destruction. He judged, and it was the Judge who was judged, who let Himself be judged. . . . In His doing this for us, in His taking to Himself — to fulfil all righteousness — our accusation and condemnation and punishment, in His suffering in our place and for us, there came to pass our reconciliation with God. *Cur Deus homo?* In order that God as man might do and accomplish and achieve and complete all this for us wrong-doers, in order that in this way there might be brought about by Him our reconciliation with Him and conversion to Him. (*CD* IV/1, pp. 222-23)

The heading "The Judge Judged in Our Place" could, read together with the above-quoted passages from *CD* IV/1, indicate that the atonement in the *CD* is understood within a legalistic framework in which the essence of the atonement is to be found in the idea of a necessary judgment and punishment that God had to undergo in our place to save humanity from destruction. This would not only imply that God — in order to remain God — had to judge the human being (without judgment, God would not be righteous), but also that the human being could not survive such a judgment (the creature would — as finite — be destroyed when it received the infinite God's infinite punishment). For the sake of the human being God therefore took the consequence of the judgment (the punishment) onto himself (God's mercy). The old Anselmian dilemma: *aut satisfactio aut poena,* would then — if this really is the essence of the atonement — be the pattern that lies behind Barth's theory of atonement in *CD* IV.

The aim with and the content of the incarnation would then be determined of an inner conflict in God between his righteousness (and honor — if not to say vanity) and his mercy.[1] God did for our sake in Jesus Christ take the destruction upon himself to enable the human being to live despite its self-imposed destruction. But is this really all Barth intends to say with his use of judgment metaphors? A further investigation of the content and the use of the terms "judgment," "punishment," and "wrath" will be needed to answer this question. An important question to keep in mind for this further investigation will be how the connection between judgment and punishment is established. Does the judgment of God inevitably entail an act of punishment or not? And if the answer to this question is yes, what does the actual punishment then consist of? And how does it relate to the wrath of God?

Judgment

The judgment of God is a judgment that no human being can escape. All will be judged by God. No one can plead "not guilty." All will be judged

---

1. See also Volker Stümke, "Eschatologische Differenz in Gott? Zum Verhältnis von Barmherzigkeit und Gerechtigkeit Gottes bei Karl Barth und Friedrich-Wilhelm Marquardt," in *Wendung nach Jerusalem. Friedrich-Wilhelm Marquardts Theologie im Gespräch,* ed. Hanna Lehming, Joachim Liß-Walther, Matthias Loerbroks, and Rien van der Vegt (München: Chr. Kaiser Gütersloher Verlagshaus, 1999), p. 371.

with the same outcome: destruction. This judgment is described as the judgment at the left hand of God. Barth claims that it belongs to the very essence of God to destroy his enemies.

> But those who are judged and rejected and condemned by God as wrongdoers are lost and condemned to perish, indeed they are already perishing. They stand on the *left* hand of God, under the *divine No,* in the sphere of that which God does not will, but rejects, and therefore in the sphere of that which is not, in the darkness in which there is no light, in the affliction in which there is no help, in the need from which there is no redemption. The power of God still rules over them, but as the power which holds and imprisons them, the power of His condemnation. (*CD* IV/1, p. 220; my emphasis)

> God would not be God if there could be any altering the universality and logic and completeness of what is necessarily done here, if there could be any escaping this sequence of sin and destruction. It means eternal perdition to have God against us. But if we will what God does not will, we do have God against us, and therefore we hurry and run and stumble and fall into eternal perdition. (*CD* IV/1, p. 221)

It is obvious that Barth here is heavily influenced by both Calvin and Luther, who claim that all human beings deserve eternal perdition, as all human beings are working against the will of God!

But not everything is said that needs to be said simply by the description of the eternal perdition worked by the left hand of God. At the right hand of God the Yes to the creature is spoken, and the punishment (eternal perdition) is transformed into "love out of wrath, life out of death" (*CD* IV/1, p. 221).[2] This description of the dialectic between the left and the right hand of God, between the No and the Yes of God, is similar to what has already been described in Part II, Chapter 6. What I will call attention to here is (1) Barth's description of the *a priori* of the judgment, and (2) the result of this judgment: the liberation of man.

---

2. The Yes of God is a gift the receiver has no right to claim as a right, and the giver is not obliged to give. See *CD* IV/1, pp. 221-22.

The *A Priori* of Judgment

The *a priori* of judgment is that the human being wants to be its own judge. This is what Barth defines as the sin *in nuce* of the human being. The reason why the human being's eagerness to judge (not only between good and evil but also itself, other human beings, and God) is described as the sin *in nuce* is that the human being hereby takes the place that rightly belongs to God.

> All sin has its being and origin in the fact that man wants to be his own judge. And in wanting to be that, and thinking and acting accordingly, he and his whole world is in conflict with God. It is an unreconciled world, and therefore a suffering world, a world given up to destruction. (*CD* IV/1, p. 220)

The result of this is that the human being creates boundaries not only between itself and God, but also between itself and other fellow human beings. Judgment is used as a "shield and weapon in relation to ourselves, our neighbours and God" (*CD* IV/1, p. 232). The role of judgment is then misused, as the real purpose of judgment turns out to be to enable oneself to plead not guilty.[3] In the hands of the human being judgment is misused as an instrument through which distance is kept not only to God but also to its fellow human beings.

The urge to declare oneself not guilty has a counterpart: the urge to judge other people.

> For where does our own judgment always lead? To the place where we pronounce ourselves innocent, and where, on account of their venial or mortal sins, and with more or less indulgence and understanding or severity and inflexibility, we pronounce others guilty. That is how we live. (*CD* IV/1, p. 233)

The logic behind this is that the next best thing to being innocent is to be nearly innocent in the sense of being less guilty than others. A harsh judgment of others thus becomes a way by which, despite one's own lacks and discredits, one can manage to put oneself in a favorable light in comparison with others.

---

3. According to Barth, one is able to see through this serious illusion only if one is aware of the fact that all people are guilty before God.

In describing the human being's urge for judging other people as the sin *in nuce*, Barth is defining an anthropological constant.[4] The human being cannot by its own efforts escape this urge for judging. The pattern of separation cannot only be acknowledged by the help of — but also only be broken with the help of — an intervention from the outside. Expressed within the dogmatic terminology of Barth, this means that the human being cannot — by itself — realize that by judging others in the name of God, it is judging itself. Typically the judgment of the human being ends with the result that the human being acquits itself, but judges others to be "more or less guilty" (see *CD* IV/1, p. 231). So, when the human being becomes judge, judgment is used as an instrument in each person's own attempt to obtain justification. From the perspective of divine judgment, however, the judgment of the human being, in which the human being thinks that it acquits itself, is instead a judgment in which it renders itself guilty. Human judgment serves a self-promoting purpose, whereby all others are reduced to instruments for one's own project of self-justification. The identity of the human being is hereby established by a judgment of others — which is another way to describe what I am negatively (by saying what I am not, instead of what I am). The identity and self-perception of each individual is thus established through an act of judgment. Boundaries are in this way created between me/us and others, between inside and outside. So when God judges the human being, God judges the human being's own wish to judge not only itself but also all other people.

The precondition for Barth's definition of the human striving for judgment as the sin *in nuce* is that judgment belongs to God only. By judging, the human being has taken the place of God. God takes this place back, which belonged to him from eternity, by judging human judgment in Jesus Christ.[5] This is not only a question of reversal of roles, but also of content.[6] God's judgment of the human being differs from the human be-

---

4. I am well aware that Barth himself did not use terms like "anthropological constants" or "anthropological *a priori*." Such terms would have too close an affinity to the methods of liberal theology.

5. "It is this function of God as Judge which has been re-established once and for all in Jesus Christ. What we want to do for ourselves has been taken out of our hands in Him" (*CD* IV/1, p. 232).

6. God occupies the place of judgment quite differently than the human beings. "We must say at once that He does not come to this place to do there what we ourselves do. In

ing's judgment of itself. Where human beings use judgment as a way to create boundaries, God uses judgment as a way to unite.

Barth's way of describing and using the sin *in nuce* is not without structural similarities to René Girard's demonstration of the connection between violence and the sacred. Girard claims that an opposition to this connection can be found in the Christian narrative, in which God is described as a God for victims. This, according to Girard, is what distinguishes the Christian narrative from myths and other religious narratives. But before going into a description of some of the theological implications in the work of Girard, I will present the structure of Barth's way of interrelating God's judgment of the human being, and the human being's judgment of God.

The Judgment of Jesus Christ

The judgment of Jesus Christ is a judgment that contains two overall perspectives: God's judgment of the human being and the human being's judgment of God. Both judgments are enacted in the death of Jesus Christ. In the former, God is the subject behind the death of Jesus; Jesus had to die to reestablish the relation between God and human beings. In the latter the subject behind the death of Jesus is the crowd that killed him on behalf of mankind as such. From this perspective Jesus' death has its cause in the resistance of the crowd to his proclaimed message. It might seem as if we are presented here with two mutually exclusive choices: either God or the human being is the murderer of Jesus Christ. Either God is evil (killing his own son) or the human being is evil (killing the Son of God). Either God is violent or the human being is violent. But the case might not be that simple. At least, not if the judgment of Jesus is seen in relation to the atoning act of the Trinitarian God.[7] From this perspective the judgment of Jesus, viewed under the head-

---

taking our place as Judge He takes the place which belongs to Him, which is His own from all eternity. He does not, therefore, do anything illegitimate. And it is not like ours an unrighteous but a righteous judgment which He exercises in this place. He does in this place the very opposite of what we usually do" (*CD* IV/1, p. 236).

7. Hunsinger emphasizes strongly, with references to Hans Urs von Balthasar and Thomas Torrance, that the atonement must be seen within a Trinitarian perspective. If

ing of the judgment of God, involves four distinctions: (1) God as subject,
(2) God as object, (3) Jesus as subject, and (4) Jesus as object.

(1) God is subject, insofar as he sends his Son into the world for the sake
    of the world (God's going into the far country). This mission includes
    in itself a judgment of the world. According to Barth, God is also ac-
    tive in the actual death of Jesus Christ ("yet not what I want but what
    you want" [Matt. 26:39]). But this does not imply (as we will see later)
    that God is a violent and vindictive God.
(2) God is object, insofar as he takes the suffering of Christ onto himself.
    The Trinitarian approach thereby enables the reader to see the self-
    devotion of Christ as the self-devotion of God. From this perspective
    God is actually putting himself at risk when he incarnates himself.[8]

---

not, it loses its atoning character and becomes one death of an innocent among other in-
nocents. See George Hunsinger, *Disruptive Grace: Studies in the Theology of Karl Barth*
(Grand Rapids: Eerdmans, 2000), pp. 30-34.

8. The reader will notice here a tension between my earlier description and emphasis
on the original will of God, where it seems as if there is no change in God at all, and the
description of the atonement that is given here, where the incarnation involves God putting himself at risk. This includes a reflection on how the incarnation and the atonement
are interrelated. It is not the death on the cross itself that constitutes the center of the
atonement. Instead, it is the fact that it is Jesus Christ who dies on the cross that establishes the atonement between God and human beings.

What I suggest is that the work of Barth entails a tension in the way the incarnation
and the atonement are interrelated. Does God really put himself into play in a way that
also influences the being of God himself and thereby creates a difference within God: a
before and an after? Or is it "just" the original will of God that was effectuated in time?
Does God, when he interacts within the world through the incarnation, take a risk? Is he
in danger of losing himself by this interaction — and is it the willingness to take this risk
for others that really makes him a God for the human being? What I am trying to formu-
late by adducing all these different questions and options is that Barth is not completely
clear on this point. In some passages he seems to advocate a Platonically inspired dialectic
between the original will of God (eternity) and the outliving of this original will in time.
Other passages seem to be more influenced by a Hegelian thought structure, where God
really puts himself into play through the incarnation. Barth would never claim that God
needed the world to be God, but he does at places claim that God is putting himself at risk
by this interaction. Therefore, it must also be adequate to talk about a self-willed transformation of God: a before and after. The interrelation between the incarnation and the act
of atonement, and the question of how this interrelation affects God (and vice versa), is in
other words not totally clear in the *CD*.

(3) Jesus is the subject of judgment, when he proclaims the coming of the kingdom of God. This proclamation is in itself a judgment of the way human beings live and understand themselves.

(4) Jesus Christ is object when he accepts the will of the Father and thereby takes on the destiny of the cross.

The inner-Trinitarian approach to the atonement enables Barth to maintain a classical doctrinal understanding of the death of Jesus as inevitable, willed by the Father for the sake of the human being, without picturing God as angry, revengeful, or violent. And here we come to one of the really important aspects of the heading, "The Judge Judged in Our Place." Despite the fact that Barth does not specifically use the term "non-violent God," my thesis is that this is right at the core of his understanding of God. This also comes to expression in the way he describes what is at stake when God is the judge judged in our place. The only subject who has the right to execute final judgment over human beings is God. When the human being wants to take this place itself, it takes the place of God, and thus turns itself into an idol. This is rather obvious, and has surely been heard before. What is interesting in Barth's treatment of God as the judge, however, is how — viewed from this perspective — the narrative discloses the truth that God is the only rightful judge: the judge (God) lets himself be judged (Christ at the cross). This implies not only a negation of the human being's sin *in nuce* (the ongoing tendency to judge), but it also implies a negation of its practical consequences: the "God-sanctioned" boundaries that are drawn when human beings judge each other in the name of God.

The judgment of God is an "all-uniting" judgment that can also be described as a negation of the negation. The reason for, and the content of, God's judgment can only be fully perceived when it includes a knowledge of the human being's striving to be without God — which for Barth is equal to the human being's striving to be God. In both cases the qualitative difference between God and the human being is rejected. In both cases the human being has become its own presupposition and aim. In short: the human being has become its own eschaton. From the perspective of Barth both aspects of judgment (God's judgment of the human being, and the human being's judgment of God) can be understood only when it incorporates the human being, prior to God's judgment of the human being, judging God. This all-uniting judgment may be outlined here as follows:

(1) The human being wants to judge other people. Judgment enables it to distance itself from others by creating boundaries.
(2) In Christ God takes the place of the human being.
(3) Christ is the only person who has the right to judge.
      Presupposition a: Only God has the right to make final and eternal judgments.
      Presupposition b: The sin *in nuce* is the human being's wish to judge fellow humans.
      Presupposition c: Christ is the only human person without sin.
(4) The judgment of God in Christ is non-violent in its structure.
(5) God's judgment of the human being in Christ has both an active and a passive element.
      (a) *active:* in the proclamation of the kingdom of God.
      (b) *passive:* in the obedience toward God that is ultimately expressed in the willingness to die. Note: (b) is here understood as the practical consequence of (a).
(6) The judgment is a judgment of our judgment.
(7) The judgment unites all human beings before God.
(8) The judgment is all-uniting, both in its radical rejection and in its radical acceptance of the human being.

The uniting character of God's radical judgment is expressed through the already-described dialectic between the judgment of God at the left and at the right hand. The all-inclusiveness of the judgment (which is another way of expressing the positive all-inclusiveness of the act of atonement) also comes to expression in the way that Barth separates the act of atonement and the quest for discipleship:

> The event of redemption took place then and there in Him, and therefore "for us." In Him, as that which took place then and there, it embraces us, it becomes the basis of fellowship, it call us to discipleship, but not in such a way that it becomes an event of redemption only through our obedience to this call, or is not an event of redemption through our disobedience, but in such a way that as the event of redemption which took place for us in Him it always comes before the question of our obedience or disobedience, it is always in itself the event of redemption which took place for us, whatever may be our answer to that question. (*CD* IV/1, pp. 229-30)

The fact that the act of atonement — and thereby also the judgment — embraces us, whether we respond to it in obedience or disobedience, is not the same as to say that it should be taken less seriously. In Barth's logic such a complaint lives only by the human being's wicked wish to use judgment as an instrument through which it creates self-established boundaries between "us" and "them," between the righteous and the unrighteous. In fact, such a complaint is just a perfect illustration of the fact that judgment, in the hands of the human being, serves a self-righteous purpose.

Theological Implications in the Work of René Girard: Girard and Barth

It is, as said, possible to see some structural similarities between Barth's rejection of the human being's right to judge other people and René Girard's understanding of mimesis, the connection between violence and the sacred, and the need for an unveiling of these structures from the *outside*.[9] The presupposition for Girard's analysis of the connection between the sacred and violence is that all cultures have one common pattern: mimetic desire.[10] The result of this is mimetic rivalry.

9. For a more detailed description of the theological implication of Girard's anthropology and its structural affinity to Barth's theology, see Hans Vium Mikkelsen, "Offer og forsoning. Dogmatiske perspektiver og konsekvenser af René Girards antropologi" [Sacrifice and atonement: Dogmatical perspectives and consequences of René Girard's anthropology], in *Syndens Sold — en antologi om den mimetiske teori* [The wages of sin: An anthology regarding the mimetic theory], ed. Jørgen Jørgensen (Frederiksberg: Aros Forlag, 2006), pp. 141-73. See also S. Mark Heim, *Saved from Sacrifice: A Theology of the Cross* (Grand Rapids: Eerdmans, 2006). Heim offers in this book a theory of atonement that takes Girard's critique of a sacrificial interpretation of the death of Jesus into account without neglecting the central role of the cross. The traditional theory of substitution is substituted by a Girardian-inspired "anthropology of the cross," where the substitution no longer consists in a righteous punishment of the innocent. The perspective of the passion story has hereby changed radically from the persecutor(s) to the victim. It is God who in Jesus suffers on the cross for our sake, but that does not imply that the suffering is an act of God's righteous punishment of sinful human beings. As Heim states it at the very end of his book (p. 329), "The God who paid the cost of the cross was not the one who charged it."

10. See René Girard, *Things Hidden Since the Foundation of the World*, trans. Stephan Bann and Michael Metteer (Stanford, CA: Stanford University Press, 1987), p. 18: "That

Girard sees mimetic desire as an anthropological constant. One of the basic characteristics of the human being is its ability to imitate other human beings. In fact, human culture is based on this ability. The desire is not directed at the object (in opposition to Freud). The object in itself is not the reason for mimetic desire. Instead, the reason is to be found in the rivalry for the object. "To untie the knot of desire, we have only to concede that everything begins in rivalry for the object."[11] One of Girard's favorite examples to illustrate this is the Judgment of Solomon. By pretending that he will divide the child in two, the king is able to reveal which of the two "mothers" really loves the child and therefore is willing to lose it, and which of them lacks a genuine love for the child and therefore is willing to accept the death of the child. The latter is a prime example of mimetic rivalry, where the rivalry is constitutive for the desire.[12]

The question is then: How is it possible to maintain a community despite this mimetic rivalry? The answer to this is the "establishing" of a common enemy (a scapegoat) that unites the community in its opposition to this particular outsider. Chaos is transformed into cosmos through a swift movement from an all-against-all to an all-against-one structure. The unification of a community that takes place through an "invention" of a common enemy becomes ritualized in religion, in such a way that religion plays a constitutive role within a community. Religion is thus in itself violent, as — despite its ability to "glue" the community together by establishing a common scapegoat — it serves to consolidate the community's violent structure. On the one hand, the scapegoat may be said to have a

---

cause [the cause of the conflictual aspect of mimesis], we repeat, is rivalry provoked by an object, the acquisitive mimesis which must always be our point of departure." In *Violence and the Sacred* Girard expresses it in the following way: "Rivalry does not arise because of the fortuitous convergence of two desires on a single object; rather, the subject desires the object because the rival desires it." René Girard, *Violence and the Sacred*, trans. Patrick Gregory (Baltimore: Johns Hopkins University Press, 1977), p. 145. See also Girard, *Things Hidden*, pp. 283-98.

11. Girard, *Things Hidden*, p. 294.

12. "The only thing that counts for her [the second woman] *is possessing what the other one possesses.* In the last resort, she is ready to accept being deprived of the child as long as her opponent is deprived of it in the same way. Quite clearly, mimetic desire impels her to speak and act; things have reached such a pitch of exasperation with her that the object of the quarrel, the living child, no longer counts; all that counts is her fascination with the hated model and rival" (Girard, *Things Hidden*, pp. 238-39).

positive function within the community, as this ritualization of violence serves to save the community from dissolution (and thereby to reduce the actual amount of violence). But, on the other hand, a religious justification of violence has taken place in which the roots of violence are left unquestioned. In short: the preservation of a community is based on violence/sacrifices.[13] According to Girard, this is a common feature for all religions except for Christianity.[14] What we find in the history of religions is a combination of sacredness and violence, whereby violence is legitimized, at least in a cultic form.

In Christianity there is no legitimized connection between the sacred and violence. Consequently, the idea of a sacrifice must be an alien thought in Christianity. Instead it is the victim — the one who is sacrificed — that is defended. In the Bible the scapegoat is unveiled as what it is: a scapegoat. It is the victim — and not the community that enacts the sacrifice — who is innocent. The death sentence of Jesus is an ostracizing of the one person who revealed that the Jewish religion — like any other religion — is a religion that legitimizes violence through its sacred acts. The death of Jesus on the cross showed that God is on the side of the victim and not on the side of those who victimize. In the preaching of Jesus violence is revealed as such, including its cultic forms. From this point of view the difference between God and human beings can be explained by the fact that God — in contrast to human beings — is non-violent. This is revealed in

13. "We have seen that, in *the founding murder, the victim is held responsible for the crisis;* the victim polarizes the growing mimetic conflicts that tear the community apart, the victim breaks the vicious cycle of violence and becomes the single pole for what then becomes a unifying, ritual mimesis. The experience of *disorder* and the *return to order,* for which such a victim is made responsible, constitute an experience too intolerable and incomprehensible to allow for rational understanding. Since the victim seems to be capable of first causing the most disastrous disorder and then of re-establishing order or inaugurating a *new order,* it seems legitimate to return to that victim whenever it is a question of deciding what one must and must not do, as in ritual and prohibitions, the resolution and the crisis" (Girard, *Things Hidden,* p. 40; my emphasis).

14. "We will see now that not only the prohibition but also ritual and ultimately the whole structure of religion can be traced back to the *mechanism of acquisitive mimesis*" (Girard, *Things Hidden,* p. 18; my emphasis). The distinction between Christianity and other religions is anchored in the claim that Christianity is the only religion in which there is no legislation of sacred violence. On the contrary, the Christian God takes the side of the victim instead of the side of the perpetrator. See René Girard, *Job: The Victim of His People,* trans. Yvonne Freccero (Stanford, CA: Stanford University Press, 1987), pp. 154-68.

and through the incarnation. The consequence of this approach to sacrifice is that it is no longer possible to interpret the actual death of Jesus on the cross as a willed act of God. God did not have to kill his own Son to avoid having all other human beings judged to eternal damnation in hell.[15] If God really were the subject of the death of Jesus, it would, according to Girard, have served as a legitimation of the anthropological constants: mimetic desire, rivalry, and the scapegoat function. The connection between the incarnated Jesus and God, who is incarnated, is instead established through Jesus' own life and work, which can be summarized in the proclamation of the kingdom of God.

Girard views the death on the cross as the result of this proclamation. God is not the hidden subject behind the death of Jesus. Jesus did not have to die to pay any kind of *satisfactio* back to God, so as to enable God to let human beings live despite their sin against him. Instead the death on the cross is the almost too-obvious result of the proclaimed message of Jesus.[16] Jesus could, perhaps, have anticipated that this would very likely be the consequence of his preaching. In Jesus' preaching of the kingdom of God the violent structure of the community (due to mimetic rivalry), the connection between sacrality and violence, and the way religion functions as a legislator of this violence are unmasked. God is instead portrayed as a non-violent, merciful God. The crowd's response to this proclamation of a non-violent God, who cannot be used to legitimate any kind of violence, is to kill the "messenger." The one who draws attention to the general structures in and behind the ongoing expulsion within a community is expelled from the community. In a Girardian perspective Jesus did fully what was already anticipated in Job: revealing that God is the God of the victims (instead of the oppressors).[17] The consequences of this reading are many. Here I will just draw attention to three of them:

---

15. "If the fulfilment, on earth, passes inevitably through the death of Jesus, this is not because the Father demands this death, for strange sacrificial motives. Neither the son nor the Father should be questioned about the cause of this event, but all mankind, and mankind alone" (Girard, *Things Hidden*, p. 213). See also pp. 182-85, 193.

16. "The events that followed the preaching of the Kingdom of God depended entirely on the response of Jesus' audience. If they had accepted the invitation unreservedly, there would have been no Apocalypse announced and no Crucifixion" (Girard, *Things Hidden*, p. 202).

17. See Girard, *Job*, pp. 154-68.

(1) An interpretation of Jesus' death as a sacrifice willed by God would, according to Girard, be to destroy the whole message from within. If this is regarded as the key to understanding the death of Jesus, then the unveiling of mimetic desire, the phenomenon of the scapegoat, the structure of sacred violence and the non-violent God — who is the God of victims — have not been heard. All of this is made known from and through the biblical narrative. Instead, the extra-textual dogmatic idea that Jesus must die on behalf of human beings to give God satisfaction — and thereby enable God to live out his love toward human beings — has become determining for the way the biblical narrative is read.

(2) The judgment of God is interpreted without any kind of revenge or "lack-of-reward motif." Instead the judgment of God is rooted in the human being's rejection of the preaching of the kingdom of God. When human beings reject this preaching and its inherent unveiling of the structure of violence, they remain stuck within the structure of violence. And this in itself is the judgment.[18] The apocalyptic parts of the New Testament are, according to Girard, a description of reality as it is when this unveiling of the structure of violence is left unheard.

(3) The narrative of the gospel contains all the aspects of a scapegoat phenomenon. The same crowd that previously adored Jesus now sentences him to death. It is only because the gospel includes all the elements of the scapegoat mechanism that it is possible to see it revealed as such through the narrative of the passion. This disclosure of the scapegoat mechanism happens through a reversal of the usual characteristics of the scapegoat. *First,* the scapegoat refuses to be a scapegoat. The scapegoat (Jesus Christ) does not accept the blame placed on him by the crowd.[19] *Second,* the passion story tells the reader/listener that what is a failure in the eyes of the world (that the one who himself claimed to be the witness of God's kingdom died on the cross) is a victory in the eyes of God. The connection between the sacred and violence is hereby revealed as a false connection. In the suffering of Jesus Christ God has revealed himself as a non-violent God.

18. See Girard, *Things Hidden,* pp. 202-5, where he describes this as the relation between the kingdom of God and the Apocalypse.

19. Take for example Matthew 26:59-66. At first Jesus does not respond to the accusations. And when he finally does, his answer is: "You have said so."

God as the Subject of Jesus' Death?
A Comparison Between Barth and Girard

Barth's understanding of the atonement can be reconstructed as a dogmatic version of Girard's literary and anthropological analysis of the death of Jesus. Many of the practical consequences of Girard's theory of the scapegoat and the relation between the sacred and violence can also be traced within Barth's approach to the atonement. Both Girard and Barth operate, as demonstrated above, with an anthropological *a priori*. In the case of Girard we have seen how mimetic desire and mimetic rivalry are the *a priori* for the description of the scapegoat mechanism. In Barth's description of the atonement, the human being's urge to judge not only itself but also others is the *a priori* for the description of God's judgment of the human being's judgment. According to both Barth and Girard the *a priori* must be revealed from the outside. It is the acts of God in Christ that reveal and unmask — and thereby also break — the anthropological structure.

Both see that the narrative of the gospel is playing an important role in this revelation. In and through the gospel (the proclamation of the kingdom of God) the basic anthropological structure is revealed. In the case of both Girard and Barth the kingdom of God is personalized in Jesus Christ. In the work of Girard the scapegoat is revealed by a victim (an "apparent-scapegoat") who refuses to be the scapegoat. In the work of Barth a judge who is letting himself be judged reveals the judgment. The result is in both cases that God is a God who cannot be used to legitimate violence, i.e., a loving, non-violent God.[20]

But, with these parallels in mind, we also have to take note of some of the main differences in Barth's and Girard's approaches. In Girard's perspective God cannot be the subject of the death of Jesus. This would imply that God remains a violent God who needs sacrifice in order to be satisfied. For Girard, the judgment of the human being that happened at the death of Je-

---

20. For a further description of the similarities between Barth and Girard — especially regarding their use of revelation, the distinction between Christianity and religion, and the way they use love as the most adequate description of the being of God, see Adrianus van Egmond, "Triumph der Wahrheit und Triumph der Gnade. René Girard und Karl Barth über Offenbarung, Religion, Kreuz und Gott," *Zeitschrift für Dialektische Theologie* 6, no. 2 (1990): 185-205.

sus Christ did not have to take place. It was the result of human beings' rejection of the proclamation of the kingdom of God. Thus, the subject behind the death of Jesus Christ is human and not divine. The atonement consists in a disclosure of the immanent structure of violence that is given within any kind of community. Girard's approach therefore deliberately avoids a Christology from above, since such an approach would be purely speculative.

The main difference between Barth and Girard has thus already been stated: in Barth's theology God remains both the subject and the object of the atonement. The death of Christ takes place due to the will of the Father. God sacrifices his Son for the sake of human beings. The Son lets himself be sacrificed. However, the sacrifice of the Son is a self-surrendering sacrifice that has only one purpose: to reestablish the human being as the covenant partner of God. God is not doing this for the sake of obtaining any satisfaction or having revenge or anything of the kind.[21]

According to Barth the universal implications of the atonement can only be fully understood when seen from the perspective of the Trinity. Christ is not "just" revealing the truth about life, nor is he "just" revealing an aspect of God; he is revealing the very being of God from all eternity. What happens in the life, death, and resurrection of Jesus Christ is not merely a revelation of the structures of human existence, or a revelation of what has been hidden beneath these structures since the foundation of the world; it is the revelation of the human being as a sinner and God's all-embracing grace toward the human being (the reconciled human being).

The God who is revealed in Christ is the triune God. The death of Christ implies not only the obedience of the Son toward the Father, but also the Father's self-surrender of the Son. Both the Father and the Son are subject(s) and object(s) in the act of the atonement.[22] According to Barth's

---

21. Hunsinger's main argument against Girard is that Girard falsely sees non-violence and sacrifice as mutually exclusive. According to Hunsinger, God can both be non-violent and sacrifice his Son, as the sacrifice at stake is a self-sacrifice. See Hunsinger, *Disruptive Grace*, p. 29.

22. Barth is here close to Jürgen Moltmann's interpretation of the relation between the Father and the Son. For Moltmann the relation between the Father and the Son can be described as following. The Father is the subject, as he gives his Son away. The Father is the object as Jesus is praying to him. The Son is the subject as he obeys the Father (whereby he unites his own will with the will of the Father). The Son is the object as he lets himself be captured and crucified. However, one main difference between Barth's and

logic, Christ had to die due to the fact that the mercy of God and the judgment of God cannot be separated. The human being can only be free through the judgment of God. The liberation of the human being takes place through an annihilation of the human being, an annihilation that God takes on himself. By sacrificing his own Son, he is also sacrificing himself. The one who is elected for all is reprobated for all.

From Girard's perspective, this might sound like a reinstatement of the scapegoat category, with the difference that God — instead of the human being — is the subject (which would just make it worse). But the question is, is this an adequate critique of the form and content of Barth's teaching of the atonement? In Barth's understanding, the content of the atoning death of Jesus Christ is

(1)   that the annihilation of Jesus Christ, the Son of God and Son of Man, serves the annihilation of sin;
(2)   that the annihilation of sin frees the human being from its own self-destruction;
(3)   that the human being by the help of God has been transformed from an enemy of God to a partner of God;
(4)   that this transformation has taken place due to God's self-donation;
(5)   that this self-donation is most clearly an expression of God's love.

Girard would agree that God is love and that this love is most strongly expressed in the death of Christ. He too refers to the passage in John 15:13: "No one has greater love than this, to lay down one's life for one's friends." For both Girard and Barth the death of Christ is a death that reveals the truth about the human being, and a death that enables the human being to escape the spiral of mimetic rivalry/the spiral of self-justifying judgments (in the case of Girard by realizing the structural pattern of mimetic desire; in the case of Barth by God's all-uniting judgment). The result of Jesus' reconciling death, according to Girard, is that the power of violence has

---

Moltmann's descriptions of the inner relation between the Father and the Son in the passion is that Barth refrains from giving an inner description (one might even say a kind of psychological profile) of the Father's feeling towards the Son, and the Son's feelings towards the Father. Moltmann explains, for example, that the fear of Jesus in Gethsemane is a fear of being alone with the Father, who will let him die at the cross. See Jürgen Moltmann, *The Way of Jesus Christ: Christology in Messianic Dimensions*, trans. Margaret Kohl (London: SCM Press, 1990), pp. 165-67.

been broken. The result of the atonement, according to Barth, is that the power of nothingness has been broken, as the human being — through Jesus Christ — has been reinstated in the covenant with God.

Barth's sacrificial understanding of Christ's death (that Jesus has to die due to the will of God) must be seen in relation to the dialectic between the judge and the one who is judged, a dialectic that has been discussed above and will be developed in the following. At this point I will merely note that this dialectic implies a distinction between God as the one who wants to reconcile the world due to his free love toward the world, and Christ as the one who in his obedience toward God is willing to live out this love within the world.

The obedience of Christ contains two aspects: an active and a passive obedience.[23] In the former, Christ is the subject. It is this side of Christ that according to Barth is described in the first parts of the synoptic gospel.[24] Here Jesus Christ is the one who, in words and deeds, proclaims the kingdom of God. In the latter, Jesus Christ is instead the object. His obedience consists here in his willingness to accept the judgment. This judgment has, as already noted, two sides: it is at one and the same time God's judgment of the human being (a judgment of the human being's wish to judge) and the human being's judgment of God (the judgment of the one who by his proclamation of the kingdom of God opposes the human being's wish to judge). The relationship between the judge and the ones who should be judged is thus turned around. It is God who is prosecuted by the human being. It is God (the Judge) who, due to his free will, lets himself be judged by those who were to be judged by God. In the words of Barth:

> And although in the real second part of the Gospels we have the description of a judgment which falls on Israel, the surprising thing is that it is not a judgment which falls directly on the guilty — as formerly on Samaria and Jerusalem. The One who is prosecuted according to this story, the One whose passion is enacted in all its stages, is the only innocent One, the One who has indeed divine authority to accuse in the midst of sinful Israel, the "King of the Jews." There is, in fact, *a complete reversal,* an exchange of roles. Those who are to be judged are given space and freedom and power to

23. See Hunsinger, *Disruptive Grace,* p. 143.
24. See *CD* IV/1, pp. 224-25.

judge. *The Judge allows Himself to be judged.* That is why He came to Jerusalem, entering it as a King. He is, in fact, judged. (*CD* IV/1, p. 226; my emphasis)

With the help of terms from Girard the above quote can be described as an unveiling of the scapegoat mechanism. The emphasis here is not on the crowd who choose a scapegoat, but on the one who by letting himself be the scapegoat is revealing this mechanism as such.

Despite their differences, the result of Barth and Girard's teaching of the atonement is in practice very much the same. Barth's dialectical theology of revelation makes it possible at one and the same time to claim that God is the subject behind the death of Jesus Christ, and that God is the God for the victims. In Barth's own terminology this can be described as the relation between a Christology from above and a Christology from below. I will now give a more thorough description of the content of the judgment with the help of two headings: "Substitution" and "Solidarity."

Substitution

There are, as already noted, several phrases in *CD* IV where Barth seems very close to an Anselmian point of view on the atonement, where both the wrath and the punishment of God seem to play a major and constitutive role in the act of atonement. One similarity in the structure is that God, as we have seen above, is both the subject and the object in the atonement. In this section I will investigate further what is implied in God's being both the subject and the object of the atonement, when it is looked at from the perspective of substitution and solidarity.

The substitution has a double aspect: Jesus Christ has taken the place of both God and of the human being. Jesus Christ is both the Judge (active) and the accused (the one who is judged — passive). This interaction between the active and the passive side of the judgment plays a vital role in Barth's complex approach to substitution. Even when Jesus is passive (when the Son of Man is judged on behalf of the human being), he is also active, as he (the Son of God) lets himself be judged.

Because He was a man like us, He was able to be judged like us. Because He was the Son of God and Himself God, He had the competence and power to allow this to happen to Him. Because He was the divine Judge come amongst us, He had the authority in this way — by this giving up of Himself to judgment in our place — to exercise the divine justice of grace, to pronounce us righteous on the ground of what happened to Him, to free us therefore from the accusation and condemnation and punishment, to save us from the impending loss and destruction. (*CD* IV/1, pp. 222-23)

This interaction between the active and the passive side of the judgment is made possible through the Chalcedonian approach to Christology, whereby the dialectic between Jesus as the Son of God and Jesus as the Son of Man is maintained as the filter through which the life of Jesus of Nazareth is interpreted. The connection between the atonement and God's judgment is worked out in the framework of a theistic understanding of God. Through the dialectic between the active and the passive side of the judgment, Barth is able to emphasize the aspect of God's suffering very strongly, without ending up in a pure kenosis-Christology. For Barth this would imply the rejection of a theistic understanding of God.[25]

Jesus Christ as the Judge

God's judgment of the human being takes place in Jesus Christ. The judgment has thus acquired a concrete content. The judgment of God can no longer be associated with, for example, fear of eternal damnation and an unknown hell. Instead the judgment of God can only be known through the life, death, and resurrection of Jesus Christ. For Barth there is a strong connection between Jesus' proclamation of God's kingdom, the death of Jesus on the cross, and the resurrection on the third day, through which God reveals that the words and acts of Jesus are the words and acts of Christ, and thus God's own words and acts. It is thus confirmed that the death of Jesus Christ is not only expressive of a willingness to take on the judgment of the public, but also that it first and foremost reveals an acceptance of God's judgment of the human being. The content of this judgment is, as shown above, a judgment of the human being's inclination to

25. For further insight into Barth's critique of a "pure" kenosis-Christology see Chapter 11 and *CD* IV/1, pp. 179-85.

judge itself and others. So Jesus Christ is not only object (the one who is judged), but also subject (the one who judges) in the judgment.

> This tells us that God acknowledged this Jesus of Nazareth, the strange Judge who allowed Himself to be judged, by raising Him from the dead. (*CD* IV/1, p. 227)

> He Himself, He alone: He who was alone and superior and majestic in Galilee; He who was again alone but beaten and humiliated in Jerusalem, in the very midst of Israel. He, the Judge who allowed Himself to be judged, lives and rules and speaks and works. He is Himself the word which is to be proclaimed to all creatures as the Word of God. That is what the Easter narrative tells us. (*CD* IV/1, p. 227)

It is through the proclamation of the kingdom of God that the connection between the life and death of Jesus is established. In Jesus Christ the kingdom of God is personalized: "He comes as the kingdom of God in person. He comes to reconcile the world with God, i.e., to convert it to God" (*CD* IV/1, p. 216). In other words it is the judgment given within Jesus' proclamation of the kingdom of God that enables us to see the judgment of the human being in the death of Jesus Christ (a revelation from the outside).[26] That Jesus is judge means that he removes the human being from the judging role, which is in itself a judgment of the human being. This sets the human being in a two-sided situation.

First, it "means the abasement and jeopardising of every man" (*CD* IV/1, p. 233). When the human being is unable to judge others in the name of God, it stands isolated before God. In this confrontation the whole previous life of each individual human being is under the judgment of God. The judgment cannot be turned into any kind of power instrument, nor can it be turned into a harmless kind of abstract judgment from an abstract God.[27] *Second,* the judgment in and by Christ creates liberation and

---

26. Girard also states very clearly the connection between Jesus' proclamation of the kingdom and the judgment of Jesus. See Girard, *Things Hidden,* pp. 196-215.

27. "It is a matter of the very man Jesus of Nazareth in whom God has crossed our path and by whom we find ourselves deposed. Abasement by an abstract 'god' is a safe enough matter which we can turn to our own glory. But abasement by God in the flesh, in the person of this fellow-man, is a dangerous matter" (*CD* IV/1, p. 233).

hope. The human being has been set free. It is no longer its own judge, nor is it the judge of others. This freedom enables the human being to live. Barth interprets the warning in Genesis 2:17 ("but of the tree of the knowledge of good and evil you shall not eat, for in the day that you eat of it you shall die") as a description of how life has been reduced and narrowed — and thereby transformed into its own opposite: death (here understood as absence of life) — if it is lived from the perspective of judgment.[28]

This setting free of the human being could not take place by means of a new prohibition (such as: Do not judge!). For what would prevent the human being from transgressing this prohibition, as it had already done just that? Instead, liberation is brought about through the life, death, and resurrection of Jesus Christ. The freedom of the human being in relation to God as well as to all other human beings is thereby related to the fact that God is the sole and final judge of the human being. And his judgment is a merciful and righteous judgment (in opposition to the human being's self-righteous judgment).

> That means, therefore, in fear before the Judge on whose good and redemptive will I can already count, whose decision I can look forward to with trust whatever it may be, in whose hands I can know that my own case and that of others is at least safe. In a fear, therefore, which at bottom is hope. (*CD* IV/1, p. 234)

Jesus Christ as Judged in Our Place

Jesus Christ is not only at one and the same time the electing God and the elected human being, but he is also the rejecting God and the rejected human being.[29] The one who is free of sin has taken the place of the human being (who is not free of sin) before God for the human being, and the place of God (who has the right to judge) in the sight of the human being for the human being. To take the place of the human being for the human being implies that he has taken the sin of the human being onto himself. The sin *in nuce* has been described above as the human being's self-righteous judgment. Christ, the one who does not judge self-righteously,

---

28. See *CD* IV/1, p. 234.
29. See *CD* IV/1, p. 237.

has therefore taken the consequence of the human being's self-righteous judgment onto himself: death. Christ, the one man who has the right to judge, is the one who lets himself be judged. This judgment has two subjects: God and the human being. God, in the sense that it is God who sends his Son to "convert the world to himself, and therefore genuinely to reconcile it" (*CD* IV/1, p. 237). To obtain the conversion of the human being, the sinful self-righteousness of the human being must be broken, which happens in Christ's willingness to take on the human being's judgment of God (the rejection of Jesus' proclamation of the kingdom of God — which in this phraseology could be described as the human being's judgment of God's judgment of the human being) and God's judgment of the human being (which is a judgment of the human being's wish to be its own eschaton). The result of human beings' judgment is that Christ died on the cross as a malefactor, blasphemer, and political agitator.

To sum up: the one who has the right to judge (God) has through the incarnation placed himself in the place of the human being (who does not have the right to judge). Jesus Christ is therefore the only man who has the right to judge. But this right is executed in a rather strange way, as the Son of God lets himself be judged (both by God and other men). The qualitative difference between the judgment of the human being and the judgment of God is hereby revealed. The substitution thus not only consists in the fact that Jesus Christ takes God's judgment of the human being onto himself, but also in the fact that by doing this he is judging the human being (a judgment of the human being's judgment). Jesus Christ is hereby substitute for both God and the human being.

Solidarity

The act of substitution includes a strong aspect of solidarity. God shows in Jesus Christ his solidarity with the human being.

> The way of His humiliation is simply the way which leads Him to us, the way on which He draws near to us and becomes one of us. And this means first that the mortal peril in which man stands becomes and is His peril, the need of man His need. The Son of God exists with man and as man in this fallen and perishing state. We should be explaining the incarnation docetically and therefore ex-

plaining it away if we did not put it like this, if we tried to limit in any way the solidarity with the cosmos which God accepted in Jesus Christ. (*CD* IV/1, p. 215)

Another way to express this is to describe Christ as the brother of the human being.[30] That Christ really is a human being like any other human being is expressed in the temptations. In *CD* IV/1, pp. 259-73, Barth emphasizes the connection between the temptations at the beginning of Jesus' public life and teaching (after the forty days in the wilderness) and the temptation at the end of his public life (in the garden of Gethsemane). The latter is read as the climax of the first. The first three temptations (in the wilderness) are a kind of extension of the prelude to Jesus' life and work, which is given at his baptism. The three temptations share one common feature: the attempt to break the unity between the will of God and the will of Jesus. The aim of the temptations is to dissolve the solidarity between Jesus and human beings that is expressed in Jesus' baptism. Jesus rejected the wish of John to become baptized by Jesus (which can be read as a first temptation). Instead Jesus asked John to baptize him. In the river Jordan Jesus starts his way as a repenting sinner on his way to the final destination at the cross. Thus the temptations in the wilderness are not only attempts to break the unity of the will of God and the will of Jesus, they are also attempts to dissolve the solidarity between Jesus and his fellow human beings, whereby the human being would be left to its final destruction. However, Jesus' resistance demonstrates what it is that makes this particular human being different from all other human beings: his obedience to the will of God. Jesus is not different from all other human beings in the sense that he cannot be tempted. He really is tempted: "My Father, if it is possible, let this cup pass from me; yet not what I want but what you want" (Matt. 26:39). But he is different because he is the only human person who was able to withstand the temptation. It is this ability to live in full obedience to God that reaches its climax in the temptation at Gethsemane: "My Father, if this cannot pass unless I drink it, your will be done" (Matt. 26:42). The passion of Jesus is thereby a passion that includes an action: the willingness to die at the cross, the willingness to suffer for the sake of others.

At this point Barth wants to make sure that the uniqueness of Jesus' death is preserved. Other people have been willing to die for their beliefs,

---

30. See for example *CD* IV/1, p. 215.

and some of them seem even to have taken their destiny more stoically. Barth mentions as examples many a Christian martyr, Socrates, many Communists, and even the German general Jodl, who was executed by the Nuremberg War Crimes Tribunal.[31] Furthermore, the suffering of Jesus cannot in itself be said to exceed other people's sufferings. Barth notes in passing (one might say a bit cynically) that Jesus' suffering after all took place in only a few days.

What really makes the suffering of Jesus special is that it is the Son of God who suffers. It is thereby both the person and the God-given task of this person that make this suffering unique. It is unique in the way that this particular person's suffering can be claimed to have a saving significance for all human beings both before and after the event. If Jesus had not been obedient, the wrath of God would still have resulted in the destruction of the cosmos and the extinction of the human being.[32] In Jesus the first Adam perished, while the second Adam was born. Through the act of the second Adam the human being has been reinstated as the covenant partner. What is important to note here is twofold. *First,* that this act of Jesus Christ has taken place in solidarity with the human being: to stop the human being from perishing. *Second,* that it *had* to take place, if the human being should be reinstated in the covenant.

---

31. See *CD* IV/1, p. 265.
32. See *CD* IV/1, pp. 222 and 261.

CHAPTER 10

The Double Outcome

Rejection of a Spatial and Chronological Separation Between Salvation and Damnation

Traditionally the doctrine of the double outcome, as it is worked out in the Western tradition in the wake of Augustine, is used as a rubric for a description of the final eternal judgment, where God will judge some people to eternal damnation and others to eternal salvation. Both the Lutheran and the Reformed traditions emphasize a final and eternal judgment, and both operate also with a spatial division between salvation and damnation. Under the heading of the return of Christ to judgment the doctrine of the double outcome is expressed as following in *Confessio Augustana*, Article XVII:

> It is also taught among us that our Lord Jesus Christ will return on the last day for judgment and will raise up all the dead, to give eternal life and everlasting joy to believers and the elect but to condemn ungodly men and the devil to hell and eternal punishment.

Some people will be saved in eternity (obtain "eternal life and everlasting joy"); others will be eternally damned (condemned "to hell and eternal punishment"). This implies not only that a spatial division is established between heaven and hell, but also that resurrection, judgment, and salvation or damnation are perceived as three serial events (the chronological separation). The resurrection from the dead does not in itself imply salvation, as "ungodly men and the devil" will be resurrected to eternal punishment. Neither Luther nor Calvin sees any conflict within God due to the fact that God judges some people to eternal damnation and other people to eternal salvation. God executes this judgment. Thus, it must be a righteous judgment. What God does is always right.[1]

For Calvin the understanding of the double outcome is combined with a strict and clear teaching of a double predestination.[2]

> We call predestination God's *eternal decree,* by which he compacted *with himself* what he willed to become of *each* man. For all are not created in equal condition; rather, *eternal life is foreordained for some, eternal damnation for others.* Therefore, as any man has been created to one *or* the other of these ends, we speak of him as predestined to life *or* to death. (Calvin, *Institutes,* p. 926; my emphasis)

> As Scripture, then, clearly shows, we say that God once established by his eternal and unchangeable plan those whom he long before determined once for all to receive into salvation, and those whom, on the other hand, he would devote to destruction. We assert that, with respect to the elect, this plan was founded upon his freely given mercy, without regard to human worth; but by his just and irreprehensible but incomprehensible judgment he has barred the door of life to those whom he has given over to damnation. Now among the elect we regard the call as a testimony of election. Then we hold justification another sign of its manifestation, until they come into the glory in which the fulfillment of that election lies.

1. "For God's will is so much the highest rule of righteousness that whatever he wills, by the very fact that he wills it, must be considered righteous. When, therefore, one asks why God has so done, we must reply: because he has willed it." John Calvin, *Institutes of the Christian Religion,* trans. Ford Lewis Battles, ed. John T. McNeill (Philadelphia: Westminster, 1960), p. 949; "For it is not because he is or was obliged so to will that what he wills is right, but on the contrary, because he himself so wills, therefore what happens must be right." Martin Luther, *The Bondage of the Will,* in *Luther's Works. American Edition. Volume 33, Career of the Reformer III,* trans. Philip S. Watson and Benjamin Drewery, ed. Philip S. Watson (Philadelphia: Fortress Press, 1972), p. 181.

2. For a more detailed analysis of Luther's and Calvin's teaching of election, see Walther Kreck, *Grundentscheidungen in Karl Barths Dogmatik. Zur Diskussion seines Verständnisses von Offenbarung und Erwählung* (Neukirchen-Vluyn: Neukirchener Verlag, 1978), pp. 284-315.

> But as the Lord seals his elect by call and justification, so, by shut-
> ting off the reprobate from knowledge of his name or from the
> sanctification of his Spirit, he, as it were, reveals by these marks
> what sort of judgment awaits them. Here I shall pass over many fic-
> tions that stupid men have invented to overthrow predestination.
> (Calvin, *Institutes*, p. 931)

Some people are elected to eternal salvation from eternity, others to eternal
reprobation. But again, this cannot be unrighteous, since God decrees it.
Neither Calvin nor Luther finds it problematic that not all people will be
saved. This is regarded as a simple, non-disputable fact along the lines of,
for example, the existence of God. Actually, it is viewed the other way
round. All people deserve to receive eternal punishment.[3] No one deserves
eternal salvation. That God saves anybody at all (be it few, or be it many) is
in itself an act of pure grace![4] Thus, one cannot criticize God for not saving all human beings. Such a critique would be estimated as an anthropomorphic type of argument, where God is evaluated with the help of the
human being's perception of justice. The human being gladly accepts the
fact that God justifies the ungodly, despite their many demerits. They only
accuse him of injustice when he damns the ungodly. Against this line of
thought Luther states for example:

> Observe, therefore, the wickedness of the human heart! When God
> saves the unworthy without merits, or rather justifies the ungodly
> with their many demerits, it does not accuse him of injustice; it
> does not demand to know why he wills this, which in its judgment
> is most unjust, but because it is advantageous and pleasing to itself
> it deems it just and good. But when he damns those without merit,
> then since this is disadvantageous to itself, it is unjust, it is intolera-

---

3. "But if all whom the Lord predestines to death are by condition of nature subject
to the judgment of death, of what injustice toward themselves may they complain?" (Calvin, *Institutes*, p. 950).

4. "Because God metes out *merited penalty* to those whom he condemns but distrib-
utes *unmerited grace* to those whom he calls, he is freed of all accusation — like a lender,
who has the power of remitting payment to one, of exacting it from another. 'The Lord
can therefore also give grace . . . to whom he *will* . . . because he is *merciful*, and not give to
all because he is a *just* judge. For by giving to some what they do not deserve, . . . he can
show his free grace. . . . By not giving to all, he can manifest what all deserve'" (Calvin, *Institutes*, p. 959; my emphasis).

ble, and here there is protesting, murmuring, and blaspheming. (*The Bondage of the Will*, pp. 207-8)

When therefore Reason praises God for saving the unworthy, but finds fault with him for damning the undeserving, she stands convicted of not praising God as God, but as serving her own interests. That is to say, what she seeks and praises in God is herself and the things of self, not God or the things of God. But if God pleases you when he crowns the unworthy, he ought not to displease you when he damns the undeserving. If he is just in the former case, why not in the latter? (*The Bondage of the Will*, p. 208)

According to this kind of logic, God is just when he delivers the human being to damnation, and unjust when he saves human beings — in spite of their demerits.

The emphasis on the relation between the double outcome and the double predestination is much weaker in the theology of Luther than in the theology of Calvin — but is not totally absent. In his polemic against Erasmus in *The Bondage of the Will* Luther seems forced at places to operate with a double predestination.[5] When the human being has no influence on how it is judged finally, when there is no power alongside God, and when an eternal separation must take place between the ones

---

5. Luther is not as explicit as Calvin on the theme of the double predestination. It is not a central theme in Luther's elaboration of the doctrine of justification by faith alone. But it is, nevertheless, at several places in *The Bondage of the Will*, the inevitable result of Luther's argument. Luther states for example: "For who can resist his will? Who can obtain mercy when he does not will it? Who can melt if he wills to harden? It is not in our power to change, much less to resist, his will, which wants us hardened and by which we are forced to be hardened, whether we like it or not" (*The Bondage of the Will*, p. 187); "But the elect and the godly will be corrected by the Holy Spirit, while the rest perish uncorrected. Augustine does not say that no man's or all men's good works are crowned, but that some men's are. So there will be some who correct their life. Who will believe, you say, that he is loved by God? I answer: No man will or can believe this; but the *elect* will believe while the rest perish in unbelief, indignant and blaspheming as you are here. So some will believe. As to your saying that a window is opened for impiety by these dogmas, let it be so; such people belong to the above-mentioned leprosy of evil that must be endured. Nevertheless, by these same dogmas there is opened at the same time a door to righteousness, an entrance to heaven and a way to God for the godly and the elect" (*The Bondage of the Will*, pp. 60-61; my emphasis).

who are judged to eternal salvation and the ones who are judged to eternal damnation, God must be the one who has predestined the destiny of each individual human being. Foreknowledge is interwoven here with the idea of predestination. What God wants is what God does; what God does is what God wants. Thus, there is no space for an interpretation of God's foreknowledge, where a possible gap is established between the foreknowledge of God and the actual events in the world. Such a God, according to Luther, would be a ridiculous God.[6] This said, Luther's use of double predestination does not primarily serve him as an attempt to give a rational account of the logic behind the divine judgment, and thereby to explain how the idea of a merciful God can correspond with the seemingly brutal fact that some are damned and others are saved. This remains for Luther a mystery of faith.[7] Instead, the aim of the indirect references to double predestination is to comfort the human being in despair. Salvation happens solely due to the grace of God. The human being cannot — due to its own acts (or failure to act) contradict the eternal decision of God.

Both in the Lutheran and the Reformed traditions, the teaching of the double outcome is linked to the teaching of justification by faith alone. A strictly logical perception of belief in justification by faith alone implies that the human being can do nothing either for its own salvation or against its own reprobation. Both salvation and damnation are grounded in God's inscrutable grace. Four different options then seem available:

(1) Some people are destined to salvation, whereas others are destined to damnation.
(2) All human beings are destined to damnation.
(3) All human beings are destined to salvation.
(4) The judgment contains in itself both salvation and damnation, and both aspects relate to all human beings.

---

6. "Yet natural reason itself is forced to admit that the living and true God must be one who by his freedom imposes necessity on us, since obviously he would be a ridiculous God, or idol rather, if he foresaw the future uncertainly, or could be proved mistaken by events, when even the heathen have given their gods an 'ineluctable fate'" (*The Bondage of the Will,* p. 189).

7. See for example Luther, *The Bondage of the Will,* p. 62.

Only the first option is viewed as an option by the reformers. The positive *raison d'être* behind the teaching of the double outcome is that no one can obtain the grace of God on the basis of any self-motivated act or deed. Salvation is due solely to the will of the gracious God, which for Luther was the radical answer to the despairing question: How can I obtain a gracious God?

But if the human being can do nothing to deserve eternal salvation, it logically follows that the human being can do nothing either to deserve or to escape eternal damnation. The latter presupposes that all human beings deserve eternal damnation. The former presupposes that the human being is unable to "qualify" for damnation by its own acts or lack of acts. If this were the case, the human being would be able to exclude itself from salvation in such a way that the human being would, albeit indirectly, have been granted the ability to qualify for its own salvation. In short: by its own acts the individual can do nothing to determine whether it will be damned or not. Otherwise, the human being would minimally possess the possibility to reject or to withdraw itself from the gracious act of God.

This leaves us with the question as to who is going to be saved and who is not. From the perspective of the individual human being this question takes the form: Will I be saved or not? And furthermore, how can I obtain certainty about my salvation?

Luther's and Calvin's answers to these questions differ. Luther demonstrates at this point a very mature psychological insight, as he warns the individual against a speculative approach to the question of who is going to be saved and who is going to be damned.[8] Such a speculative approach,

---

8. "Twelfth, you must not regard hell and eternal pain in relation to predestination, not in yourself, or in itself, or in those who are damned, nor must you be worried by the many people in the world who are not chosen. If you are not careful, that picture will quickly upset you and be your downfall. You must force yourself to keep your eyes closed tightly to such a view, for it can never help you, even though you were to occupy yourself with it for a thousand years and fret yourself to death. After all, you will have to let God be God and grant that he knows more about you than you do yourself." Martin Luther, "A Sermon on Preparing to Die," in *Luther's Works. American Edition. Volume 42. Devotional Writings I*, trans. Martin H. Bertram, ed. Martin O. Dietrich (Philadelphia: Fortress Press, 1969), p. 105; see also pp. 102-3. In his polemic against Erasmus, Luther is at places forced to take such a speculative approach, which he himself warns against. The reasoning for his warning is that in the speculation one can no longer see the difference between God and the Devil.

which would try to sort out the God-given criteria for the double outcome (God's motivation), would inevitably lead to a life in fear of God's final judgment. Instead, the human being should look at the cross and have faith in Christ, who died for the sake of human beings.[9] The answer to the question of the reasoning behind the final judgment is here placed at the mystery of the cross, whereas in the theology of Calvin it is placed at God's eternal decision (regarding who is predestined for salvation, and who is predestined for damnation).[10]

To understand both Luther and Calvin on their own premises, one should notice that their aim is the same. Calvin's teaching of the double predestination also serves to emphasize the free mercy of God. God is the one and only subject of the human being's salvation. From this perspective, the teaching of the double predestination should also be interpreted as a comfort to those who believe in God. Both Luther and Calvin stress that a final and eternal judgment will take place in which some people will be judged to eternal damnation, others to eternal salvation. This not only implies that judgment and salvation/damnation are chronologically separated, but also that salvation and damnation are spatially separated. The difference between Luther and Calvin on this subject consists in their use of the meta-level. How are the eternal will of God and the human being's fear of eternal damnation related to the teaching of the double outcome? Is the emphasis on the practical aspect of pastoral care ("Gleubstu, so hastu.

---

9. "Thus you must concern yourself solely with the death of Christ and then you will find life. But if you look at death in any other way, it will kill you with great anxiety and anguish. This is why Christ says, 'In the world — that is, in yourselves — you have unrest, but in me you will find peace' [John 16:33]" ("A Sermon on Preparing to Die," p. 104).

10. "So then, gaze at the heavenly picture of Christ, who descended into hell [1 Peter 3:19] for your sake and was forsaken by God as one eternally damned when he spoke the words on the cross, 'Eli, Eli, lama sabachthani!' — 'My God, my God, why hast thou forsaken me?' [Matt. 27:46]. In that picture your hell is defeated and your uncertain election is made sure. If you concern yourself solely with that and believe that it was done for you, you will surely be preserved in this same faith. Never, therefore, let this be erased from your vision. Seek yourself only in Christ and not in yourself and you will find yourself in him eternally" ("A Sermon on Preparing to Die," pp. 105-6); "Behold! Since the disposition of all things is in God's hand, since the decision of salvation or of death rests in his power, he so ordains by his plan and will that among men some are born destined for certain death from the womb, who glorify his name by their own destruction" (Calvin, *Institutes*, p. 954).

Zweiffelstu, so bistu vorloren") or on the theoretical aspects (a rational account of the mystery of the will of God)?[11]

A Twofold Election in Jesus Christ

I will now go on to a more detailed description of how Barth uses — or better: reuses — the teaching of double predestination and double outcome. Barth — in quite a different way from Calvin — combines the teaching of a twofold election with a teaching of double outcome.[12] Here it should be noted that in Barth's perspective election and predestination are synonymous. Both election and predestination are first and foremost placed in Jesus Christ and not in a nation or in any individual human person. The question of salvation and reprobation is no longer viewed as a question that takes place at the level of the individual human being — in the sense that some are damned while others are saved.[13] Thus, the classical questions of *Anfechtung* (am I elected to eternal salvation or damnation? Am I saved or damned?) are avoided. In Jesus Christ God has elected each individual human being to both damnation and salvation. God in Christ has taken the damnation of the human being onto himself. At the cross damnation has taken place. In the resurrection salvation is fulfilled in such a way that damnation has been damned. To understand Christ as the one human being whom God has elected to both damnation and salvation therefore implies an understanding of the relation between the cross and the resurrection.

Salvation and damnation are not understood as purely futuristic and spatially independent events but are instead dialectically interwoven. They are both part of one and the same judgment. There is no judgment without grace; there is no grace without judgment. Consistently, judgment cannot be split up into two independent parts: salvation or damnation. One consequence of such a chronological and spatial separation would have been that the resurrection would become a value-free event. The resurrection would then not in itself be an act of salvation. Instead all the deceased would first be

---

11. Martin Luther, "Ein Sermon von dem Sakrament der Taufe," in *Martin Luther Werke. Kritische Gesamtausgabe 2* (Weimar, 1884), p. 733.

12. See for example *CD* IV/2, p. 32.

13. See also Henning Thomsen, "Prædestinationen — et centralt element i Karl Barths teologi" [Predestination — a central element in Karl Barth's theology], *Dansk Teologisk Tidsskrift* 49, no. 2 (1986): 123.

resurrected, and then — when they are all resurrected — judged, some to eternal salvation, others to eternal reprobation. In this way the resurrection would have been turned into a neutral precondition for the realization of the final judgment. The judgment would then not be a judgment that would necessarily abolish the human being's distance from God. Instead the judgment could just as well confirm the human being's God-forsakenness!

This said, the election of all human beings in Jesus Christ can only be fully understood when it is seen in relation to the two natures of Christ. As true God, Jesus Christ is the one who elects all human beings to salvation. Calvin's doctrine of *decretum absolutum* is replaced here by the "assertion that Jesus is the electing God."[14] In Jesus Christ we see the real essence of God: the willingness to be in partnership with the human being, a willingness that leads God into self-destruction in the sense that Jesus Christ, the Son of God, dies at the cross. The election of all human beings happens through the reprobation of this one man. The love of God toward humanity is seen here in relation to (and not in contrast to) the will of God. As true human being, Jesus Christ is the one who is elected to both damnation and salvation. The former is, as said, seen at the cross, the latter in the resurrection. Again, we see how this enables Barth to reinvent the use of the double outcome, as it is God himself who takes on the punishment for all and who thereby overcomes death (and thereby the absence of God) for all. The election is universal.[15] There is no room for a split between people elected for salvation and people elected for condemnation (the split would in that case be based on the free will of God), nor is there any room for a final and deci-

---

14. See Colin Gunton, "Karl Barth's Doctrine of Election as Part of His Doctrine of God," *Journal of Theological Studies* 25, no. 2 (1974): 381-85, esp. 385.

15. Barth's advocacy of universal salvation is expressed dogmatically in his way of combining a teaching of universal election in Jesus Christ with a theory of the two states and a reinterpretation of the double outcome. This is further combined with an emphasis on the claim that the obstacle against atonement is placed in the human being and not in God himself. Consequently, the aim of the atonement is to enable the human being to move toward God (through God's move toward the human being), and not to enable God to enter into a relation with the human being again. But Barth has connected his opposition against a teaching of the atonement, where the emphasis is laid on God's overcoming of an inner conflict in God (between the righteousness and the mercy of God), with an understanding of God's inability to change. The incarnation does not affect God himself. This is, in my view, the proper place to address one's critique against Barth's teaching of the atonement. I shall pursue this issue further in Chapter 13.

sive split between the offer of salvation and the acquisition of salvation (here the gap would instead be caused by the free will of the human being).

Prenter is very critical of this latter point, as he wants to maintain a sharp distinction between God's offer of salvation *(Heilsangebot)* and the human being's acceptance of it *(Heilsaneignung)*. The offer of salvation concerns all, but not all accept it. Prenter is not trying to explain why this is so. If he were, he would have to reopen the question as to how God's judgment and God's predestination are connected. Instead, he wants to maintain the fact that not all human beings hear or understand themselves under the Word of God. The offer of salvation is potentially for all, but not all actually want to receive it. They have — so to speak — only themselves to blame for their reprobation. Prenter hereby supports — willingly or not — what I have described above as a value-free understanding of the resurrection, as the resurrection is a resurrection to both eternal damnation and eternal salvation. From a Barthian perspective, such an emphasis on an eternal separation is, to say the least, very dubious. Who can have full trust in a God who resurrects people for the purpose of eternal damnation? Would such an understanding of God not be in conflict with the radical message of Christianity: to love one's enemy? It is one thing to claim that it is impossible for the human being to measure up to this command, but can one claim that it is not possible for God?

Excursus

In the final paragraph above, I write *"from a Barthian perspective* such an emphasis on an eternal separation is, to say the least, very dubious" deliberately. In the *CD* Barth himself rejects the idea that he teaches *apokatastasis* (see for example *CD* II/2, pp. 417, 422-23, 476-77). Prenter nevertheless claims, rightly, that it is the inevitable consequence of Barth's teaching of the atonement.[16] Thus, I disagree with Krause's "traditional" rejection of the accusation of *apokatastasis* in Barth's theology (rooted in his monism of grace) due to its eschatological character.[17]

In *The Humanity of God* Barth asks rhetorically if his theology ends up with universalism. Unfortunately he does not give a really sharp and profiled answer (at

16. See Regin Prenter, "Karl Barths Umbildung der traditionellen Zweinaturlehre in lutherischer Beleuchtung," in *Theologie und Gottesdienst. Gesammelte Aufsätze*, ed. Erik Kyndal, Gerhard Pedersen, and Anna Marie Aagaard (Aarhus: Aros, 1977), pp. 92, 113.

17. See Burghard Krause, *Leiden Gottes — Leiden des Menschen. Eine Untersuchung zur Kirchlichen Dogmatik Karl Barths* (Stuttgart: Calwer Verlag, 1980), pp. 132-33, 146-47.

least not directly). Instead, he urges a reconsideration of the matter once again under the heading: Why could it not be so? Why is it regarded as such an impossible thought? Barth's answers to these rhetorical questions can be summed up in three points. *First,* he asks for calmness when the question of universalism is at stake. One should not reject it without reconsidering it. *Second,* he argues that passages such as Colossians 1:19 could at least "promote" a reconsideration of universalism as a legitimate Christian thought. *Third,* he opposes any kind of theological right to limit the loving-kindness of God. Instead "our theological duty is to see and understand it [the loving-kindness of God which has appeared in Jesus Christ] as being still greater than we had seen before."[18]

On the last pages of *CD* IV/3, part I, Barth states: "there is no good reason why we should forbid ourselves, or be forbidden, openness to the possibility that in the reality of God and man in Jesus Christ there is contained much more than we might expect and therefore the supremely unexpected withdrawal of that final threat, i.e., that in the truth of this reality there might be contained the super-abundant promise of the final deliverance of all men. To be more explicit, there is no good reason why we should not be open to this possibility. If for a moment we accept the unfalsified truth of the reality which even now so forcefully limits the perverted human situation, does it not point plainly in the direction of the work of a truly eternal divine patience and deliverance and therefore of an *apokatastasis* or universal reconciliation?" (*CD* IV/3, pp. 477-78).

In relation to the discussion of the double outcome, it is important to note that for Barth there is no difference between what God wants and what God is able to do. If God wants to save the human being, he does so. It is an "unthinkable thought" for Barth, that God wants to save the human being, but that he — due to the human being's refusal — is either unable or unwilling to do so. The salvation of the human being would then — at the end of the day — be dependent on the human being's willingness to receive it or not.

Due to his emphasis on God's absolute free and sovereign will Barth could only claim universalism within the category of hope. But this is not a plausible objection against the *apokatastasis* as such, as all theology is a theology written within the language of hope. In the words of Carl Braaten: "Barth's universalism is highly nuanced and qualified. It is not a dogma, not a piece of knowledge, and not something which humans have a right to claim. We may, however, cautiously and distinctly pray and hope that in spite of everything that seems to point conclusively in the opposite direction, God's mercy will not cast off his world forever."[19]

18. See Karl Barth, *The Humanity of God* (Louisville: John Knox Press, 1960), pp. 61-62.

19. Carl E. Braaten, *No Other Gospel! Christianity Among the World's Religions* (Minneapolis: Fortress Press, 1992), p. 60.

CHAPTER 11

The Punishment and Wrath of God

The Wrath of God Demonstrated in the Death of Christ

At this point we need to take a closer look at Barth's understanding of punishment and its interrelation with the understanding of the wrath of God. Barth opposes the view that there might be any split between God's righteousness and mercy (as in Anselm). The mercy of God is not restricted by any extrinsic rules (as for example a general concept of righteousness). The death of Jesus does not serve to satisfy God, to enable God to live out his love toward human beings. If this were the case, the atonement would then primarily be concerned with God's own need for reconciliation. God himself would then be the main obstacle that had to be conquered to enable an establishment of a renewed relation between God and human beings. Such a standpoint is rooted in an emphasis on the righteousness of God, where God to remain God must be righteous, for which reason punishment has to take place. Barth states for example:

> If Jesus Christ has followed our way as sinners to the end to which it leads, in outer darkness, then we can say with that passage from the Old Testament that He has suffered this punishment of ours. But we must not make this a main concept as in some of the older presentations of the doctrine of the atonement (especially those which follow Anselm of Canterbury), either in the sense that by His suffering our punishment we are spared from suffering it ourselves, or that in so doing He "satisfied" or offered satisfaction to the wrath of

God. *The latter thought is quite foreign to the New Testament.* And of the possible idea that we are spared punishment by what Jesus Christ has done for us we have to notice that the main drift of the New Testament statements concerning the passion and death of Jesus Christ is not at all or only indirectly in this direction. (*CD* IV/1, p. 253; my emphasis)

The key to understanding the punishment is the mercy of God. Thus, the righteousness and the mercy of God are not viewed as two mutually excluding movements within God. The divine mercy is first and foremost revealed in the passion of Jesus Christ. Could it therefore be that, despite his sometimes rather extensive use of a traditional wrath-punishment language, Barth is closer to what I will define as a compassion-mercy structure? What does he actually mean when he uses the term "punishment"? In what does punishment consist and for what is it a punishment? And finally, what is achieved through the punishment?

In this chapter I will investigate whether the punishment (Jesus' death on the cross) can be interpreted as an experience of God-absence.[1] At several places in the *CD* Barth refers to the importance of Jesus' cry from the cross: "My God, my God, why have you forsaken me?" (Matt. 27:46). If it is plausible to interpret Jesus' experience of the absence of God as the wrath and punishment of God, God has taken on himself his own wrath and punishment. Thus, it is not death itself but the experience of death as the absence of God that expresses the wrath and punishment of God. But this absence of God has, in Jesus' death on the cross, been absorbed into the being of God. Death separates the human being from life, but death does not segregate the human being from the power of life (God). The power of death has hereby been broken. That the cross is the place where the power

---

1. My interpretation here is inspired by Dietrich Bonhoeffer's emphasis on the experience of the absence of God at the cross. See especially Dietrich Bonhoeffer, *Ethics*, trans. Reinhard Krauss, Douglas W. Stoot, and Charles C. West, ed. Ilse Tödt, Heinz Eduard Tödt, Ernst Feil, and Clifford Green (München: Chr. Kaiser Verlag, 1991), and Dietrich Bonhoeffer, *Widerstand und Ergebung. Briefe und Aufzeichnungen aus der Haft*, ed. Christian Gremmels, Eberhard Bethge, Renate Bethge, and Ilse Tödt (Gütersloh: Chr. Kaiser/Gütersloher Verlagshaus, 1998). For an analysis of Bonhoeffer's emphasis on the outcry at the cross, see Hans Vium Mikkelsen, "Kun den lidende Gud kan hjælpe. Dietrich Bonhoeffers relationstænkning," *Dansk Teologisk Tidsskrift* 59, no. 4 (1996): 266-87.

of death is broken, rather than manifested, is revealed to the human being in the resurrection of Jesus Christ.

The wrath of God, which Barth often refers to in *CD* IV, is a wrath directed against the human being's rejection of God:

> Because he negates God, the man elected by God, the object of the divine grace, is himself necessarily, and logically, and with all that it involves, the man negated by God. It is also true that God has sworn to be, and actually is, faithful, that God's grace does not fail but persists toward him. But within these limits it is unconditionally the case that as a sinner he is rejected by God, that he not only stands under the wrath and accusation of God, but because this wrath is well-founded and this accusation is true, he stands under His sentence and judgment. (*CD* IV/1, p. 173)

The aim of the wrath of God is not to destroy the human being as such but to destroy the human being's self-destruction. The latter consists in the human being's own rejection of being a person in relation to God. To reject God is to reject the real ground of the human being. Without God the human being is lost in its own hopeless attempt to become its own eschaton. By rejecting God the human being is not being free. Instead "man" becomes

> a prisoner of the world-process, of chance, of all-powerful natural and historical forces, above all of himself. He tries to be his own master, and to control his relations with God and the world and his fellow-men. And as he does so, the onslaught of nothingness prevails against him, controlling him in death in an irresistible and senseless way and to his own loss. This is the *circulus vitiosus* of the human plight presupposed and revealed in and with the grace of God. And there is no man who, whether he experiences it or not, is not in this plight. (*CD* IV/1, p. 173)

The wrath of God has thereby, as said, an implicit aim: to destroy the self-destruction of the human being. This wrath is inclusive, as all human beings need the judgment of God (in which the wrath is unfolded) to escape their own self-righteous judgments. Through the wrath of God the human being becomes a new being.

The wrath of God is not righteous in the sense that it distinguishes between the unrighteous, who are to be destroyed, and the righteous, who are to be rewarded. This would imply a spatial distinction between the saved and the reprobated that corresponds to the distinction between the righteous (the ones who are not destroyed by the wrath of God) and the unrighteous (the ones who are righteously destroyed by the wrath of God). Such an interpretation of the wrath of God would have led Barth back into a traditional Reformed teaching concerning the double outcome. Instead, the wrath of God is universal, as all human beings are under this wrath — no single person can escape it. In Jesus Christ each person is under both the wrath and the mercy of God (which also no one can escape). The final judgment of God consists thereby of both God's wrath and God's mercy.

According to Barth, the wrath of God is a topic that can serve to clarify the difference between the picture of God in the Old and the New Testament. In both the Old and the New Testament, the human being is under the wrath of God. But in the Old Testament this is worked out in "the antithesis between the righteous God and the bitter things which man has to accept from Him without murmuring" (*CD* IV/1, p. 175). Job is mentioned here as a prime example of this antithesis. In the New Testament a radical change has taken place, as the antithesis is eliminated in the story of the Passion. The wrath of God is not eliminated, but the wrath of God is no longer expressed in opposition to human beings. In the New Testament the wrath of God does not strike arbitrarily, nor does it fit into any kind of individual punishment/reward scheme. Instead the wrath of God strikes all, as it strikes God himself in Jesus Christ.

> In Him God has entered in, breaking into that *circulus vitiosus* of the human plight, making His own not only the guilt of man but also his rejection and condemnation, giving Himself to bear the divinely righteous consequences of human sin, not merely affirming the divine sentence on man, but allowing it to be fulfilled on Himself. He, the electing eternal God, willed Himself to be rejected and therefore perishing man. That is something which never happened in all the dreadful things attested in the Old Testament concerning the wrath of God and the plight of man. (*CD* IV/1, p. 175)

The wrath of God and the effectuation of this divine wrath (the punishment), which is a part of the prophecy in the Old Testament, have thus been fulfilled in Jesus Christ. Therefore the death of Jesus Christ can be looked at both as the end (continuity) and as the new beginning (discontinuity).[2] The annihilation of the human being has taken place in Christ, as Christ has taken upon himself the punishment that belongs to us.[3] In Jesus Christ God has taken the wrath of God upon himself. The election of this one human being contains also the reprobation of this one human being. Jesus Christ is reprobated for the sake of all humanity. Not only the salvation but also the reprobation is universal within Barth's theology. The reprobation serves an aim of transformation. Through the reprobation of all human beings in Jesus Christ, all human beings are saved. Viewed from this angle one could say that in Jesus Christ the human being has received its "life-sentence," in the sense of "sentence to life" (as opposed to a death-sentence).

We saw in Chapter 9 that God's judgment of the human being consists in a judgment of the human being's striving to become God. The root of all sin consists in the human being's striving for self-justifying judgments. Except for Jesus Christ no human being can withdraw from this sin *in nuce*.[4] God's judgment of the human being is therefore most clearly expressed in the passion of Jesus Christ, where God in Jesus Christ lets himself be judged by human beings. The sin of the human being is not only revealed but also broken in Christ's readiness for self-sacrificing himself. By virtue of the Son's obeying the will of the Father, the kingdom of God breaks through — not only in preaching, but also in action. By allowing other people to judge him, Jesus Christ — and thereby also God — is actually judging the people who judge him.[5]

Within the *CD* the love of God toward the human being is most often

---

2. See *CD* IV/1, p. 257.

3. See *CD* IV/1, pp. 253-55.

4. "Not all men commit all sins, but all men commit this sin which is the essence and root of all other sins. There is not one who can boast that he does not commit it. And this is what is revealed and rejected and condemned as an act of wrong-doing by the coming of the Son of God. This is what makes His coming a coming to judgment, and His office as Saviour His office as our Judge" (*CD* IV/1, p. 220).

5. ". . . that because it is a matter of the appearance and work of the true Judge amongst those who think they can and should judge and therefore exalt themselves, therefore the abasement of the Son to our status, the obedience which He rendered in humility as our Brother, is the divine accusation against every man and the divine condemnation of every man" (*CD* IV/1, p. 220).

described in the language of a Christology from above: God loved the world so much that he sent his Son into the world to die for the sake of the world. But this might turn into some kind of self-evident, high-Christological "language game," where the content of the message is absorbed (and thereby eroded) by the form of the message. I will therefore try to describe the character of this radical love as Barth might have explicated it, if he had phrased it within the language of a Christology from below: God's ultimate love toward the human being is revealed in the passion of Jesus Christ, a love that is different from the love of human beings in the sense that it cannot turn into hate. Jesus did not curse the men who killed him. Instead he said: "Father, forgive them; for they do not know what they are doing" (Luke 23:34).

Jesus is hereby living out his own proclamation of the kingdom of God to its very end, whereby a connection between the life and the death of Jesus is established. Jesus' death on the cross is a fulfillment of the proclamation of the kingdom of God. The death of Jesus Christ reveals in one and the same act both God's Yes and God's No toward the human being. The No implies a judgment of the human ability to turn love into hate. This is what it means when Jesus is described as the one who dies under the wrath of God. Jesus takes the wrath of God upon himself, in his willingness to obey God even unto death. The proclamation of the kingdom of God is lived out in its most radical consequence. The wrath of God is thereby still connected with the death of Jesus Christ. But the death of Jesus Christ cannot then be described as the punishment of God in a traditional legalistic sense. Jesus did not have to die so that God could love the human being again. Jesus died because God loved the human being. Jesus did not have to die in order for God to once again enter into the covenantal relation with the human being (in order to remove any internal obstacles within God). Jesus died in order that the human being again could be installed as the covenant partner of God (in order to remove obstacles that prevent the human being from entering into the covenant).[6]

---

6. "Here is the place for the doubtful concept that in the passion of Jesus Christ, in the giving up of His Son to death, God has done that which is 'satisfactory' or sufficient in the victorious fighting of sin to make this victory radical and total. He has done that which is sufficient to take away sin, to restore order between Himself as the Creator and His creation, to bring in the new man reconciled and therefore at peace with Him, to redeem man from death. God has done this in the passion of Jesus Christ. For this reason the divine judgment in which the Judge was judged, and therefore the passion of Jesus

Acknowledging this, the question that still remains to be answered is: In what do the punishment and wrath of God consist? I will in the following opt for one possible interpretation, which is worked out in a continuation of my interpretation of the judgment as God's judgment of our judgment.

A Possible Interpretation: Punishment as Absence of God?

We have seen that Jesus Christ is both subject (the electing God) and object (the elected human being) in the election. Concerning the atonement this implies that Jesus Christ is both the God who judges the human being and the human being who is judged by God. As in all judgments where the accused is judged guilty, the judgment is followed by some kind of punishment. The CD also describes this punishment as God's wrath toward the human being. This leads to the question: Is the death of Jesus on the cross the punishment of God? And if so, how?

An understanding of the atonement according to which God sacrifices his own Son (let it be for the sake of others or not) is in the eyes of Dorothee Sölle disqualified, as God would then be evil. The distinction between the victim and the executioner would be abolished.[7] Sölle rejects such an understanding of God, interpreting it as an obsolete, pre-modern, and theistic understanding of God. According to Sölle, this God is really dead on the cross. A self-limited, impotent, and suffering God, who at the cross demonstrates his solidarity with the human being, has replaced the almighty, all-powerful, omniscient, and omnipresent God. God is not the Lord who stands in a Master-slave relation to the human being. Instead God is the Lord who lives in solidarity with the oppressed.

Christ, is as such the divine action of atonement which has taken place for us" (CD IV/1, pp. 254-55).

7. See Dorothee Sölle, "Gott und das Leiden," Diskussion über Jürgen Moltmanns Buch "Der gekreuzigte Gott," ed. Michael Welker (München: Chr. Kaiser Verlag, 1979), pp. 114-17. Sölle's critique of Moltmann would also, from her perspective, include Barth's teaching of the atonement. Here the critique of Sölle serves as an eye-opener to the problems involved in the teaching of the atonement, namely: How can both God and Jesus be the subject of the atonement, and what is the content of the punishment and wrath of God? Nevertheless, I shall not enter into a detailed analysis of the content and adequacy of Sölle's own analysis.

The type of "God-is-death-theology" that Sölle advocates, in opposition to Barth among others, is ebionitic. The "old" concept of God (a theistic God) has been replaced by a "new" concept of God (an a-theistic God).[8] God has become historicized both internally and externally. This historicization of God not only relates to the human being's perception of God (noetic), but implies also an inner development within God himself (ontological). God cannot — due to the incarnation — be described as an inhuman God. God cannot — for the same reason — be interpreted as a pre-ethical God. Gone is the almighty and all-powerful God in the Old Testament, who was God for a specific people. God is instead a God for the victims. The key words in interpreting the essence of God's being are "suffering" and "solidarity." In the theology of Sölle, one might conclude that Jesuology has replaced Christology.

The question now is: Where does Barth stand in relation to this alternative (the omnipotent versus the impotent God), and how would he have evaluated the alternative as an alternative? Do we really have to choose between the two alternatives: a suffering or an almighty God? Following Barth's line of arguing in *CD* IV/1, the stated alternative is false. I will, through the use of his argument here, also be enabled to answer my question: What is the material content of the punishment of God that Jesus Christ suffers as a substitute for all humankind?

In the *CD* Barth is in direct polemic against a purely kenotic understanding of God in which the crucifixion of Jesus Christ is used as an argument for a self-willed transformation within God from an almighty and powerful God to a powerless and suffering God. Barth is not opposing the view that God suffers on the cross (if this were the case, his Christology would be docetic), but he is opposing the view that the essence of God should hereby have changed. Barth finds that a Marcionite distinction between "God 1" and "God 2" would have been established if this were the case. Such a distinction would not only separate God the Reconciler from God the Creator, but would also disconnect the act of incarnation from the act of atonement. What happens at the cross is really a fulfillment of what has already happened in the incarnation, by which God due to his love toward the human being has become a human being. The humiliation of God already takes place in the incarnation and not first on the cross.

---

8. See Dorothee Sölle, *Atheistisch an Gott glauben. Beiträge zur Theologie* (Olten: Walter-Verlag, 1969), pp. 77-96, esp. 79.

To clarify Barth's point, I will draw attention to his way of using the distinction between the immanent and the economic Trinity.[9] According to Barth, suffering is not a part of the immanent Trinity. If this were the case, the suffering of the man Jesus would just be a repetition of God's a-historical suffering in the immanent Trinity prior to time. Suffering would then be necessary, in the sense that it was actively willed by God (in contrast to passively).[10] Barth wishes to avoid a "motif of eternal tragedy within the doctrine of God."[11] Further, if suffering did belong to the eternal being of God, the cruelty of the suffering would be relativized. The suffering of God belongs instead within the economic Trinity. God chooses to suffer in solidarity with human beings.

> God is moved and stirred, yet not like ourselves in powerlessness, but in his own free power, in his innermost being: moved and touched by Himself, i.e., open, ready, inclined *(propensus)* to compassion with another's suffering and therefore to assistance, impelled to take the initiative to relieve this distress. It can be only a question of compassion, free sympathy, with another's suffering. God finds no suffering in Himself. And no cause outside God can cause Him suffering if He does not will it so. But it is, in fact, a question of sympathy with the suffering of another in the full scope of God's own personal freedom. This is the essential point if we are really thinking of the God attested by Scripture, and speaking only of Him.[12]

The suffering of Jesus is the suffering of God, in which the will of God to be God for the human being is revealed. In the incarnation God takes on the finitude of humanity. Thus, the eternal election of the human being is revealed in the suffering of God (placed in the economic Trinity). Jesus' suffering on the cross belongs within the realm of the eternal covenant be-

---

9. See Burghard Krause, *Leiden Gottes — Leiden des Menschen. Eine Untersuchung zur Kirchlichen Dogmatik Karl Barths* (Stuttgart: Calver Verlag, 1980), pp. 153-54.

10. The distinction between God's active and passive sides may be seen in relation to my description of the difference between the *opus proprium* and the *opus alienum* in Chapter 6.

11. See Krause, *Leiden Gottes — Leiden des Menschen,* p. 154.

12. Karl Barth, *Church Dogmatics* II/1 (Edinburgh: T. & T. Clark, 1957), p. 370; hereafter cited as CD II/1. See also *CD* II/1, p. 307.

tween God and humanity.[13] This *passio dei* should be interpreted within the eternal will of God *(actio dei)*, instead of *reactio dei* (in that case, the incarnation would be God's accidental answer to the episode of the fall).[14] It is the connection between the immanent and the economic Trinity that establishes God's excess in the suffering of Jesus, whereby God can suffer without emptying himself out on the cross.

As previously noted, God need not first become a human being and then — as a human being — humiliate himself on the cross. The incarnation would in that case be reduced to the necessary precondition for the cross. Instead, the cross is the climax of what has already happened in the incarnation — that God has acted in solidarity with the human being for the sake of the human being. What happens at the cross — including the scream of God-forsakenness — must then be interpreted with the help of a Trinitarian framework. At the cross it is evident that God is present in all his self-differentiations at one and the same time. God is one subject with three modes of being.[15] If not, God would either be against God, or one God would die and another God would rise.[16] God has not limited himself by entering into time in a particular person at a particular place, nor has he changed his essence by becoming incarnated in time. What God reveals in the incarnation is what God always has been, even prior to the creation. Barth therefore describes the Son in the Trinity as the substitute *(Platzhalter)* for Jesus Christ. God has entered history without subjugating himself to history. Instead God is the presupposition for all history. Thus God is able to show solidarity with the human being without losing his excess and sovereignty in relation not only to the human being, but also to the

---

13. Krause, *Leiden Gottes — Leiden des Menschen,* pp. 118-23.

14. Krause, *Leiden Gottes — Leiden des Menschen,* pp. 118-20.

15. See *CD* IV/1, pp. 204-5, 65. Some critiques have found that Barth hereby overemphasizes the unity of the Trinity, whereby his interpretation becomes modalistic. Exponents for such a critique are for example Catherine Mowry LaCugna and E. P. Meijering. See Alan Torrance, "The Trinity," in *The Cambridge Companion to Karl Barth,* ed. John Webster (Cambridge: Cambridge University Press, 2000), p. 81.

16. Barth's critique of what he defines as a "modern" kenosis-theology can be summarized in the position that a kenosis-theology inevitably (again according to Barth) leads into an understanding of either two opposing wills within one God, or two independent gods. In either way the unity of God has disappeared. Barth will instead solve the question of transformation by the help of the distinction between the immanent and the economic Trinity. See *CD* IV/1, pp. 179-85.

cosmos as such. In short: the alternative between a self-sufficient God and a suffering God, who on the cross empties himself out, is false.

The main thesis of the "modern" kenosis is that God has limited himself freely. From the standpoint of Barth the "modern" kenosis-theology can be characterized as a "God-willed secular theology," meaning that God on the cross has anticipated the secularization of himself. But to see the act on the cross as a self-limitation is, from the perspective of Barth, to presuppose an anthropomorphic picture of God. It is likewise an anthropomorphic picture of God if the suffering of Jesus is not perceived as the suffering of God.[17] The *theologia crucis* belongs to the being of God (in the economic Trinity). Jesus' suffering on the cross is the self-revelation of God's self-humiliation.[18] God does not limit or restrict himself on the cross. Instead God shows who he really and eternally is at the cross: "the *crucified* Jesus is the 'image of the invisible God'" (*CD* II/2, p. 123). The passion of Jesus is the passion of God. The suffering of Jesus is at the very center of Jesus' divinity. It is God who enters into the far country.[19] What is really important here is that God takes the human experience of death into himself. This experience includes the experience of being forsaken by God. In Jesus Christ God has also taken up the experience of God's absence.

I will therefore, against Barth's own explicit statements, add that one consequence of God's absorbing of human finitude must be that God not only is able to change, but also that God actually did change during the incarnation.[20] I find that Barth at this point of his thought structure is much more

17. See *CD* IV/1, p. 186.

18. See Bertold Klappert, *Die Auferweckung des Gekreuzigten. Der Ansatz der Christologie Karl Barths im Zusammenhang der Christologie der Gegenwart* (Neukirchen-Vluyn: Neukirchener Verlag, 1981), pp. 180-81.

19. I agree with Krause, who states: "In the *CD* the suffering of Jesus becomes the center of interpreting Jesus' divinity, it becomes the methodically reflected place of specifying the concept of God. By doing so, Barth thoroughly 'inscribes the cross into the act of speaking of God'" (Krause, *Leiden Gottes — Leiden des Menschen*, p. 94).

20. Barth uses a distinction between the *unchangeability* of God and the *immovability*. Exactly as unchangeable, God can move and be moved. See *CD* II/2, p. 185. In *CD* IV/1, pp. 179-80, Barth states: "God is always God even in His humiliation. The divine being does not suffer any change, any diminution, any transformation into something else, any admixture with something else, let alone any cessation. The deity of Christ is the one unaltered because unalterable deity of God. Any subtraction or weakening of it would at once throw doubt upon the atonement made in Him. He humbled Himself, but He did

Hegelian inspired than he himself knows. The reason that Barth is unable to take this final step within his theology of incarnation is his emphasis on protology. In this way Barth can avoid any distinction of content between the hidden and the revealed God. We have seen, in Chapter 7, how the protology is worked out in the description of the relation between λόγος ἄσαρκος and λόγος ἔνσαρκος. But the price Barth pays for his emphasis on protology is that he is unable to give up the idea of divine unchangeability.

My claim that Barth is closer to the thought of Hegel than he himself knows is also connected to his awareness that God is taking a risk in the incarnation (see also Chapter 13). The project of the incarnation could have failed. Jesus could have sinned. As noted in Chapter 9, Barth operates with a fourfold differentiation between God the Father and Jesus the Son as being both subject and object in the act of atonement. The act of atonement implies then a unity between the free will of God and the man Jesus. In the following I draw a different conclusion from this model of unity and difference than Barth himself did, but I will, nevertheless, claim that Barth's text — at least at places — allows for such a reading.

Barth unites the will of God and the will of the man Jesus in the eternal, original will of God that comes to expression in the incarnation. God could have done otherwise, but he didn't. Thus, God is unchangeable, but moveable. It is my claim, however, that this unity between the free will of God and the free will of the man Jesus also implies a move from below, which is most clearly seen in the rejections of the temptations in the beginning and the end of the narrative of Jesus' life — an insight I owe to Barth's own excursus on the theme of temptation in *CD* IV/1, pp. 259-73 (see also Chapter 9). The emphasis on the actual temptation, and the despair in which the final rejection takes place, makes way for an interpretation of the incarnation in which the incarnation includes a risk. Jesus could have acted otherwise; he could have chosen to let the last cup pass from him. He could have been tempted by the last temptation. The man Jesus could have reacted to his own will instead of the will of God. The difference between Jesus and other men does not consist in the fact that he is not tempted like any other human being, but that he, as the one human being, resists all temptations — even the last one, for which reason he died on the cross.[21]

---

not do it by ceasing to be who He is. He went into a strange land, but even there, and especially there, He never became a stranger to Himself."

21. See *CD* IV/1, pp. 215-16, 258-73.

Such a reading works out the full potential of the interaction between a Christology from below and a Christology from above. But if God is really taking a risk, this must also — despite the actual result (success or failure) — involve at least a potential change in the being of God.[22] The risk is situated in the relation between God and the man Jesus. Jesus could have deserted the task he was given. In the relation between God and Jesus we not only have to take the will of the Father into account but also that of the Son. And that Jesus Christ is truly human and truly God consists in the fact that he — as the one and only person — was able to obey the will of the Father until death. He is, as earlier noted, the personification of the kingdom of God.

But — and here we are back to the question of the meaning of the death of Jesus Christ — he died in uncertainty. Barth does not state this explicitly, but he emphasizes the tension and the despair of Jesus' cry from the cross so strongly that it would destroy the depth and gravity of Jesus' cry of fear and bitterness if it were not so.

> And even more striking is the fact that in Mark (15,34) and Matthew (27,46) His only word on the cross, and therefore His final word, is the despairing question: 'My God, my God, why hast thou forsaken me?' The Gospels do not conceal the fact, but state it, that His death is a problem of the first magnitude. It is, in fact, the problem of all the problems of His existence and relationship to God and His life's work. The darkness of His end is a true and final darkness. It is a darkness which even He Himself could not see through directly, but which had to be traversed like a tunnel. (CD IV/2, pp. 250-51)

Further, Barth states that God could have let the cross at Golgotha be the last word. The final word of judgment could have been said here. "Ruling as the Judge, He might have given death and nothingness the last word in rela-

22. Jürgen Moltmann's Christology, *The Way of Jesus Christ,* can be read as an attempt to explore and broaden Barth's understanding of the strong interrelation between the incarnation and cross. In fact, it seems to me as if Moltmann at places finds himself so close to Barth that he needs to create room for his own conception with the help of a simplified presentation of Barth's theology, where the *CD* one-sidedly is interpreted in the light of the early Barth's commentary on Romans. See also Henning Thomsen, "Moltmanns teologiske historieopfattelse som et trinitarisk formuleret svar på lidelsens problem" [Moltmann's theological perception of history as a Trinitarian way of answering the problem of suffering], in *Verbum Dei — Verba ecclesiae,* ed. Theodor Jørgensen and Peter Widmann (Aarhus: Det teologiske Fakultet, Aarhus Universitet, 1996), p. 99.

tion to the creature. He would still have been in the right" (*CD* IV/1, p. 306).
Read in connection with Barth's emphasis on the cry on the cross, this implies that at the time of the cry, "My God, my God, why have you forsaken
me?" (Mark 15:34; Matt. 27:46), Jesus did not know that he would be resurrected on the third day. At the point of death he did not know if God was
with him or not. The feeling of God's absence was not just apparent but
real. Had God abandoned him? Had he himself failed in his task? Or had he
simply been mistaken? Had his proclaimed message of the kingdom of God
been nothing more than empty words? For both the disciples and the
crowds it must certainly have looked like that. A symptomatic reaction here
is the statement of the chief priests: "He saved others; he cannot save himself" (Mark 15:31). And for Jesus himself — according to the testimony of
Mark 15:34 and Matthew 27:46 — it also looked as if he had failed.

As said, Barth refers in the *CD* at several places to the cry from the
cross. I will proceed here with an analysis of four of the places in *CD* IV/1
where Barth refers to Jesus' cry. Each of them has its own accent: God's solidarity with the human being, the self-willed finitude of God, death as the
end, and finally the end of death.

God's Solidarity with the Human Being

> But the *self-humiliation* of God in His Son is genuine and actual,
> and therefore *there is no reservation in respect of His solidarity with
> us.* He did become — and this is the presupposition of all that fol-
> lows — the *brother of man,* threatened with man, harassed and as-
> saulted with him, with him in the stream which hurries downward
> to the abyss, hastening with him to death, to the cessation of being
> and nothingness. With him He cries — knowing far better than any
> other how much reason there is to cry: "My God, my God, why hast
> thou forsaken me?" (Mk. 15,34). *Deus pro nobis* means simply that
> God has not abandoned the world and man in the unlimited need
> of his situation, but that He willed to bear this need as His own, that
> He took it upon Himself, and that He cries with man in this need.
> (*CD* IV/1, p. 215; my emphasis)

Barth says, with no reservation, that Jesus was not spared any of the
threats, anxiousness, temptations, and sufferings that life — in all its ambi-

guity — contains. Neither is it likely that he missed the brighter side of life such as happiness, joy, knowledge of a call, and *joie de vivre*. In short, what makes the life of Jesus special is that he is a man with a God-given mission. Further, it was not a given that the mission would be completed. The "agent" might have failed the task that he had been given. He might have wanted to escape his "destiny." And not only might he have wanted to escape his destiny, he might also himself have been in doubt as to whether he really had completed it or not. In the case of Jesus the doubt of the fulfillment of his call can be seen in his fear of the absence of God, which is at stake in the cry from the cross.[23]

That God in Jesus has become the brother of human beings implies, as stated above, that God has been "threatened with man, harassed and assaulted with him, with him in the stream which hurries downward to the abyss, hastening with him to death, to the cessation of being and nothingness." God has hereby not only taken death onto himself, but he has also taken the fear of death onto himself. This fear is expressed most clearly in the cry at the cross, where the feeling of the absence of God and the fear of death are connected. To die as a blasphemer hanging on the cross is to die a death in the feeling of God-abandonment: therefore the cry. The solidarity of God thereby reaches into the human being's experience of God-absence. The punishment then consists in an act of grace:

---

23. My stressing of the element of risk or insecurity might confuse some readers, since it emphasizes a strain within Barth's Christological teaching that is normally neglected. Usually the entire focus of the interpretation is on the connection between the original will of God prior to time and the outliving of this will in the incarnation (including the atonement). And this, as it also appears from this thesis, is the overall framework. But within this framework, Barth does interrelate the Christology from below with the Christology from above and vice versa. And the places where this is most daringly expressed are in the analysis of the relation between the Son and the Father in the temptations of the man Jesus (in the wilderness and Gethsemane, see *CD* IV/1, pp. 259-73), and in the emphasis on Jesus' cry to God on the cross. And it is then my claim that within Barth's theology, there is a potential for an interpretation that reduces the emphasis on the radical free will of God, and instead accentuates God's ability to take on human experience in Jesus Christ. As long as the ability of God to experience human experiences could be interpreted as the enacting of the original will of God, Barth himself would probably agree with this interpretation, but when, as I do, it is used in connection with a critique of Barth's stressing of the *majestas Dei*, that God could just as well have been a self-sufficient God without the "need" for any relation — he would, surely, have been unsatisfied with this reading and critique.

that God himself takes on the experience of God-absence, whereby there really is no place for the human being where it can set itself outside of the reach and love of God.

However, Barth does not follow this line of thought far enough, as he is unable to see that the relation between the incarnation and the cross inevitably must allow for possible changes within God himself. What happens in the life and death of Jesus cannot leave God unchanged. God cannot really be the same as before (a point I will pursue in Chapter 13). Here it is enough to emphasize the connection between the punishment of God and the absence of God. The death of Jesus can be described as the punishment of God in the sense that it contains a God-willed absence of God. But it is an absence that God himself absorbs as it is his Son who feels it (if not, the Trinitarian understanding of God would be suspended).

Taking the resurrection into account we must at this point in the argument further distinguish between the feeling of the absence of God and the reality of the absence of God. The feeling of the absence of God was real, but this does not make the absence of God real. The latter is demonstrated in the resurrection. The resurrection on the third day is only possible because Jesus had never been without God. Throughout the whole time of Easter, God was there as the Sustainer of life. When God as the infinite takes on the finite, the finite is absorbed within God. This leads me to the second subheading: God's self-willed experience of finitude. But before entering into this let me just make a final exploration of the act of solidarity that is at stake in the last words of Christ on the cross.

I have demonstrated here that the incarnation also entails a risk. And this openness to the future is included in God's solidarity with the human being, which also demonstrates that Jesus is fully human and fully God. Fully human, as he does not know the final result of what will happen after death. If this were not the case, the cry "My God, my God, why have you forsaken me?" (Mark 15:34; Matt. 27:46) would have been fake. Fully God, Jesus was the one and only man able to live his life in full obedience toward the future of God. The solidarity that is at stake here is a solidarity that is broader than "just" a solidarity with the oppressed. It is not enough to state that God suffers together with the ones who suffer. God is more than a kind of "transcendental spiritual adviser" who can offer to go a mile or two with the oppressed. It is a solidarity that lives out of the hope for and longing after a new world. This new world consists of the final breakthrough of the coming of the kingdom of God. This breakthrough has partly happened in the life, death, and resurrection of Jesus Christ. The hope for and longing after the new world lives therefore not only out of the future (that God may let his kingdom come), but also out of the past, as the content of the future is known in and through Jesus Christ.

God's Self-Willed Experience of Finitude

> The incarnation, the taking of the *forma servi,* means not only God's becoming a creature, becoming a man — and how this is possible to God without an alteration of His being is not self-evident — but it means His giving Himself up to the contradiction of man against Him, His placing Himself under the judgment under which man has fallen in this contradiction, under the *curse of death* which rests upon Him. The meaning of the incarnation is plainly revealed in the question of Jesus on the cross: "My God, my God, why hast thou forsaken me?" (Mk. 15,34). (*CD* IV/1, p. 185; my emphasis)

The cry from the cross is the clearest example that God — by taking on the *forma servi* — has delivered himself up to his own finitude. In the incarnation God has placed himself under the curse of death. He has taken the punishment of God — which inevitably leads to the destruction of the human being — upon himself. And this destruction can, as shown above, be interpreted as the experience of absence of God.

To really grasp the logic behind Barth's way of combining the death of Jesus and the death of God it is important to look at the relation between the *forma dei* and the *forma servi.* God's love *(forma dei)* toward the human being is so strong that it includes the willingness to give himself away. For the sake of the human being, God became a servant of the human being *(forma servi).* But that God is willing in his love to become a human being is not the same as God thereby — willingly or not — giving up being God. What help would God be for the human being if, in his movement toward the human being, he had given himself up?[24] In fact, only God could do what Jesus did. Jesus did not become Christ through his words

---

24. "Of what value would His deity be to us if — instead of crossing in that deity the very real gulf between Himself and us — He left that deity behind Him in His coming to us, if it came to be outside of Him as He became ours?" (*CD* IV/1, p. 185).

and acts, but he did what he did due to the fact that he was Christ. There-fore, again, it is very important for Barth to maintain a Chalcedonian pat-tern in his Christology. In Christ God became his own instrument to fulfill his own aim: the reestablishment of the partnership between God and the human being.

But a problem remains when God is seen as the subject of the death of Jesus. How does this not end up in an inner conflict, in which God be-comes "God against God"? One way to try to solve this problem is to maintain that God does not alter. God can — if he wants to — let his being take another form. This other form might look like a paradox from the point of view of the human being, or perhaps even a self-contradiction: God is at one and the same time omnipresent and limited in time and space; God is at one and the same time the one who cannot be tempted and the one who is tempted.[25]

This way of arguing might at a first sight seem to be really Barthian. Barth nevertheless opposes it in the *CD* as a false track, since it ends up in a division of God. Thus, the problem is that a very sharp distinction be-tween God, as God is in and for himself, and God, as God is for the human being, is established. The former is unaffected by the latter. In himself God is still the omnipresent, almighty, and all-powerful God. But in Jesus of Nazareth he was limited in time and space, vulnerable and impotent. A connection is then not really established between the Redeemer and the Creator, God in himself and God for us. The consequence is that noetically and logically God can only be described with the use of the term "para-dox." Ontically there would then be a "gulf in God Himself, between His being and essence in Himself and His activity and work as the Reconciler of the world created by Him" (*CD* IV/1, p. 184). The problem here is that the act of redemption is not seen as constitutive for the being of God in and for himself. God could then possibly be a God in self-contradiction. Under the next heading ("Death as the End") I will demonstrate that Barth's own critique of a division of God against God can be used against his own emphasis on God's free will in the sense that God could have done otherwise than he did.

Barth's emphasis on the incarnation, as the place where both the true God and the true human being are revealed to the human being, is one way of uniting the teaching on the Trinity and Christology. Christology

25. See *CD* IV/1, p. 184.

and Trinity are viewed as two different ways of describing the same theological reality: the being of God as a being in act. The reference to one and the same reality (God) is so strong in the *CD* that there is no space for a dichotomy within God, whereby God would become a "God against God." If this were the case, God would consist in an "inner and outer antithesis to Himself" (*CD* IV/1, p. 184). Instead, there is only space for one single motif behind the various acts of God: God's love toward human beings. There is one link between God as God is in himself independently of the human being, and God as God is in relation to the human being (for the human being): the Creator's sustaining love toward his creation. It is this love that "urges" God to become his own instrument toward a finalization of finitude. According to Barth, this can only happen if God maintains his superiority, if God maintains an excess in relation to the history into which he himself intervened in the man Jesus of Nazareth.

At the cross God is not emptying himself out, but he is taking on the pain and suffering of human beings. God is not restricting himself in the sense that the God-predicates are transformed from, for example, almightiness and omnipresence to impotence and limitation.[26] God does not lose his power at the cross, but at the cross God is instead able to absorb the human being's experience of finitude. The reason why Barth at one and the same time can emphasize the cry from the cross so strongly and still dissociate himself from the modern kenotic theories is that the latter approach (according to Barth) results in God's own self-destruction. Against these modern kenoticists Barth states:

> God gives Himself, but He does not give Himself away. He does not give up being God in becoming a creature, in becoming man. He does not cease to be God. *He does not come into conflict with Himself.* He does *not sin* when *in unity with the man Jesus* He mingles with sinners and takes their place. And when He dies in *His unity with this man, death does not gain any power over Him.* He exists as God in the *righteousness* and the *life*, the *obedience* and the *resurrection* of *this* man. He makes His own the being of man in contradiction against Him, but He *does not make common cause* with it. He also makes His own the being of man under the curse of this con-

26. See *CD* IV/1, p. 184.

tradition, but *in order to do away with it as He suffers it.* He acts as Lord over this contradiction even as He subjects Himself to it. (*CD* IV/1, p. 185; my emphasis)

I will underline two points from this passage:

(1) The reason why God can become incarnated without ceasing to be God is that this particular man (Jesus of Nazareth) is different from all other human beings in the sense that he does not sin.[27] He lives — in contrast to all other human beings — fully out of his trust in God. He is the true human being.[28] Even in the death of the incarnated one God retains an excess in relation to history. However, this excess can first be recognized retrospectively: from the point of the resurrection.[29]

(2) God defines his own predicates. There is no speculative gulf between God prior to the incarnation and God in the incarnation. They are connected by the will of God to incarnate himself.[30]

27. See for example also *CD* IV/1, p. 215.

28. Barth expresses it in the following way in *CD* IV/2, pp. 27-28: "But the fact that He is not only *a* true man, but *the* true man, is not exhausted by His likeness with all other men. He is not only completely like us, but completely unlike us — and it is only when we add this complementary truth that we realise the full meaning of the *vere homo* as it applies to Him. But the unlikeness consists in what must necessarily become, and has become, of 'human nature' when He assumed it in likeness with us, of flesh when it became His. It relates to the particularity of the history, which took place when He became man, and still takes place as He, the Son of God, is man.

"His unlikeness with us does not consist, of course, only in the fact that He is something that we are not — the Son of God, very God. Rather, because He is the Son of God, it consists in the unlikeness of His humanity and ours. Because and as He is the Son of God, He is exactly the same as we are, but quite differently."

29. See also my reference to Jüngel's use of the distinction between the an- and the enhypostasis in Chapter 7.

30. In the original German text Barth distinguishes between *hingeben* on the one hand and *weggeben* and *aufgeben* on the other hand. "Gott würde sich nach dieser Konzeption in der Fleischwerdung des Wortes nicht nur hingeben, sondern weggeben, als Gott aufgeben." Karl Barth, *Die Kirchliche Dogmatik* IV/1 (Zollikon-Zürich: Evangelischer Verlag A.G., 1953), p. 201; hereafter cited as *KD* IV/1. The English translation is not really able to express these distinctions so precisely: "On this view God in His incarnation would not merely give Himself, but give Himself away, give up being God" (*CD* IV/1, p. 184).

In short: God can give himself to the human being without giving himself up. Jesus can die without God dying. God can, due to his Trinitarian structure, become a human being (experience finitude) and still be God (being infinite). God does not cease to be God through the incarnation. The incarnation is, rather, the most explicit demonstration of God's excess.

Death as the End

> According to the disposition and in the service of God death and nothingness are brought in and used for the reconciliation of the world with God, as instruments in His conflict with the corruption of the world and the sin of man — but death and nothingness in all their evil and destructive power. It is also to the wrath of God which permits this force and judges evil by evil that Jesus commits Himself and in and with Himself the world and the individual sinner. The reconciliation of the world with God which took place in Jesus Christ had therefore the meaning that a radical end was made of Him and therefore of the world.
>
> And that might have exhausted its meaning. The saying: "My God, my God, why hast thou forsaken me?" (Mk. 15,34) shows how close was this frightful possibility. It might have been that God turned away His face finally from us. (CD IV/1, p. 306)

Barth emphasizes here — as in so many other places — that the final judgment of the human being could have ended otherwise. The story could have stopped at the cross. God could have chosen to turn his face from the human being, and thereby to give the human being the judgment that it really deserved. God was fully in his right to let nothingness triumph over the human being. In fact, an echo of this terrible judgment can be heard in Jesus' cry from the cross. In the death of Christ, nothingness seemed to have won. But it did not.

I find, however, that Barth's emphasis on the radical freedom of God is problematic. Barth stresses the majesty of God so utterly that he falls into the very pitfall he wants to avoid: the fear of an unknown God. The freedom of God has here been taken *ad absurdum*. I have described the strong rejection of the teaching of the double outcome in Chapter 10, where we saw that the election of Jesus Christ includes reprobation of and salvation for all human beings in Jesus Christ. There is no hidden God to fear, who might have other motives than the ones that are already revealed in Jesus Christ. However, it is problematic that Barth is still operating with the option that God could really have acted otherwise toward the human being. Barth uses this type of scholastic argument as a way of emphasizing the grace of God, but he does it in a way that presupposes an odd logic: the bigger the uncertainty (the emphasis on God's potential options), the greater the grace (the emphasis on God's actual choice).

This line of thought is really absurd, as Barth's whole way of interpreting the grace of God is based on the presupposition that the grace of God is qualitatively — and not "just" quantitatively — different from the grace of the human being. And if God really could have acted otherwise; if God really could have turned his face away from the human being, the grace of God would not have been qualitatively different from the grace of human beings. A very human perception of righteousness, with a clear symmetry between act and reward/punishment, would have been in play instead. To claim that God really could have done otherwise is a way of retaining the practical impact of the double outcome: the fear of reprobation. Of course, it has been transformed here from an actual threat: that some will end up in a state of eternal torment (whereas others will end up in a state of eternal joy) to a kind of "flashback fear," where the reflection of what could have happened can still fill one with dread. It could have gone wrong! We could all have been eternally doomed. In fact, we did all deserve it. Thanks be to God that it did not happen![31]

But a reflection on this reflection will inevitably lead one into the abyss: Could it still happen? Can God still change his mind? And why should he not do so? Barth claims not only that God would still have been God if he had destroyed all human beings, but he states further that the echo of this possibility can be heard in the cry from the cross. The dichotomy in God

---

31. I am aware that my critique is not shared by the followers of Barth who see no problem in the tension between the constant reminding of the absolute freedom of God, who without ceasing to be God could have chosen to be God without humanity, and the accentuation of the actual election of the human being in Christ. See for example Bruce L. McCormack, "The Sum of the Gospel: The Doctrine of Election in the Theologies of Alexander Schweizer and Karl Barth," in *Towards the Future of Reformed Theology: Tasks, Topics, Traditions*, ed. David Willis and Michael Welker (Grand Rapids: Eerdmans, 1989), p. 491.

("God against God"), which we have seen was rejected by Barth, is, despite his strong critique, at play in his own distinction between what God actually did, and what he could have done. The difference between what God actually did and what he righteously could have done (potentiality) is a reminiscence of a traditional distinction between the hidden and the revealed God. Of course, a fundamental change has happened, as the distinction is no longer used as a way through which the eschatological future is kept unknown. The eschatological future is already given a known content by Barth in the revelation of Jesus Christ. And, according to the main tendency of Barth's thought, the content of this future can no longer be envisaged otherwise than as salvific. But then there is really no reason for stating so loudly that God could have acted otherwise.

Barth could at least have avoided the fear of such a change by stating loudly and clearly that God, after his decision to be the God who shows mercy and grace toward the human being, had no other option but to stay within his decision. God is bound to his own decisions, his own will, his own love. But Barth could also have stated — consistent with his emphasis on the relation between being and acts, where it is the will of God that constitutes the acts and thereby the being of God — that if God really had done otherwise, he would really have been another God. The reference to a potential other choice would then have had no other function than to demonstrate that it was the free will of God that was behind the actual choice of God. But looked at retrospectively, God could not have done otherwise and still be the same God.

The End of Death

> In so doing [raising Jesus Christ from the dead] He answered the question which in Mark and Matthew forms the last words of the Crucified. But we can and must say that in so doing He has shown that as recorded in St. Luke's account Jesus commended His spirit into His hands, and that only in so doing did He subject Himself to death, that He bowed His head before Him, and only because He bowed before Him did He also bow before the claim and power of nothingness, that He was obedient even unto death only in this way and in this order (and to that extent as already the secret Lord of the death to which He subjected Himself). (*CD* IV/1, p. 307)

The last question of the crucified is answered in the resurrection. It thus becomes clear that Jesus was never without God. God had never ceased to be in relation with him. Even at the cross the relation between the Father and the Son is still intact, even if the Son at this point is no longer able to believe it. To avoid a dichotomy between the content of the cross and the content of the resurrection Barth combines the cry at the cross as it is described in Mark and Matthew (Mark 15:34 and Matt. 27:46) with the less dramatic version of Luke, where Jesus' final words at the cross are: "Father, into your hands I commend my spirit" (Luke 23:46). Barth wishes hereby to stress not only that death is conquered in and through death, but also that the resurrection was not necessary for the justification of the death of Jesus. At the cross God judges the world by letting himself be judged. The resurrection does not outdo the cross; rather it confirms it. Thus God would also have been a righteous and loving God even if he had let the mission of the man Jesus be completed on Good Friday. What the resurrection adds to the cross is the revelation of the hidden love of God at the cross.[32]

God incarnates himself into the reality of the fallen human being. From this perspective the incarnation can be read as an incarnation into

---

32. "But then, and at an even higher level, He did it [justified himself] in the revelation of His faithfulness as the Father of this Son, in the revelation of the love with which He loved Him from all eternity and all along His way into the far country, at Jordan and in the wilderness and in Gethsemane, and never more than when the Son asked Him on the cross (Mark 15:34) whether He had forsaken Him, and when He then cried with a loud voice and gave up the ghost. His whole eternal love would still have been His even if He had acquiesced in His death as the Judge who was judged, if His mission had concluded at that ninth hour of Good Friday, if it had been completed with His fulfilling and suffering in His own person the No of the divine wrath on the world. But then, like His right as Creator and Lord of the world, it would have been, and remained, a completely hidden love: without witnesses, without participants, because without proclamation, without outward confirmation and form, concealed in the mystery of the inner life and being of the Godhead. It pleased God, however, to justify Himself, that is, to reveal and give force and effect to His faithfulness and love in this supreme sense, by an ὁρίζειν (Rom. 1:4) of His Son which the disciples of Jesus could see and hear and grasp, and which was ordained to be publicly proclaimed. He willed to give to His eternity with Him and therefore to Himself an earthly form. He willed to give to the inner and secret radiance of His glory an outward radiance in the sphere of creation and its history. He willed to give to His eternal life space and time. And that is what He did when He called Jesus Christ to life from the dead" (*CD* IV/1, p. 308).

God-absence. At the cross this absence is lived out in its most radical form, as Jesus cries out at the cross. But the absence of God has hereby also reached its limits. When God himself has taken on the experience of the absence of God, this experience is absorbed within God. It is thus the experience of the absence of God, and not God, that is absorbed on the cross. The resurrection is a confirmation of what happened at the cross. The power of death is broken, but it is broken already at the cross and not first at the resurrection. The sustaining power of God has never ceased to be at work. This does not turn the resurrection into an appendix to the incarnation and the cross, since it is first in the resurrection that the relation between incarnation, death, and resurrection can be perceived.

To sum up the four aspects of the cry on the cross: Barth's theology operates within a speculative, theistic, and Trinitarian framework. Within this framework he has been able to incorporate elements of thought that were later emphasized much more strongly (and also more one-sidedly) in secular, "God-is-dead" theologies. I have in my analysis of the punishment of God opted for a reading of the *CD* in which punishment is interpreted as the experience of the absence of God. The connection between the incarnation, the cross, and the resurrection becomes hereby explicit, as God, by taking on the "destiny" of the human being, changes the "destiny" of the human being in a profoundly radical way. This change is revealed in the act of resurrection.

CHAPTER 12

The Humanity of Jesus Christ

The Interrelations Between the Life and Death of Jesus Christ

I will here follow up on one of the themes that was analyzed in my interpretation of the atonement: the reason why Jesus had to die. I have demonstrated that there is no solid foundation within the *CD* for interpreting the death of Jesus as a necessary sacrifice that aims to overcome internal obstacles within God. The aim of the sacrifice is not to please God. God is not a God who seeks revenge, nor is he a God who is torn between his urge for righteousness and his love and mercy toward human beings. But the question that needs further investigation is: How do the life and the death of Jesus Christ interrelate? This question plays an important role in Prenter's analysis of Barth's Christology. I will therefore use Prenter's approach to this question as a way of structuring my own evaluation of how this question is treated in the interrelation between Christology and atonement in the *CD*.[1]

According to Prenter there are only two options: either the death of Jesus explains his life, or the life of Jesus explains his death. The life of Jesus is in the former case reduced to nothing more than the necessary precondition for his death. He had to live, so that he could die and become resur-

---

1. See Regin Prenter, "Karl Barths Umbildung der traditionellen Zweinaturlehre in lutherischer Beleuchtung," in *Theologie und Gottesdienst. Gesammelte Aufsätze,* ed. Erik Kyndal, Gerhard Pedersen, and Anna Marie Aagaard (Aarhus: Aros Forlag, 1977), pp. 60-70.

rected. The humanity of Jesus is hereby devalued, which is why Prenter claims that such an understanding of the connection between Jesus' life and death inevitably will end up in docetism. In the latter case it is instead the life of Jesus that explains the meaning of his death. His death is viewed here as the positive fulfillment of his life — or one might even say — as the climax of his life.

Prenter states that Barth's teaching on Christology and the atonement is worked out within the framework of the first approach, since the death of Jesus is explained with the help of references to the immanent Trinity. In Christ God has demonstrated his eternal election of the human being. This election, despite its eternal foundation, is first fully visible for the human being in the incarnation. Thus, Jesus is the illustration of God's eternal acceptance of the human being in predestination.[2] The humanity of Jesus seems hereby to acquire a very vague role in Barth's Christology. The life of Jesus is reduced to a "replay" of God's eternal decision. In Jesus the eternal God repeats himself in time.[3]

It is not my aim to enter into a detailed discussion of Prenter's "two-options" scheme here. (I find, however, that Prenter's model is far too simplistic, as it does not take sufficiently into account the difference between the ontological and the noetical aspects of the relation between the life, death, and resurrection of Jesus Christ.) What really concerns me is whether — given the two options as he has defined them — Prenter has chosen the right one in his description of Barth's Christology. I have in my use of Girard demonstrated that there is a strong connection between the life, death, and resurrection of Jesus Christ in Barth's teaching of the atonement. This connection is established through the proclamation of the coming of the kingdom of God, which strongly unites all three aspects (the life, death, and resurrection of Jesus). In fact, Barth's teaching on the atonement manages to emphasize all three aspects in such a way that none of them merely serves as a precondition for or result of the others. If this is

2. See Prenter, "Karl Barths Umbildung der traditionellen Zweinaturlehre," pp. 67-68.

3. "The death of Jesus — including his life seen from this perspective — and the resurrection after his death has only one meaning: to be analogy, 'representation, image, and counterpart' of the immanent Trinitarian relationship between father and son. This immanent Trinitarian relationship is the eternal reason for everything which happens in the history of the revelation" (trans. Michael Waltemathe). Prenter, "Karl Barths Umbildung der traditionellen Zweinaturlehre," p. 67.

correct, it is no longer manifest that the humanity of Jesus Christ plays no important role within Barth's Christology.

The Interrelation Between the Cross and the Resurrection

It is evident that neither the cross nor the resurrection can be understood independently. The cross and the resurrection are two individual acts of God that must be seen in relation to each other to be fully understood. Or phrased otherwise: there is no real alternative between a *theologia gloriae* and a *theologica crucis*. They are both dependent on each other. Without the latter, the former will be empty. Without the former, the latter will turn into an abstract magnification of the passion and death of Jesus Christ.[4] The questions are: (1) How are they related? and (2) What is the content of this relation?

Noetically, the resurrection is the ground and starting point for any Christological claims. It is through the resurrection that it is revealed that Jesus is Christ. However, this does not mean that Jesus first became Christ in the resurrection event. But it is first in and through the resurrection and ascension of Jesus that human beings are enabled to see that Jesus is Christ. What was hidden from human beings before is now revealed to them through God's own act. The resurrection thereby confirms what was already at stake before the resurrection: that Jesus is the Son of God.[5] We have previously seen that the actual content of this Sonship consists in the proclamation of the kingdom of God. The immediate result of this proclamation was the death of the proclaimer. The connection between the life,

---

4. See *CD* IV/1, pp. 557-58. As a curiosity it can be mentioned that Barth ironically refers to a specific Scandinavian emphasis on the *theologia crucis*, where it "at a certain point which is hard to define, become[s] a pagan instead of a purely Christian seriousness, changing suddenly into a Nordic morbidity, losing the direction in which alone it can have any Christian meaning, suddenly beginning to look backwards instead of forwards, transforming itself into the tragedy of an abstract *theologia crucis* which can have little and finally nothing whatever to do with the Christian knowledge of Jesus Christ" (*CD* IV/1, p. 559). One should add that the term "Nordic morbidity" is a quite misleading translation of "nordische Schwermut" (*KD* IV/1, p. 623).

5. See also Eberhard Jüngel, "Der königliche Mensch. Eine christologische Reflexion auf die Würde des Menschen in der Theologie Karl Barths," in *Barth Studien* (Gütersloh: Gütersloher Verlagshaus, 1982), p. 242.

death, and resurrection of Jesus Christ is hereby established through the proclamation of the kingdom of God. Viewed from this perspective, Barth can be claimed to be in opposition to the often-used theological distinction between the historical Jesus and the proclaimed Christ. From Barth's perspective an unsubtle use of this distinction must be problematized due to at least the following three reasons:

(1) Jesus is Christ throughout his whole life and death.[6]
(2) A too-firm theological use of the distinction between the historical Jesus and the proclaimed Christ operates on the presupposition, expressed explicitly or not, that Jesus first became Christ in the resurrection.
(3) It implies an inescapable conflict between Jesus' self-understanding and the community's understanding of Jesus. And according to Barth, there is no such schism between Jesus' self-understanding and the congregations' proclamation of Jesus as the Son of God.

The problem with a Christology that accepts this schism is that it presupposes not only a noetic but also an ontological schism between pre- and post-resurrection. But Jesus is, both before and after the resurrection, Christ. The new *aeon* (the coming of the kingdom of God) had already started in the life and the death of Jesus Christ — and not first in the act of resurrection. The new covenant between God and the human being is established through the life and the death of Jesus Christ. Nothing new needed to be added to this covenant, nor had anything new actually been added to this covenant in the resurrection:

> The humiliation of God and the exaltation of man as they took
> place in Him are the completed fulfilment of the covenant, the

---

6. "It is impossible to make the abstract distinction sometimes made between the sequence which precedes Easter and the event which follows the death of Jesus Christ, which means between the ground of the *reality* of His being and the ground of its *knowledge*. For the former sequence is not entirely devoid of the character of revelation. In it Jesus Christ is not absolutely concealed and unknowable and actually unknown as the One He was and is. The being of Jesus Christ in it is not abstractly that of the humiliated Son of God who was necessarily unknowable as the One He was. . . . This is only, of course, in the light of the event of Easter and the ascension, which means that this light is not entirely absent even in the pre-Easter sequence" (*CD* IV/2, p. 135).

completed reconciliation of the world with God. *His being as such* (if we may be permitted this abstraction for a moment) *was and is the end of the old and the beginning of the new form of this world even without His resurrection and ascension. He did not and does not lack anything in Himself.* What was lacking was only the men to see and hear it as the work and Word of God — the praise and thanksgiving and obedience of their thoughts and words and works. What was lacking was only their service of witness and proclamation. (*CD* IV/ 2, pp. 132-33; my emphasis)

The new in the resurrection is from this perspective "only" noetical. What nobody had ears to hear and eyes to see can now be heard and seen due to God's own self-communication. "The resurrection and the ascension of Jesus Christ are the event of His self-declaration" (*CD* IV/2, p. 133). Without the resurrection and the ascension Jesus would have "gone under in world history," as he would have been remembered as "an obscure and unsuccessful Jewish eccentric and revolutionary like so many others" (*CD* IV/ 2, p. 168). From this perspective the resurrection can be described as a necessary and independent act, the primary function of which consisted in its power to reveal what had already happened in the life and death of Jesus Christ: the "completed fulfilment of the covenant" (see *CD* IV/2, p. 132) and thereby "the completed reconciliation of the world with God" (*CD* IV/ 2, p. 132). What was prior to resurrection can only be understood as what it really was in the light of the resurrection.[7]

If the men of the New Testament could think and speak at all of Jesus Christ, if they had any right to do so, it was only as He had given Himself to be known as the One He was in His resurrection and ascension, as His being was manifested to them in the revealing power of this event. In this event of His revelation He became for them what He had been in Himself, in the secret of His previous history, *even without* this event, but what He could be for them only in this event — the Son of God and Son of Man, and in His existence as such the event of salvation for them and for Israel and for the world. In His resurrection and ascension He gave Himself to be

---

7. Here we are back at Barth's fundamental claim: that God is the real subject of any knowledge about God. For a further elaboration of the epistemological content and consequence of this emphasis on revelation, see Chapters 2 through 4.

seen and heard and understood by them as the One He was and is.
(*CD* IV/2, p. 134)

Noetically, the emphasis is on the resurrection, but ontologically the incarnation is the foundation. Barth connects all these elements within his Christology, as he operates with what I will define as a "three-step scheme": the divine election of grace (prior to time), the historical fulfillment of this divine election in Jesus Christ, and the revelation of it in the resurrection and ascension of Jesus Christ.[8]

But can the resurrection really become reduced to being "nothing more" than a revelation of what has already happened in the incarnation?[9] No! In the above description the resurrection is to be interpreted as prolongation of the incarnation. But my former description of Barth's understanding of the connection between the resurrection and the incarnation does not give the whole picture of how Barth interrelates these two. The second half has yet to come, which claims that something new really has happened in the resurrection. It is a new act, which not only confirms the latter, but also leads the latter to its climax.

> We have to emphasise that in relation to the happening of the cross it [the resurrection] is an *autonomous, new act* of God. It is not, therefore, the noetic converse of it; nor is it merely the revelation and declaration of its positive significance and relevance. It is this, as we have seen. And obviously it is in fact related to that first event. But in spite of this it is distinguished from it as an event of *a particular character*. It is not enclosed in it, but follows on it as *a different happening*. On the other hand, it is not a light which makes that first happening a meaningless shadow. The *theologia resurrectionis* does not absorb the *theologia crucis,* nor *vice versa*. The event of Easter in its indissoluble connexion with the event of the cross is an event which has its own content and form. (*CD* IV/1, p. 304; my emphasis)

8. See *CD* IV/2, p. 118.

9. According to Pannenberg the answer is yes: "Also, according to Karl Barth, Jesus' resurrection is not a completely new event with its own decisive importance, but still only the 'revelation' of Jesus' history consummated on the cross." Wolfhart Pannenberg, *Jesus — God and Man,* 2nd ed., trans. Lewis L. Wilkins and Duane A. Priebe (London: SCM Press, 2002), p. 110.

Death has, so to speak, been broken twice. *First,* it has been broken in Jesus' willingness to obey his Father and to take on the judgment of death, which was fulfilled at the cross. The power of death is broken in and through death. *Second,* it has been broken in the Father's resurrection of Jesus, who really was dead and buried. God has in "the resurrection of Jesus Christ from the dead confronted His being in death, that is, His non-being as the One who was crucified, dead, buried and destroyed, as the One who had been and had ceased to be" (*CD* IV/1, p. 305). The being in death is described here as the non-being of the one who was crucified, dead, buried, and destroyed. Even in death, the death of Jesus is determined by his willingness to bow his head under death (self-sacrifice). Again, a clear connection between the life, death, and resurrection of Jesus Christ is established. This means that the awakening of Jesus Christ can be claimed to be both an act in extension of Jesus' own act, and an act of God that is new and autonomous. The self-sacrifice of Jesus is verified as a God-willed act, but the resurrection is more than "just" a verification. In the resurrection the saving significance of the life and death of Jesus is expressed in a way that it could not have been in the acts of Jesus alone.[10] If this were the case, the death of Jesus could not have included Jesus' despair over death. I will use the following quote to sum up the formal relational character of the crucifixion and the resurrection:

> A *theologia gloriae,* the magnifying of what Jesus Christ has received for us in His resurrection, of what He is for us as the risen One, can have no meaning unless it includes within itself a *theologia crucis,* the magnifying of what He has done for us in His death, of what He is for us as the Crucified. But an abstract *theologia crucis* cannot

---

10. "His [Jesus'] raising, His resurrection, His new life, confirmed His death. It was God's answer to it, and to that extent its revelation and declaration. But as God's answer to it, it was distinct from it. It was God's acknowledgment of Jesus Christ, of His life and death. As a free act of divine grace, it had formally the character of an act of justice on the part of God the Father in His relation to Jesus Christ as His Son, just as the obedience of the Son even to the death of the cross, as a free act of love, had formally the character of an act of justice of the Son in His relation to God the Father. . . . It was a second act of justice after the first to the extent that it was the divine approval and acknowledgment of the obedience given by Jesus Christ, the acceptance of His sacrifice, the proclamation and bringing into force of the consequences, the saving consequences, of His action and passion in our place" (*CD* IV/1, p. 305).

have any meaning either. We cannot properly magnify the passion and death of Jesus Christ unless this magnifying includes within itself the *theologia gloriae* — the magnifying of the One who in His resurrection is the recipient of our right and life, the One who has risen again from the dead for us. (*CD* IV/1, pp. 557-58)

CHAPTER 13

Discussion

The Need for an "Earthly" Jesus

Barth demonstrates no systematic theological interest in the search for the historical Jesus. This lack of interest is partly grounded in the character of the sources and partly anchored in the inherent logic of the basic claim: that Jesus is Christ.[1] We have earlier noted that Barth warns against a misrecognition of genre. The Bible is not to be read as a historical textbook. The Bible is a narrative that expresses the community's faith in the proclamation of Jesus as Christ. The connections between the life and the

---

1. I here agree with Ford, who states: "He [Barth] never denies that the Gospels refer to historical events, but he does deny that critical investigation of the events should be coordinated with exegesis of the biblical text in order to arrive at the text's meaning. The meaning of the text and the meaning of an account of events reconstructed by an historian are not systematically related, and attempts to combine them will only yield a third account." David F. Ford, *Barth and God's Story: Biblical Narrative and the Theological Method of Karl Barth in the Church Dogmatics* (Frankfurt am Main: Peter Lang Verlag, 1981), p. 52. Barth's rejection of a systematic theological interest in the search for the historical Jesus is rooted in the claim that God not only is the precondition of history, but that it is this God who is revealed in Christ. Thus, a distinction must be made between a strict historical approach to the revelation in Jesus Christ, which due to the noted precondition is unable to describe Christ as Christ, and the actual historical context of this revelation. See also Kjetil Hafstad, "Åbenbaringen — den umulige mulighet for fornuften. Karl Barths løsningsforsøk" [Revelation — the impossible possibility according to reason. The attempt of Karl Barth to solve the problem], *Norsk Teologisk Tidsskrift* 88, no. 2 (1987): 74.

death of Jesus are established with the help of a literary approach to the biblical text (including an awareness of the function of the text), and not through a search for a historical core in the description of Jesus' life and death. The biblical text consists of an intertwining of different traditions. It is therefore impossible to clearly separate Jesus' own self-understanding, the disciples' interpretation of Jesus prior to and after his death, and the first Christian communities' interpretation of Jesus in the light of their own situation.

In the case of Barth, I think it would be fair to say that not only does the life of Jesus — as it is narrated in the various texts within the New Testament — inform us about the content of the cross, but the cross also fills out the life of Jesus. The life of Jesus cannot be fully perceived without taking its end into account. In both cases, the cross is seen as the climax of Jesus' life. Thus, the life of Jesus does not just serve as the necessary precondition for his death (as Prenter claims was the case in Barth's theology). Rather, both the life and the death of Jesus must be seen in their internal connection to the resurrection and ascension of Jesus Christ.[2]

Barth has, as already shown, established the connection between the life and the death of Jesus by underlining the proclamation of the kingdom of God. It is this personalized proclamation of the coming of God's kingdom that leads to Jesus' death. His death is thereby the final confirmation of his message about the non-violent structure of God's kingdom. Thus, the life of Jesus is of theological importance. But this positive approach to the life of Jesus should not in itself be equated with a positive approach to the search for a historical Jesus behind the text. To equate the Christology from below with the search for the historical Jesus is one of the most common mistakes in recent Christology. If a Christology from below implies that Christology is equated with the historical search for the man Jesus of Nazareth, Barth's Christology cannot, for sure, be described as such. But such a point of view would from Barth's perspective be stuck in historical materialism. Barth's way of operating with a Christology from below is

---

2. Again, I agree with Ford, who states: "The unity that Barth proposes is held together by the central character, Jesus Christ, and the plot of his life. In generalising this man's story (to embrace not only the O.T. but also the rest of history before and since) the resurrection plays the vital role. . . . The way C.D. IV.1 sums up that role is as 'the verdict of the Father,' and this can be clarified with the help of Stern's concept of the 'realism of assessment'" (Ford, *Barth and God's Story*, p. 52).

much closer to what Hans Frei, inspired by literary criticism (especially Erich Auerbach), has described as realistic narrative.[3] The basis of the search for a Christology from below is then the story of Jesus.

Barth's Christology from below consists in a search for the "earthly Jesus," rather than in a search for the historical Jesus.[4] The "earthly Jesus" is in itself a theological construction in which, in the shape of a narrative, the first Christian communities give witness to their Christian faith: that Jesus is Christ. In contrast to the search for the historical Jesus, the search for the "earthly Jesus" does not intend to find a basis outside the story through which its faith-claim can be defended (what Frei defines as the text's ostensive reference).[5] Thus, the search for the "earthly Jesus" differs from the search for the historical Jesus in its unapologetic exercise. The question of truth is not equated with the question of historical authenticity. The search for the earthly Jesus regards the biblical text as a narrative unit that reflects the first communities' belief in Christ. The climax of the text is the resurrection and ascension, for which reason this must be the key to the interpretation of the whole story. The approach of narrative realism in the works of the late Frei is combined with an increasing awareness of the function of the text then and now.[6] The search for the "earthly Jesus" then includes an investigation of how the first Christian communities interpreted the story, and why they told it as they did.

The arguments for the replacement of a search for the historical Jesus

---

3. See Hans W. Frei, *The Eclipse of Biblical Narrative: A Study in Eighteenth and Nineteenth Century Hermeneutics* (New Haven: Yale University Press, 1974), pp. 1-16; David Ford, "Barth's Interpretation of the Bible," in *Karl Barth: Studies of His Theological Method*, ed. S. W. Sykes (Oxford: Clarendon Press, 1979), pp. 76-87.

4. I have borrowed the distinction between the earthly and the historical Jesus from the Danish New Testament scholar Geert Hallbäck. See Geert Hallbäck, "Den historiske Jesus som teologisk projekt — en kritisk betragtning" [The historical Jesus as a theological project — a critical view], in *Den historiske Jesus og hans betydning* [The implications and consequences of the historical Jesus], ed. Troels Engberg-Pedersen (Copenhagen: Gyldendal, 1998), p. 166.

5. Frei, *The Eclipse of Biblical Narrative*, p. 12.

6. The late Frei combined the insight of literary criticism with the social anthropological emphasis on the communities' use of a text, which in the case of the Bible means the Christian church. See Hans W. Frei, *Types of Christian Theology*, ed. George Hunsinger and William C. Placher (New Haven: Yale University Press, 1992), pp. 8-18; Hans W. Frei, *Theology and Narrative: Selected Essays*, ed. George Hunsinger and William C. Placher (New York: Oxford University Press, 1993), pp. 17-18.

with a search for the "earthly Jesus" have so far been in line with the insights of literary criticism. However, Ford notices correctly that Barth's final argument on this matter is purely theological. The final and ultimate reason why the historical gap between the reader and the Bible is not identified as the major hermeneutical problem is that the main story (the story of Jesus Christ) refers to a living person, who is risen and alive.[7] The ostensive reference is then not to a person, there and then, but to a living person here and now, "who is in a position to confirm their message."[8]

In short: the search for an "earthly" Jesus would from Barth's perspective be viewed as a more promising project than the search for the historical Jesus. My emphasis on the search for an "earthly" Jesus is an attempt to qualify how, within Barth's theology, it is possible to claim that Jesus can only be understood as Christ in and through the resurrection and ascension, without thereby neglecting the importance of the life and death of Jesus Christ. In Barth's own terminology, this could be described as a way through which Christology is explored in an ongoing dialectic between a Christology from above and a Christology from below. Barth's Christology is worked out within the overall framework of a Christology from above, without having the Christology from below diminished to a Christological appendix. In fact, it is only through the story of Jesus that the Christology from above gains its content.

7. Ford, "Barth's Interpretation of the Bible," pp. 70-76.

8. See Ford, *Barth and God's Story*, p. 52; Ford is here working along the line of Frei, who in his book *The Identity of Jesus Christ* states that one should ask: "Who is Jesus Christ?" rather than "How is Christ present?" or "How can we believe in his presence?" The focus should not be placed on the individual's belief or disbelief (which would turn hermeneutics into an apologetic exercise), but instead it should be placed on the presence of Christ as it is witnessed in the Bible. In his introduction Frei states: "The governing conviction in this essay is that in Jesus Christ identity and presence are so completely one that they are given to us together: We cannot know *who* he is without having him present. But I also want to suggest that if we begin with the often nagging and worrisome questions of *how* Christ is present to us and *how* we can believe in his presence, we shall get nowhere at all. It is far more important and fruitful to ask first, *Who* is Jesus Christ?" Hans W. Frei, *The Identity of Jesus Christ: The Hermeneutical Bases of Dogmatic Theology* (Philadelphia: Fortress Press, 1975), p. 4.

The Framework for a Christology from Below:
Barth and Pannenberg

In his 1964 book *Grundzüge der Christologie*, Wolfhart Pannenberg states that Christology must start from below, from the historical person Jesus of Nazareth.[9] Only through the history of Jesus of Nazareth can theology gain any knowledge of Christ. In opposition to dialectical theology Pannenberg states that any Christology is faced with an important choice: Does it want to start with the *kerygma* of the first Christian communities or with Jesus himself?[10] Following Pannenberg the choice is not really a choice, since it is only the latter that enables us to obtain any real knowledge of this particular man, Jesus of Nazareth — who, in continuity with the first Christians, the church confesses to be Christ. It is only in and through a historical analysis of the life of Jesus of Nazareth that we can gain access to the Christological titles (and thereby also to the God-attributes).[11] Thus a Christology should not start with the idea of the incarnation, but rather with a historical investigation of the person Jesus of Nazareth.

Barth and the young Pannenberg thus share a strong Christological accent in their approach to the doctrine of God, but where Barth can only operate with a Christology from below within the frame of a Christology from above, Pannenberg can only operate with a Christology from above developed out of a Christology from below. Both Barth and Pannenberg understand the revelation of Jesus Christ as God's own self-revelation within history. But where this leads the young Pannenberg to a search for the historical Jesus, this leads Barth to an exploration of the motive behind the actual revelation in history: the eternal love of God toward the human being. The motive of God is known through the narration of the first community's faith in Jesus as Christ (as it is revealed in the Bible). Consequently, Barth's interest is focused on what I have defined as a search for

---

9. "Thus the task of Christology is to establish the true understanding of Jesus' significance from his history, which can be described comprehensively by saying that in this man God is revealed." Wolfhart Pannenberg, *Jesus — God and Man*, 2nd ed., trans. Lewis L. Wilkins and Duane A. Priebe (London: SCM Press, 2002), p. 12.

10. "The question is this: Must Christology begin with Jesus himself or with the kerygma of his community?" (Pannenberg, *Jesus — God and Man*, p. 2).

11. "As Christians we know God only as he has been revealed in and through Jesus. All other talk about God can have, at most, provisional significance" (Pannenberg, *Jesus — God and Man*, p. xxvii).

the "earthly" Jesus. The narrative investigation of the Jesus-portrait in the biblical text serves the same dogmatic purpose as the search for the historical Jesus: namely to fill out the relation between the life and death of Jesus Christ. According to both Pannenberg and Barth, this is first revealed to the human being in the resurrection.

In the work of Pannenberg the connection between history and revelation takes its starting point in the historicity of Jesus' life, death, and resurrection. Pannenberg does not claim that it is possible by a rational investigation of the life, death, and resurrection of Jesus to convince anybody about the truth in the statement that Jesus is Christ. (Pannenberg is not, despite his emphasis on the historical Jesus, stuck within historical materialism.) When the theologian embarks upon the quest of the historical Jesus, this is done with the prior assumption that Jesus is Christ.[12] But Pannenberg claims that the only way the theological assertion — that Jesus is Christ — can obtain content is through a search for the historical Jesus. In this sense Christology must start from below. Further, the history can only be understood as such when it has reached its end. The "only" problem with Pannenberg's eschatological understanding of history is, of course, that history has not yet reached its end. But according to Pannenberg the end of history has already been anticipated in the resurrection of Jesus Christ. Therefore, on the one hand, the resurrection is necessary to understand history as such. This claim can first be finally verified at the very end of history. At the end of history it will be shown whether what is claimed to be the anticipation of the end of history really *is* the end. Thus Pannenberg will claim that he avoids decisionism, as he operates with a hypothesis in contrast to a claim of faith. On the other hand, the resurrection cannot be understood in and of itself. As an act in history it must be understood with the help of both the expectation of what is to come and the knowledge of what has already been. The latter is in the case of the resurrection expressed in the search for the historical Jesus, as the resurrection is God's verification of Jesus' proclamation: that in him the kingdom of God has arrived. In short: the revelation is revealed in and through history. For Pannenberg this implies that Christology must start from below.

---

12. That Jesus is Christ is based on the faith and the confession. But what it means that Jesus is Christ is derived from the knowledge we can obtain about the historical person Jesus of Nazareth. See Pannenberg, *Jesus — God and Man*, pp. 1-12.

Where Pannenberg in his early work operates with a strong differentiation between a Christology from above and a Christology from below, he wants to overcome this distinction in his later works.[13] Instead he claims that there are three different ways of approaching Christology (headings mine):[14]

(1) *Theological approach.* This type of Christology starts with doctrines of God that are developed independently of Christology. Christology is worked out from the idea of the incarnation; the pre-Christian understanding of God is determining the perception of the revelation of God in Christ. Thus the history of Jesus is not determining for the essence of God. God is from start to end perceived as a God above history, as an a-historical God. The precondition for this model is that a natural revelation of God is possible. Jesus' proclamation of God is not special in the sense that it is the only way to grasp the identity of the Christian God, nor is it a necessary reference in the sense that it is the touchstone for all other references to God. What Jesus proclaims can also be heard and seen elsewhere, if one only had the ability to hear and see. This model's defect is that Christology can very easily be turned into an appendix that is not essential to the essence of God. Christology becomes external to the being of God. And how does this connect with the Christian claim that it is first in Christ that God restores his fellowship with human beings? This type of Christology tends to be stuck in pre-Christian perceptions of God as for example immutable (Greek) or omnipotent (Jewish). A variation of this model can be found in a traditional dogmatic where the relation between incarnation and Christology is worked out within a Trinitarian frame that urges maintaining the a-historical identity of God — in spite of the historical impact of the incarnation. Thus the historical fulfillment of the incarnation (the actual event) seems to be secondary for the being of God.

13. The following is based on Wolfhart Pannenberg, "Christologie und Theologie" and "Die Subjektivität Gottes und die Trinitätslehre," *Grundfragen Systematischer Theologie. Gesammelte Aufsätze,* Band 2 (Göttingen: Vandenhoeck & Ruprecht, 1980), pp. 129-45, 96-111; Wolfhart Pannenberg, *Problemgeschichte der neueren evangelischen Theologie in Deutschland. Von Schleiermacher bis zu Barth und Tillich* (Göttingen: Vandenhoeck & Ruprecht, 1997).

14. See Pannenberg, "Christologie und Theologie," pp. 129-45.

(2) *Christological approach.* The human being can only gain access to the reality of God through the historical person Jesus of Nazareth. In this person God has revealed himself for human beings. This implies not only that it is only possible to understand who Jesus of Nazareth is when the relation between Jesus and God is taken into account, but also that it is only possible to describe who God is through this particular man. One must take fully into account that the self-revelation of God first took place in Jesus of Nazareth. Thus, the Trinitarian unity between the Father, the Son, and the Holy Spirit cannot be established a-historically, nor can the unity between God and human beings, which is established in Jesus Christ, be perceived as an a-historical event. This emphasis on the actual historical event implies that God cannot be thought of as a God who in eternity prior to history decides to incarnate himself, so that the incarnation is an external repetition of an already-happened internal act in God.

The stated emphasis here on the historical Jesus of Nazareth is not to be equated with the methods of the history of religion — as it presupposes a unity (hypothetically, at least) between the life and acts of Jesus and God. Christology as a topic is from the very outset normative. Any attempt to understand Jesus of Nazareth independently of his eschatological claims, which are rooted in his special relation to God, is doomed to fail.

That we must take into account the special relation between Jesus and God (and vice versa) to understand the identity of Jesus is a statement that not only concerns Jesus but humanity as such. It is the Trinitarian God who is revealing himself in Jesus of Nazareth — whereby the creation also must be looked at from the perspective of the Son. Creation is not a "Christological-free-zone," nor is Christology thinkable without creation. Creation belongs to the very essence of God. The creed illuminates God's ability of self-differentiation; eternity and time not only meet in the incarnation, but the latter is absorbed into the former in the historical revelation of the triune God in Jesus of Nazareth. The life, death, and resurrection of Jesus are a part of God's own movement, a part of his own self-realization. Thus the incarnation cannot be described adequately as God's entering into a foreign country (as Barth does).[15]

---

15. The English version of the *CD* does not clearly demonstrate Barth's position at

(3) *Historical approach.* The third type, in accordance with the Christological approach, states that there is no access to God without Jesus. But the emphasis is strictly focused here on the historical person Jesus of Nazareth. Jesus' relation to God is a secondary question that can only derive from an investigation of the historical Jesus. In fact, the precondition for this approach is that it is (only?) possible to understand who Jesus was without his relation to God. What Jesus proclaims about God must be viewed from his historical and religious context and structures: a Jew living in the Middle East around the years 0-33 CE. Further, if God is only known to us through the words of Jesus Christ, God may not exist outside of these words. The idea of God may then be a part of the historical and social structure that Jesus is part of. Is it then necessary to maintain the word "God" as a part of Jesus' proclamation? Do not the word "God" and the associations this word brings to mind prevent us from hearing the real message of Jesus? Is the task not rather to purify the content of Jesus' message from its embeddedness in two-thousand-year-old ideas of God? If Jesus preached love and understanding, why can we not just restrict ourselves to this message? Typologies that interpret Jesus as a healer, a Stoic, a socialist, or a good humanist all work along these lines. Finally, if Jesus can be understood without God, the result of this option would be that Jesuology replaces Christology, whereby the word "God" (from a Christian perspective) becomes empty.

While option one treats Christology as an appendix to theology, option three treats theology as an appendix to Christology (if not to say: Jesuology).

From the above description it is not hard to see that Pannenberg sympathizes with the second model for doing Christology. Two things are to be noted here. *First,* that Pannenberg's typology includes a critique of his own critique of Barth in 1964. *Second,* that within the second alternative Pannenberg still displays a strong critique of Barth's Christological ap-

---

this point, as it translates the subtitle, "Der Weg des Sohnes Gottes in die Fremde," as "The Way of the Son of God into the Far Country." Not only is "Fremde" inadequately translated with "far" (instead of, for instance, "foreign"), but the word "Country" also implies a kind of national interpretation of "die Fremde," whereby God might be misperceived as our God compared to theirs.

proach. Pannenberg does not state this difference between him and Barth so explicitly in the above-quoted article "Christologie und Theologie," but read together with the article "Die Subjektivität Gottes und die Trinitätslehre," a clear picture arrives. Pannenberg argues that Barth is stuck much deeper in Hegelian soil than he himself was able to see. Barth's theology, despite his loud aversion to such a type of theology, is speculative, as the perception of God is worked out within a paradigm of the sovereign subject and the self-consciousness of the subject. The revelation of God in Jesus Christ is strictly connected with the Trinity, and it is furthermore described as God's own self-revelation. God is thereby both the one who reveals himself, the one who is revealed, and the very event of revelation.[16] The three persons in the Trinity are a unity (in the immanent Trinity) prior to its revelation (in the economic Trinity); it is one absolute subject (God) who has three modes of being (Father, Son, and Holy Spirit). Further, the economic Trinity is rooted in the decision of God to incarnate himself in the person Jesus of Nazareth. Thus, the immanent Trinity (the eternal unity of God prior to creation) is the fundament for the absolute free and sovereign will of God.[17] But Barth's way of interrelating the immanent and the economic Trinity must then, again according to Pannenberg, imply that there is an internal hierarchy within the immanent Trinity, where the Father is the "Author of His other modes of being" (*CD* I/1, p. 393).[18] The logic behind this statement is that the inner-Trinitarian unity is rooted in the will of the Father to be in unity with

16. See *CD* I/1, p. 296: "*God* reveals Himself. He reveals Himself *through Himself*. He reveals *Himself*." See also Pannenberg, "Die Subjektivität Gottes und die Trinitätslehre," p. 98.

17. "Immanent Trinity is the foundation for Barth's concept of the autonomy of God in His revelation" (trans. Michael Waltemathe). Pannenberg, "Die Subjektivität Gottes und die Trinitätslehre," p. 98.

18. Pannenberg states: "If — indeed — the teaching of Trinity according to Barth shall represent the unabolishable subjectivity of God in His revelation, then God's self as being the Lord has to be the 'root' of the Trinity. Thus the three modes of being have to be understood as moments of self-unfolding of this very self. And as such it can hardly be avoided — taking into account the emphasis on the equality of the divineness of the three modes of being — that the father is perceived as the primary form of the godly self and as the 'origin of the forms of His other ways of being'" (trans. Michael Waltemathe). Pannenberg, "Die Subjektivität Gottes und die Trinitätslehre," p. 100. See also Christoph Schwöbel, "Trinitätslehre als Rahmentheorie des christlichen Glaubens. Vier Thesen zur Bedeutung der Trinität in der christlichen Dogmatik," *Zeitschrift für Dialektische Theologie* 14, no. 2 (1998): 148-49.

the Son and the Holy Spirit. Thus, the unity of the Trinitarian God is worked out within the framework of "a single thinking and willing I."[19]

In short: Barth's conception of the Trinity as three modes of being leaves no place for a dynamic conception of God's inner being. Thus, the dynamic of God, the ability of God to change, has been externalized. Following Barth's differentiation between the immanent and the economic Trinity, and the supremacy of the Father within the immanent Trinity, God cannot take the suffering of Jesus Christ on the cross up into his own inner-Trinitarian being. Therefore Barth does not, despite his intentions, manage to fulfill his own task: to fully take into account the radical thought that the life of Jesus is a part of God's own history (that is, letting it be determinative for God's own being).

A question that can serve to illustrate the difference between the Trinitarian constructions of Barth and Pannenberg is: Does the suffering of Jesus really become an essential part of the being of God, or is it supplementary?[20] If the former is the case, God must be able to change — not "only" in his economic but also in his immanent Trinity. Thus, the "function" of the Trinity cannot be to secure the basis for an eternal and immutable God; instead it serves as an explanation of how God, due to his inner Trinitarian being, is able to actualize himself in and through the history of Jesus of Nazareth. The history of Jesus is the history of God himself.[21] With regard to the issue of suffering, this implies that God really suffers in his own inner being; there is no God beyond the God who suffers. Thus, God can

19. See Pannenberg, *Problemgeschichte der neueren evangelischen Theologie in Deutschland,* p. 250.

20. See Pannenberg, "Christologie und Theologie," p. 139. The suffering of Jesus Christ cannot, according to both Pannenberg and Barth, be viewed as a self-willed act of *kenosis.* The suffering of God is not in contradiction of his almightiness and omnipotence. Pannenberg describes the suffering of Jesus Christ as a Christian qualification of the Jewish emphasis on the omnipotence of God, whereas Barth states that the *passio dei* is to be interpreted within the eternal will of God *(actio dei).* The suffering of Jesus belongs then to the eternal covenant between God and human beings. But where this qualification of the suffering of Christ by Pannenberg is based on the idea of God's self-actualization, Barth roots it in the distinction between the immanent and the economic Trinity. Barth hereby places the actual suffering of Jesus Christ within the economic Trinity, whereby he wants to avoid having it become a part of the eternal being of God. See also Chapter 11.

21. See Pannenberg, "Christologie und Theologie," p. 137.

change, as God in his incarnation is taking on his own self-actualization in history through the history of Jesus of Nazareth.

To conclude: Barth's use of the differentiation between the immanent and the economic Trinity serves to protect the absolute freedom of God, for which reason God must be immutable. Pannenberg avoids the consequence of immutability due to his emphasis on the history of Jesus Christ. The history of Jesus Christ is the history of God. God can suffer in his most inner being, as the subjectivity of God first is the result of the mutual relations between the three persons of the Trinity, and not (as by Barth) the condition for the Trinitarian relations.[22]

Critical Remarks: Development of and within God?

The main problem with Barth's interpretation of the atonement is that it does not give room for any real development within God himself. God is the precondition for history, which according to Barth implies that he cannot undergo any changes during his interaction with history. The way Barth uses and describes the eternal being of God entails that God is a God who does not change in and through his interaction with the world. God remains the same before, during, and after the incarnation. If Jesus really is Christ, and if Christ is the revelation of the eternal God's graceful election of the human being prior to time and creation, Christ has to be the revelation of the eternal being of God. The eternal being of God cannot include changes that are rooted in a mutual interaction between God and the world. Instead, the change that happens in the incarnation serves to describe the eternal being of God.

The essence of God has therefore not been changed in the incarnation. When the incarnation expresses the eternal will of God, and when the act of the atonement is constituted by the incarnation, there seems to be no

22. Barth's critique of Pannenberg's position would be similar to his critique of Hegel, namely, that God might lose his freedom and thereby perish within history. From Barth's point of view this is the inevitable result of Hegel's speculative approach to the Trinity. Whether this is a correct objection, I will not discuss here. Here I will just draw attention to Pannenberg's rebuttal of such an objection by stating that Hegel avoided this pitfall by differentiating between an inner and external necessity, where the former is identical with the freedom of God. See Pannenberg, *Problemgeschichte der neueren evangelischen Theologie in Deutschland*, p. 259.

room for an externally based change within the being of God. According to Barth's kind of logic this would question the sovereignty of God. In short: the idea of God's immutability is combined with the often-mentioned idea of God's radical freedom. To claim that God is immutable is another way of stating that God is subjected to nothing except his own radically free will. In the words of Barth, the argument goes as following:

> If we shake off the spell, and try to think of the Godhead of God in biblical rather than pagan terms, we shall have to reckon, not with a mutability of God, but with the kind of *immutability*, which does not prevent Him from humbling Himself and therefore doing what he willed to do and actually did do in Jesus Christ, i.e., electing and determining in Jesus Christ to exist in divine and human essence in the one Son of God and Son of Man, and therefore to address His divine essence to His human, to direct it to it. Even in the constancy (or, as we may calmly say, the *immutability*) of His divine essence He does this and can do it (new and surprising and alien though it may be to human eyes blinded only by their own pride) not only without violation but in supreme exercise and affirmation of His divine essence. It is *not* that it is part of His divine essence, and therefore *necessary*, to become and be the God of man, Himself man. That He wills to be and becomes and is this God, and as such man, takes place in His freedom. It is His own decree and act. . . . On the other hand, it is indeed a part of the divine essence to be free for this decree and its execution, to be able to elect and determine itself in this form. (*CD* IV/2, p. 85; my emphasis)

But is this way of describing the dialectic between the immutability and the mutability of God satisfactory? Barth does not develop this distinction in a way that leaves space open for a real mutual interaction between God and the world, the world and God. The essence of God remains the same, but how can it do so if God's being really is a being in act? Must the being of God then not also be influenced by the acts of God? If it is the acts that constitute the being of God, must God's being then not be a being in an ongoing development (at least potentially)? The result of Barth's rejection of any real development within the being of God is that God seems at places in the *CD* to be in danger of becoming an ideal God.[23]

23. It is my claim that Barth, despite his Christocentric approach, at places is in dan-

If God is left unchanged by the incarnation, if it is only the situation between God and the human being that is changed, then God is unable to absorb the experience of the actual encounter with the world within the world. If God cannot comprehend this actual encounter, God cannot change. This a-historical understanding of God serves to avoid a Hegelian weakness (where God can be claimed to be fully absorbed by history), but it risks leaving us with a God who is unable to absorb his own history.

The passion of God's love seems to disappear into a concept of ideal love. The result is that the incarnation — willingly or not — is hereby reduced to an outpouring of God's eternal essence in time. The act of the incarnation does not change God, nor do the life and death of Jesus Christ. The distinction between an essentialistic and an actualistic understanding of God's essence, which plays a fundamental role in McCormack's analysis of Barth (see Chapter 7), seems from this perspective not to make any major difference at all, as the intention of the incarnation can be traced back to God's original essence (whether it be in the form of an original being or an original will).[24] Nothing new then has really happened to God in the incarnation. The world seems hereby to be nothing more than the stage on which God can perform his act. God seems thereby to be turned into a kind of an ideal — and thereby speculative — principle.

The speculative approach in Barth's theology consists in the fact that all that happens in the interaction between God and the world is described as an outpouring of the original will of God. The Platonic inspiration of

ger of idealizing God. The speculation arises through the emphasis on God's freedom and a speculative distinction between what God actually did, and what he could have done instead. One could define this as a theological version of contra-factual thinking. Thus it is not fully adequate to describe the difference between Barth and Schleiermacher on the doctrine of God as a difference between a realistic and an idealistic conception of God, where the main issue is if the starting point for the elaboration of the doctrine of God is "the Christian experience of redemption" or "the Self-revelation of God in Jesus Christ" as Bruce L. McCormack does. The latter is no guarantee of avoiding the roots of idealism — at least not when it is combined with an abstract perception of the freedom of God. See Bruce L. McCormack, "Not a Possible God but the God Who Is: Observations on Friedrich Schleiermacher's Doctrine of God," in *The Reality of Faith in Theology: Studies on Karl Barth. Princeton-Kampen Consultation 2005*, ed. Bruce McCormack and Gerrit Neven (Bern: Peter Lang, 2007), pp. 111-39.

24. See for example Bruce L. McCormack, "Grace and Being: The Role of God's Gracious Election in Karl Barth's Theological Ontology," in *The Cambridge Companion to Karl Barth*, ed. John Webster (Cambridge: Cambridge University Press, 2000), p. 98.

the early Barth — as expressed in his use of the *Ursprungsgedanke* — is still very much at play here.[25] But how can God then be a personal God in relation? To be in relation means to be able to relate, which again means to be able to interact mutually. Thus, the incarnation must also have an everlasting impact on God himself. In short: Barth is unable to allow space for any real mutuality between God and the world due to the way in which he combines his Christology from above with the *Ursprungsgedanke*. The actual experience of Jesus Christ is not absorbed into the being of God.[26] God does not change due to the experiences of Jesus Christ.

I find that Barth is operating with too strict a distinction between the internal and the external sides of God, between *deus per se* and *deus pro nobis*.[27] In fact, I would argue that *deus per se* does not exist independently

25. For a description of the early Barth's use of Platonism and neo-Kantianism see Michael Beintker, *Die Dialektik in der "dialektischen Theologie" Karl Barths. Studien zur Entwicklung der Barthschen Theologie und zur Vorgeschichte der "Kirchliche Dogmatik"* (München: Chr. Kaiser Verlag, 1987), pp. 222-30 and Christof Gestrich, *Neuzeitliches Denken und die Spaltung der dialektischen Theologie. Zur Frage der natürlichen Theologie* (Tübingen: J. C. B. Mohr [Paul Siebeck], 1977), p. 42. A thorough analysis of Barth's neo-Kantian heritage can be found in Johann F. Lohmann, *Karl Barth und der Neukantianismus: Die Rezeption des Neukantianismus im Römerbrief und ihre Bedeutung für die weitere Ausarbeitung der Theologie Karl Barth* (Berlin: De Gruyter, 1995); Simon Fisher, *Revelatory Positivism? Barth's Earliest Theology and the Marburg School* (Oxford: Oxford University Press, 1998).

26. Falk Wagner sees very clearly that it is the self-differentiation of God that is the hermeneutic key to understand the connection between Christology and soteriology as it is worked out in *CD* IV. On the one hand Wagner is unable to give Barth any real credit for this, as he basically reads God's self-differentiation as an assault on the human being's autonomy (a lack of acceptance of the otherness of the human being). On the other hand, Wagner sees clearly that Barth has problems with letting God really absorb the experience of the human being. According to Wagner the problem is that Barth is only able to allow for a weak otherness *(schwachem anderen — das innertrinitarische andere)* in God's self-differentiation. Wagner opts for God also being able to take a strong otherness *(starken anderen — das andere als solches)* into account in his self-differentiation. See Falk Wagner, "Theologische Gleichschaltung. Zur Christologie bei Karl Barth," in *Die Realisierung der Freiheit. Beiträge zur Kritik der Theologie Karl Barths*, ed. Trutz Rendtorff and Falk Wagner (Gütersloh: Gütersloher Verlagshaus Gerd Mohn, 1975), p. 20.

27. Wagner sees correctly that it is not unproblematic that Barth always wants to refer the actual acts of God back to God's eternal decisions and thereby to God's eternal freedom. We know that the reason Barth does this is that he wants to emphasize the free grace of God. But with Wagner we learn to see that the problem, which occurs when the

of *deus pro nobis*. My claim is that this implies that the act of atonement affects not only the being of human beings but also the being of God.

I hope that my reading of Barth, including this final chapter of discussion, has served as a constructive reading in which new insights have been explored. I have aimed in this exercise to be faithful to the overall patterns of thinking in Barth's theology, without restricting myself to giving a chapter-by-chapter summary of the *CD*. My aim has not been to reproduce Barth's theology, either historically (a generic historical reading) or actually (an attempt to express things exactly as Barth did). Rather, I have tried to show how vital a dialogue partner Barth is for modern theology.

---

deus pro nobis can only come out of the *deus per se*, is that all that happens for the human being happens according to the eternal plan of God. This implies on the one hand that God cannot be influenced by the actual outcome of his acts, and on the other hand that experience is in danger of being denied any theological relevance. By experience I am not only thinking of the human being's experience of God, but also of God's experience of the human being. See Wagner, "Theologische Gleichschaltung. Zur Christologie bei Karl Barth," p. 19. However, as I have demonstrated in Chapter 4, it is possible to interpret Barth in a way that is more open to the human being's experience of God. Here I just want to take *ad notam* what risks are involved in Barth's emphasis on the freedom of God, if this is interpreted as an unlimited freedom: (1) God is not bound by his own decisions, (2) God does not have the ability to learn by his experience, and (3) God — for the sake of God (and not the human being) — is described as immutable.

Acknowledgments

So many people — colleagues, friends, and students — are directly and indirectly a part of this book. I am grateful to them all — in spite of the fact that I am unable to mention all of them by name in this brief passage. My gratitude implies all the stimulating and fruitful theological discussions I have had with my colleagues and students, both within the university and the church.

To write a book is quite a time-consuming project. I wish therefore to express my gratitude to the Dean at the Centre for Theology and Religious Education Loegumkloster, Professor Eberhard Harbsmeier, who granted me a sabbatical leave to work on the book. Thanks also to my colleagues at the Centre who took over my teaching responsibilities during that time. The generous support from the Centre also included a financial subvention, for which I am truly grateful.

I also wish to express my thanks to Princeton Theological Seminary for the possibility of studying two semesters as a Visiting Doctoral Student back in 1999. My discussions and talks with such prominent American Barth scholars as George Hunsinger, Bruce L. McCormack, William Stacy Johnson, and Daniel L. Migliore have been both inspiring and thought-provoking for the whole process of writing this book. I would also like to thank Professor Cynthia L. Rigby at Austin Theological Seminary for being an encouraging voice in my attempt to establish the basis for a constructive reading of the *Church Dogmatics*. And as all know, it is fellow students as well as professors who help you not only to develop your ideas but also to feel at home in a foreign setting. I look back at my time in Princeton with gratitude.

I would also like to thank my old Theological Faculty at the University of Aarhus, especially Professor Niels Henrik Gregersen for his support, advice, and critique throughout the writing of my book. I also want to express my thanks to Professor Anna Marie Aagaard and Professor Peter Widmann, both of whom have been very generous in using their time to read, comment on, and discuss former stages of the book with me.

Helle D. Kjeldsen, Librarian at the Center for Theology and Religious Education Løgumkloster, has been of tremendous help in my search for literature abroad. The Director of the Karl Barth Archive in Basel, Hans-Anton Drewes, was likewise very helpful when questions occurred in my research for the book. I received generous access to Barth's lectures on anthropology from 1943/44 — before they were published on CD-ROM in 2005 *(Unveröffentlichte Texte zur Kirchlichen Dogmatik).*

Michael Waltemathe, Ruhr-Universität, Bochum, has translated the quoted passages from the books of Thies Gundlach, Eberhard Jüngel, Burghard Krause, Regin Prenter, and Wolfhart Pannenberg — for which I am truly grateful. I am, of course, responsible for the final version of these translations.

Lady Margaret Professor of Divinity at Oxford University, George Pattison, and Assistant Professor at University College South, Vinnie Lerche Christensen, have kindly taken on the duty of proofreading the manuscript with respect to the English language. Anyone who has taken on that job knows how time-consuming a task it is. Thanks! However, the responsibility for any grammatical lapses and misuses of the English language is of course solely my own.

I must also mention Samuel E. Eerdmans, then Vice President of Sales and Marketing at Eerdmans Publishing Company, whom I had the pleasure to meet at the American Academy of Religion conference in San Diego in 2007. His approach to and confidence in my project was a big encouragement for me. Further, I want to thank Eerdmans editors Linda Bieze and Jennifer Hoffman for their skill and careful work on my book.

The cross on the front and back covers was created by the internationally known Danish artist Peter Brandes, whom I have had the privilege of meeting and discussing Christianity and art with. He has very graciously allowed me to use his art as cover photos.

Finally, but not least, I wish to thank my wife Inge Lindhardt Mikkelsen, who herself is a theologian and parish minister. She has encouraged me throughout the process of writing and editing this book. But my gratitude is deeper than that — it is really an appreciation of her choosing to live her life with me. The book is dedicated to her.

Bibliography

Balthasar, Hans Urs von. *The Theology of Karl Barth*. New York: Anchor Books, 1972.

Barth, Karl. *Church Dogmatics. The Doctrine of the Word of God*, vol. I, part 1, 2nd ed. Translated by G. W. Bromiley. Edited by G. W. Bromiley and T. F. Torrance. Edinburgh: T. & T. Clark, 1975.

———. *Church Dogmatics. The Doctrine of the Word of God*, vol. I, part 2. Translated by G. T. Thomson and Harold Knight. Edited by G. W. Bromiley and T. F. Torrance. Edinburgh: T. & T. Clark, 1956.

———. *Church Dogmatics. The Doctrine of God*, vol. II, part 1. Translated by T. H. L. Parker, W. B. Johnston, Harold Knight, and J. L. M. Haire. Edited by G. W. Bromiley and T. F. Torrance. Edinburgh: T. & T. Clark, 1957.

———. *Church Dogmatics. The Doctrine of God*, vol. II, part 2. Translated by G. W. Bromiley, J. C. Campbell, Iain Wilson, J. Strathearn McNab, Harold Knight, and R. A. Stewart. Edited by G. W. Bromiley and T. F. Torrance. Edinburgh: T. & T. Clark, 1957.

———. *Church Dogmatics. The Doctrine of Creation*, vol. III, part 1. Translated by J. W. Edwards, O. Bussey, and H. Knight. Edited by G. W. Bromiley and T. F. Torrance. Edinburgh: T. & T. Clark, 1958.

———. *Church Dogmatics. The Doctrine of Creation*, vol. III, part 2. Translated by H. Knight, G. W. Bromiley, J. K. S. Reid, and R. H. Fuller. Edited by G. W. Bromiley and T. F. Torrance. Edinburgh: T. & T. Clark, 1960.

———. *Church Dogmatics. The Doctrine of Creation*, vol. III, part 3. Translated by G. W. Bromiley and R. J. Ehrlich. Edited by G. W. Bromiley and T. F. Torrance. Edinburgh: T. & T. Clark, 1960.

———. *Church Dogmatics. The Doctrine of Creation*, vol. III, part 4. Translated by

A. T. Mackay, T. H. L. Parker, H. Knight, H. A. Kennedy, and J. Marks. Edited by G. W. Bromiley and T. F. Torrance. Edinburgh: T. & T. Clark, 1961.

—————. *Church Dogmatics. The Doctrine of Reconciliation*, vol. IV, part 1. Translated by G. W. Bromiley. Edited by G. W. Bromiley and T. F. Torrance. Edinburgh: T. & T. Clark, 1956.

—————. *Church Dogmatics. The Doctrine of Reconciliation*, vol. IV, part 2. Translated by G. W. Bromiley. Edited by G. W. Bromiley and T. F. Torrance. Edinburgh: T. & T. Clark, 1958.

—————. *Church Dogmatics. The Doctrine of Reconciliation*, vol. IV, part 3.1. Translated by G. W. Bromiley. Edited by G. W. Bromiley and T. F. Torrance. Edinburgh: T. & T. Clark, 1961.

—————. *Church Dogmatics. The Doctrine of Reconciliation*, vol. IV, part 3.2. Translated by G. W. Bromiley. Edited by G. W. Bromiley and T. F. Torrance. Edinburgh: T. & T. Clark, 1962.

—————. *Die Kirchliche Dogmatik. Die Lehre vom Wort Gottes. Prolegomena zur Kirchlichen Dogmatik*, Band I, Teil 1. Zollikon-Zürich: Evangelischer Verlag A.G., 1932.

—————. *Die Kirchliche Dogmatik. Die Lehre vom Wort Gottes. Prolegomena zur Kirchlichen Dogmatik*, Band I, Teil 2. Zollikon-Zürich: Evangelischer Verlag A.G., 1938.

—————. *Die Kirchliche Dogmatik. Die Lehre von der Schöpfung*, Band III, Teil 3. Zollikon-Zürich: Evangelischer Verlag A.G., 1950.

—————. *Die Kirchliche Dogmatik. Die Lehre von der Versöhnung*, Band IV, Teil 1. Zollikon-Zürich: Evangelischer Verlag A.G., 1953.

—————. *Die Kirchliche Dogmatik. Die Lehre von der Versöhnung*, Band IV, Teil 2. Zollikon-Zürich: Evangelischer Verlag A.G., 1955.

—————. "Das Wort Gottes als Aufgabe der Theologie," in *Das Wort Gottes und die Theologie. Gesammelte Vorträge*. München: Chr. Kaiser Verlag, 1925.

—————. "Des Menschen Menschlichkeit," in *Unveröffentlichte Texte zur Kirchlichen Dogmatik. Supplemente zur Karl Barth-Gesamtausgabe 1*, edited by Hans-Anton Drewes, pp. 1084-1109. Zürich: Theologischer Verlag, 2005 (CD-ROM).

—————. "Nein! Antwort an Emil Brunner," in *"Dialektische Theologie" in Scheidung und Bewährung 1933-1936*, edited by Walther Fürst, pp. 208-58. München: Chr. Kaiser Verlag, 1966.

—————. *The Epistle to the Romans*. Translated by Edwyn C. Hoskyns. London: Oxford University Press, 1933.

—————. *The Humanity of God*. Louisville: John Knox Press, 1960.

Becker, Dieter. *Karl Barth und Martin Buber — Denker in dialogischer Nachbarschaft? Zur Bedeutung Martin Bubers für die Anthropologie Karl Barths*. Göttingen: Vandenhoeck & Ruprecht, 1986.

Beintker, Michael. "Kontingenz und Gegenständlichkeit. Zu Bonhoeffers Barth-

Kritik in 'Akt und Sein,'" in *Die Aktualität der Theologie Dietrich Bonhoeffer*, edited by Norbert Müller, pp. 29-54. Halle: Martin-Luther Universität Halle-Wittenberg, 1985.

————. *Die Dialektik in der "dialektischen Theologie" Karl Barths. Studien zur Entwicklung der Barthschen Theologie und zur Vorgeschichte der "Kirchlichen Dogmatik."* München: Chr. Kaiser Verlag, 1987.

Berkouwer, Gerrit C. *The Triumph of Grace in the Theology of Karl Barth.* Grand Rapids: Eerdmans, 1956.

Bonhoeffer, Dietrich. *Act and Being: Transcendental Philosophy and Ontology in Systematic Theology.* Edited by Hans-Richard Reuter and Wayne Whitson Floyd. Translated by Martin H. Rumscheidt. Minneapolis: Fortress Press, 1996.

————. "Antrittsvorlesung: Die Frage nach dem Menschen in der gegenwärtigen Philosophie und Theologie," in *Barcelona, Berlin, Amerika 1928-1931*, edited by Reinhart Staats, Hans Christoph von Hase, Holger Roggelin, and Maathias Wünsche, pp. 357-78. München: Chr. Kaiser Verlag, 1991.

————. *Ethics.* Edited by Ilse Tödt, Heinz Eduard Tödt, Ernst Feil, and Glifford Green. Translated by Reinhard Krauss, Douglas W. Stoot, and Charles C. West. München: Chr. Kaiser Verlag, 2004.

————. *Widerstand und Ergebung. Briefe und Aufzeichnungen aus der Haft.* Edited by Christian Gremmels, Eberhard Bethge, Renate Bethge, and Ilse Tödt. Gütersloh: Chr. Kaiser/Gütersloher Verlagshaus, 1998.

Braaten, Carl E. *No Other Gospel! Christianity Among the World's Religions.* Minneapolis: Fortress Press, 1992.

Bromiley, Geoffrey W. *Introduction to the Theology of Karl Barth.* Edinburgh: T. & T. Clark, 1996.

Brunner, Emil. *Truth as Encounter.* Translated by Amandus W. Loos and David Cairns. Philadelphia: Westminster Press, 1964.

————. *Man in Revolt: A Christian Anthropology.* Translated by Olive Wyon. Philadelphia: Westminster Press, 1947.

Buber, Martin. *I and Thou.* Translated by Ronald Gregor Smith. New York: Scribner Classics, 2000.

————. *Das Dialogische Prinzip.* Gütersloh: Gütersloher Verlagshaus, 2002.

Busch, Eberhard. *Unter dem Bogen des einen Bundes. Karl Barth und die Juden 1933-1945.* Neukirchen-Vluyn: Neukirchener Verlag, 1996.

Calvin, John. *Institutes of the Christian Religion.* Edited by John T. McNeill. Translated by Ford Lewis Battles. Philadelphia: Westminster Press, 1960.

Demson, David E. *Hans Frei and Karl Barth: Different Ways of Reading Scripture.* Grand Rapids: Eerdmans, 1997.

Ebner, Ferdinand. *Das Wort und die geistige Realitäten. Pneumatologische Fragmente.* Wien: Herder-Verlag, 1952.

Egmond, Adrianus van. "Triumph der Wahrheit und Triumph der Gnade. René Girard und Karl Barth über Offenbarung, Religion, Kreuz und Gott," *Zeitschrift für Dialektische Theologie* 12 (1990): 185-205.

Fisher, Simon. *Revelatory Positivism? Barth's Earliest Theology and the Marburg School.* Oxford: Oxford University Press, 1998.

Ford, David F. "Barth's Interpretation of the Bible," in *Karl Barth: Studies of His Theological Method,* edited by S. W. Sykes, pp. 55-87. Oxford: Clarendon Press, 1979.

————. *Barth and God's Story: Biblical Narrative and the Theological Method of Karl Barth in the Church Dogmatics.* Frankfurt am Main: Peter Lang Verlag, 1981.

Frei, Hans W. *The Eclipse of Biblical Narrative: A Study in Eighteenth and Nineteenth Century Hermeneutics.* New Haven: Yale University Press, 1974.

————. *The Identity of Jesus Christ: The Hermeneutical Bases of Dogmatic Theology.* Philadelphia: Fortress Press, 1975.

————. *Types of Christian Theology.* Edited by George Hunsinger and William C. Placher. New Haven: Yale University Press, 1992.

————. *Theology and Narrative: Selected Essays.* Edited by George Hunsinger and William C. Placher. New York: Oxford University Press, 1993.

Frey, Christofer. "Zur theologischen Anthropologie Karl Barths," in *Anthropologie als Thema der Theologie,* edited by Hermann Fischer, pp. 39-69. Göttingen: Vandenhoeck & Ruprecht, 1978.

Gestrich, Christof. *Neuzeitliches Denken und die Spaltung der dialektischen Theologie. Zur Frage der natürlichen Theologie.* Tübingen: J. C. B. Mohr (Paul Siebeck), 1977.

Girard, René. *Violence and the Sacred.* Translated by Patrick Gregory. Baltimore: Johns Hopkins University Press, 1977.

————. *Things Hidden Since the Foundation of the World.* Translated by Stephan Bann and Michael Metteer. Stanford, CA: Stanford University Press, 1987.

————. *Job: The Victim of His People.* Translated by Yvonne Freccero. Stanford, CA: Stanford University Press, 1987.

Grøn, Arne. "Anerkendelsens dialektik og begreb," in *Teologi og modernitet,* edited by Peter Thyssen and Anders Moe Rasmussen, pp. 50-65. Aarhus: Aarhus Universitetsforlag, 1997.

Gundlach, Thies. *Selbstbegrenzung Gottes und die Autonomie des Menschen. Karl Barth's Kirchliche Dogmatik als Modernisierungsschritt evangelischer Theologie.* Frankfurt am Main: Peter Lang Verlag, 1992.

Gunton, Colin. "Karl Barth's Doctrine of Election as Part of His Doctrine of God," *Journal of Theological Studies* 25, no. 2 (1974): 381-92.

Hafstad, Kjetil. "Åbenbaringen — den umulige mulighet for fornuften. Karl Barths løsningsforsøk," *Norsk Teologisk Tidsskrift* 88, no. 2 (1987): 65-86.

Hallbäck, Geert. "Den historiske Jesus som teologisk projekt — en kritisk betragtning," in *Den historiske Jesus og hans betydning*, edited by Troels Engberg-Pedersen, pp. 159-81. Copenhagen: Gyldendal, 1998.

Härle, Wilfried. *Sein und Gnade. Die Ontologie in Karl Barths Kirchlicher Dogmatik*. Berlin: Walter de Gruyter, 1975.

Hart, Trevor. *Regarding Karl Barth: Toward a Reading of His Theology*. Downers Grove, IL: InterVarsity Press, 1999.

Hegel, G. W. F. *The Phenomenology of Mind*. Translated by J. B. Baillie, 2nd ed. New York: Humanities Press, 1971.

Heim, S. Mark. *Saved from Sacrifice: A Theology of the Cross*. Grand Rapids: Eerdmans, 2006.

Heron, Alasdair I. C. "The Theme of Salvation in Karl Barth's Doctrine of Reconciliation," *Ex Auditu* 5 (1989): 107-22.

Hunsinger, George. *How to Read Karl Barth: The Shape of His Theology*. New York: Oxford University Press, 1991.

————. *Disruptive Grace: Studies in the Theology of Karl Barth*. Grand Rapids: Eerdmans, 2000.

Jenson, Robert W. *Alpha and Omega: A Study in the Theology of Karl Barth*. New York: Thomas Nelson & Sons, 1963.

Johnson, William Stacy. *The Mystery of God: Karl Barth and the Postmodern Foundations of Theology*. Louisville: Westminster/John Knox Press, 1997.

Jüngel, Eberhard. "Jesu Wort und Jesus als Wort Gottes. Ein hermeneutischer Beitrag zum christologischen Problem," in *Unterwegs zur Sache*, pp. 126-44. München: Chr. Kaiser Verlag, 1972.

————. "Der königliche Mensch. Eine christologische Reflexion auf die Würde des Menschen in der Theologie Karl Barths," in *Barth Studien*, pp. 233-45. Gütersloh: Gütersloher Verlagshaus, 1982.

Kelsey, David. *The Uses of Scripture in Recent Theology*. Philadelphia: Fortress Press, 1975.

Klappert, Bertold. *Die Auferweckung des Gekreuzigten. Der Ansatz der Christologie Karl Barths im Zusammenhang der Christologie der Gegenwart*. Neukirchen-Vluyn: Neukirchener Verlag, 1981.

Krause, Burghard. *Leiden Gottes — Leiden des Menschen. Eine Untersuchung zur Kirchlichen Dogmatik Karl Barths*. Stuttgart: Calwer Verlag, 1980.

Kreck, Walther. *Grundentscheidungen in Karl Barths Dogmatik. Zur Diskussion seines Verständnisses von Offenbarung und Erwählung*. Neukirchen-Vluyn: Neukirchener Verlag, 1978.

Krötke, Wolf. *Sünde und Nichtiges bei Karl Barth*, 2nd ed. Neukirchen-Vluyn: Neukirchener Verlag, 1983.

————. "Gott und Mensch als Partner. Zur Bedeutung einer zentralen Kategorie in Karl Barths Kirchlicher Dogmatik," *Zeitschrift für Theologie und Kirche*,

Beiheft 6. Zur Theologie Karl Barths. Beiträge aus Anlaß seines 100. Geburtstags (1986): 158-75.

————. "The Humanity of the Human Person in Karl Barth's Anthropology," in *The Cambridge Companion to Karl Barth*, edited by John Webster, pp. 159-76. Cambridge: Cambridge University Press, 2000.

Leiner, Martin. "Martin Buber und Karl Barth," *Zeitschrift für Dialektische Theologie* 17, no. 2 (2001): 188-91.

Lohmann, Johann F. *Karl Barth und der Neukantianismus: Die Rezeption des Neukantianismus im Römerbrief und ihre Bedeutung für die weitere Ausarbeitung der Theologie Karl Barth.* Berlin: De Gruyter, 1995.

Luther, Martin. "Ein Sermon von dem Sakrament der Taufe," in *Martin Luther Werke. Kritische Gesamtausgabe 2*, pp. 727-37. Weimar: 1884.

————. "A Sermon on Preparing to Die," in *Luther's Works. American Edition. Volume 42. Devotional Writings I.* Translated by Martin H. Bertram. Edited by Martin O. Dietrich, pp. 95-115. Philadelphia: Fortress Press, 1969.

————. *The Bondage of the Will*, in *Luther's Works. American Edition. Volume 33. Career of the Reformer III.* Translated by Philip S. Watson and Benjamin Drewery. Edited by Philip S. Watson. Philadelphia: Fortress Press, 1972.

McCormack, Bruce L. "The Sum of the Gospel: The Doctrine of Election in the Theologies of Alexander Schweizer and Karl Barth," in *Towards the Future of Reformed Theology: Tasks, Topics, Traditions*, edited by David Willis and Michael Welker, pp. 470-93. Grand Rapids: Eerdmans, 1989.

————. *Karl Barth's Critically Realistic Dialectical Theology: Its Genesis and Development 1909-1936.* Oxford: Oxford University Press, 1995.

————. "Grace and Being: The Role of God's Gracious Election in Karl Barth's Theological Ontology," in *The Cambridge Companion to Karl Barth*, edited by John Webster, pp. 92-110. Cambridge: Cambridge University Press, 2000.

————. "Not a Possible God but the God Who Is: Observations on Friedrich Schleiermacher's Doctrine of God," in *The Reality of Faith in Theology: Studies on Karl Barth. Princeton-Kampen Consultation 2005*, edited by Bruce L. McCormack and Gerrit Neven, pp. 111-39. Bern: Peter Lang, 2007.

Migliore, Daniel L. "Karl Barth's First Lectures in Dogmatics: Instruction in the Christian Religion," in *The Göttingen Dogmatics: Instruction in the Christian Religion*, pp. xv-lxii. Grand Rapids: Eerdmans, 1991.

Mikkelsen, Hans Vium. "Kun den lidende Gud kan hjælpe. Dietrich Bonhoeffers relationstænkning," *Dansk Teologisk Tidsskrift* 59, no. 4 (1996): 266-87.

————. "Offer og forsoning. Dogmatiske perspektiver og konsekvenser af René Girards antropologi," in *Syndens sold — en antologi om den mimetiske teori*, edited by Jørgen Jørgensen, pp. 141-73. Frederiksberg: Aros Forlag, 2006.

Moltmann, Jürgen. *The Way of Jesus Christ: Christology in Messianic Dimensions.* Translated by Margaret Kohl. London: SCM Press, 1990.

Nielsen, Bent Flemming. *Die Rationalität der Offenbarungstheologie. Die Struktur des Theologieverständnisses von Karl Barth.* Aarhus: Aarhus University Press, 1988.

Oyen, Hendrik Van. "Bemerkungen zu Karl Barths Anthropologie," *Evangelische Ethik 7* (1963): 291-305.

Pannenberg, Wolfhart. *Jesus — God and Man,* 2nd ed. London: SCM Press, 2002.

———. "Die Subjektivität Gottes und die Trinitätslehre," in *Grundfragen Systematischer Theologie. Gesammelte Aufsätze, Band 2,* pp. 96-111. Göttingen: Vandenhoeck & Ruprecht, 1980.

———. "Christologie und Theologie," in *Grundfragen Systematischer Theologie, Gesammelte Aufsätze, Band 2,* pp. 129-45. Göttingen: Vandenhoeck & Ruprecht, 1980.

———. *Problemgeschichte der neueren evangelischen Theologie in Deutschland. Von Schleiermacher bis zu Barth und Tillich.* Göttingen: Vandenhoeck & Ruprecht, 1997.

Prenter, Regin. "Karl Barths Umbildung der traditionellen Zweinaturlehre in lutherischer Beleuchtung," in *Theologie und Gottesdienst. Gesammelte Aufsätze,* edited by Erik Kyndal, Gerhard Pedersen, and Anna Marie Aagaard. Aarhus: Aros Forlag, 1977.

Price, Daniel J. *Karl Barth's Anthropology in Light of Modern Thought.* Grand Rapids: Eerdmans, 2002.

Rigby, Cynthia L. "The Real Word Really Became Real Flesh: Karl Barth's Contribution to a Feminist Incarnational Christology." Ph.D. dissertation, Princeton Theological Seminary, 1998.

Sauter, Gerhard. "Mensch sein — Mensch bleiben. Anthropologie als theologische Aufgabe," in *Antropologie als Thema der Theologie,* edited by Hermann Fischer, pp. 71-118. Göttingen: Vandenhoeck & Ruprecht, 1978.

Schellong, Dieter. "Barth Lesen," in *Einwürfe 3. Karl Barth: Der Störenfried?,* edited by Friedrich-Wilhelm Marquardt, Dieter Schellong, and Michael Weinrich, pp. 6-92. München: Chr. Kaiser Verlag, 1986.

Schleiermacher, Friedrich. *The Christian Faith.* Translated by H. R. Mackintosh. Edinburgh: T. & T. Clark, 1989.

Schwöbel, Christoph. "Trinitätslehre als Rahmentheorie des christlichen Glaubens. Vier Thesen zur Bedeutung der Trinität in der christlichen Dogmatik," *Zeitschrift für Dialektische Theologie* 14, no. 2 (1998): 131-52.

Sölle, Dorothee. *Atheistisch an Gott glauben. Beiträge zur Theologie.* Olten: Walter-Verlag, 1969.

———. "Gott und das Leiden," in *Diskussion über Jürgen Moltmanns Buch "Der gekreuzigte Gott,"* edited by Michael Welker, pp. 111-17. München: Chr. Kaiser Verlag, 1979.

Sonderegger, Katherine. *That Jesus Christ Was Born a Jew: Karl Barth's "Doctrine of Israel."* University Park: Pennsylvania State University Press, 1993.

————. "Barth and Feminism," in *The Cambridge Companion to Karl Barth,* edited by John Webster, pp. 258-73. Cambridge: Cambridge University Press, 2000.

Stümke, Volker. "Eschatologische Differenz in Gott? Zum Verhältnis von Barmherzigkeit und Gerechtigkeit Gottes bei Karl Barth und Friedrich-Wilhelm Marquardt," in *Wendung nach Jerusalem. Friedrich-Wilhelm Marquardts Theologie im Gespräch,* edited by Hanna Lehming, Joachim Liß-Walther, Matthias Loerbroks, and Rien van der Vegt. München: Chr. Kaiser Gütersloher Verlagshaus, 1999.

Thomsen, Henning. "Prædestinationen — et centralt element i Karl Barths teologi," *Dansk Teologisk Tidsskrift* 49, no. 2 (1986): 117-47.

————. "Moltmanns teologiske historieopfattelse som et trinitarisk formuleret svar på lidelsens problem," in *Verbum Dei — verba ecclesiae,* edited by Theodor Jørgensen and Peter Widmann, pp. 74-100. Aarhus: Det teologiske Fakultet, Aarhus Universitet, 1996.

Torrance, Alan. "The Trinity," in *The Cambridge Companion to Karl Barth,* edited by John Webster, pp. 72-91. Cambridge: Cambridge University Press, 2000.

Wagner, Falk. "Theologische Gleichschaltung. Zur Christologie bei Karl Barth," in *Die Realisierung der Freiheit. Beiträge zur Kritik der Theologie Karl Barths,* edited by Trutz Rendtorff and Falk Wagner. Gütersloh: Gütersloher Verlagshaus Gerd Mohn, 1975.

Wolterstorff, Nicholas. *Divine Discourse: Philosophical Reflections on the Claim That God Speaks.* Cambridge: Cambridge University Press, 1995.

Index

Absolute dependence, 13, 67-70

Acknowledgment, 13, 49, 53-54, 58, 60-62, 64-67, 69-70, 72-73, 99, 245

Adam: old, 169, 202; new, 169, 202

Aeon, new, 242

Ambiguity, 11, 45n.3, 51, 53, 56-57, 59n.26, 63n.28, 82, 104, 133, 141

Anhypostasis, 15, 148-53

Annihilation, 124, 137, 194, 218

Anselm of Canterbury, 214

Anthropology: anthropological constant, 170, 182, 188; general, 9, 54n.20, 187n. 9; theological, 4, 14, 87n.1, 88-89, 92-93, 96, 98-99, 121, 123-24, 126-27, 128n.13

Anthropomorphic, 205, 224

Apokatastasis, 7, 212-13

Applicatio, 56

Ascension, 17, 241, 242n.6, 243-44, 248-50

Athanasius, 155n.16, 169

Atonement: from above, 6; from below, 6; classical, 5, 169; God as object, 5, 193-94, 196, 214, 225; God as subject, 5, 193-94, 196, 225; and judgment, 186-87, 195, 197, 220; objective, 5, 17, 178-79, 196, 214; and risk, 184n.8; sub-

jective, 5, 17, 222n.15; Trinitarian, 183n.7, 185, 193. *See also* Sacrifice and Substitution

Aulén, Gustaf, 5, 169

Augustine, 203, 206n.5

Balthasar, Hans Urs von, 24n.7, 47n.8, 183n.7

Being: actualistic, 15, 27, 146, 158-59, 163-64, 260; essentialistic, 159, 163-64, 260

Berkouwer, Gerrit C., 70n.44

Biblicism, 12, 33

Bonhoeffer, Dietrich, 46nn.5,6, 52n.18, 55n.21, 215n.1

Braaten, Carl E., 213n.19

Bromiley, Geoffrey W., 88n.3

Brunner, Emil, 10, 51n.13, 52, 71nn.44,45, 82, 97n.14, 99, 125-27

Buber, Martin, 4, 10, 14, 85, 96n.13, 97-107

Calvin, John: double outcome, 7, 204-6, 208-10; double predestination, 173, 175, 204-6, 209; election, 83, 204; eternal perdition, 180; salvation, 83, 174, 204-5, 209, 211; sanctification, 83; eternal will of God, 175, 209

275